CAPITAL AND JOB FORMATION
our nation's 3rd-century challenge

EDITORIAL ADVISORY BOARD

CAPITAL AND JOB FORMATION
our nation's 3rd-century challenge

edited by

Charles D. Kuehner

American Telephone and Telegraph Company

*This is a special edition prepared for
The Presidents Association*

Dow Jones-Irwin
Homewood, Illinois   60430

This publication is designed to provide accurate and
authoritative information in regard to the subject matter
covered. It is sold with the understanding that the
publisher is not engaged in rendering legal, accounting, or
other professional service. If legal advice or other expert
assistance is required, the services of a competent
professional person should be sought.

*From a Declaration of Principles jointly adopted by a Committee
of the American Bar Association and a Committee of Publishers.*

ISBN 0-87094-149-6
Library of Congress Catalog Card No. 77–83596

Printed in the United States of America

1 2 3 4 5 6 7 8 9 0 K 5 4 3 2 1 0 9 8

PREFACE

Capital and job formation ranks number one as America's most unrecognized and misunderstood problem. It is our nation's 3rd-century challenge. Unfortunately, however, few Americans can define capital formation—let alone appreciate its impact on their own lives.

In simplest terms, capital formation is the process of channeling investment into new plant and equipment. This process is crucial in creating new and better jobs, goods, and services. Capital formation is also essential in combatting inflation, cleaning up the environment, increasing productivity, and raising our citizens' standard of living.

These "outputs" are all high priority national goals. But, sad to say, the vital "input" of capital formation has had a very low national priority, as is documented in this book.

This volume of essays deals with various facets of this challenge, and spells out, in clear terms, how it can be resolved. It has been written by recognized experts. They have devoted most of their lives contributing to our nation's economic growth through capital investment and creating new jobs. They write from first-hand experience with the subject matter. They also write with piercing insights into the problem and with a great deal of common sense. Above all else, they write with deep compassion for the economic well-being of their fellow citizens.

High blood pressure and low capital formation

In many respects, awareness of the capital and job formation problem is similar to awareness of high blood pressure: both involve millions of people who don't know they have it.

Some 20 million Americans suffer from "The Silent Killer" and are essentially unaware of it. "A large number of patients with elevated blood pressure may have no symptoms or signs, whatever."[1]

In like manner, almost 220 million Americans suffer from a lack of awareness of the capital and job formation "disease." Evidence of this abounds in numerous public opinion surveys. As with high blood pressure, the symptoms of the capital and job formation problem are not readily apparent.

If high blood pressure goes unnoticed, its debilitating effects weaken other parts of the body: heart, liver, kidneys, and so on. Likewise, if the capital and job formation disease is unrecognized, or is incorrectly diagnosed, it spreads throughout the economy in a regressive chain of events:

- Inadequate capital formation leads to large numbers of people becoming unemployed, or underemployed relative to their training or skills. This occurs first in the construction and capital goods industries and then in consumer goods and services.

- Vociferous demands are made for increasing government intervention and spending "to create jobs and income."

- With increased government spending, and without a corresponding expansion in private industry, inflation weakens the economy.

- With the slowdown in capital investment, American industry loses ground to competition in domestic and world markets.

- A weakened industrial base triggers less spending for R&D; in turn, further capital formation problems appear.

- Industry is able to offer fewer choices of products and services to consumers; thus, industry becomes less able to solve such basic problems as energy and pollution.

- At the end of the line, the consumer sees the cost of living moving up still higher and demands *still more* government intervention, controls and spending.

This book is an effort to break the above chain of events by encouraging what its authors believe must be made a top national priority: capital formation. A special effort has been made to present the data in clear, concise terms with extensive use of easily understood charts.

---

[1] T. R. Harris, *Principles of Internal Medicine*, New York: McGraw-Hill, 1972, p. 1255.

Neglect of capital and job formation

We must recognize that it will not be easy to arouse the American people about the capital and job formation challenge. It has long been a victim of public neglect, largely because of its complexity and vagueness.

■ Neglect by the nation's news media is almost total. Of the thousands of articles published in the past year by the nation's leading magazines and newspapers, only 20 dealt with the subject of capital formation.[2] Of these articles, 17 appeared in specialized business publications. It is a case of "business talking to itself." Of the three articles in magazines of general circulation (*Time, Newsweek* and *U. S. News*), all focused on the short-term outlook, ignoring altogether the basic long-term problem. Television coverage, except for two brief network features, appears to have been nonexistent. As one TV executive explained, "The American people just won't watch what they don't understand."

■ Labor leaders, especially at the local level, are most concerned with seeking the largest possible increases in wages and fringe benefits for their members. Thus, they have no special concern for the long-run impact of their agreements on corporate earnings and how this may impinge on capital formation. Capital formation has not been a top item on the agenda of the AFL–CIO annual convention in Bal Harbour, Florida.

■ Most political leaders do not regard capital formation as a high priority item. Opinion surveys show members of Congress and their staffs rank capital formation well down the list of items considered to be the most important to the nation's welfare.[3]

■ Under political pressure to keep rates low, regulatory agencies have largely neglected capital formation. The courts have not intervened because of their tendency to defer to the agencies' "expertise." As a result, many regulated companies have been forced to sell new common stock below the nominal book value per share—and far below the real value of the assets per share in dollars of constant purchasing power.

---

[2] *Reader's Guide to Periodical Literature,* New York: The H. W. Wilson Co., July 1976–June 1977.

[3] *Opinion Research Corporation Survey,* Princeton, N.J.: Opinion Research Corporation, June 1977, p. 2.

- Even the nation's graduate schools of business virtually ignore capital and job formation in their course offerings. This may explain the findings of a recent survey of MBAs (Masters of Business Administration) who failed to mention capital formation as one of America's most important problems.[4] As one professor of a leading business school noted, "Capital formation more or less fell thru the cracks."

One possible explanation for this grim state of affairs is American provincialism. We seemingly have no desire to learn from the experience of others. For example, West Germany and Japan have given capital formation highest national priority for over a quarter of a century. The result has been called "an economic miracle": up-to-date plant and equipment, high productivity, strong currencies, and very low unemployment. In contrast, England has pursued a heavy government spending policy, intervention or ownership of business, and income redistribution. The results are not encouraging: an antiquated industrial plant, low productivity, chronic weakness in the British pound, endless labor strife, and slippage from second to fifth place among the Western world's economies.

The challenge

The significance of America's 3rd-century challenge may be underscored by a few key factors:

- *Unemployment.* Unemployment has recently been in the range of 7 million.
- *Labor force growth.* By 1985 some 12 million *additional* jobs must be created just to keep pace with the growth in the nation's labor force.
- *Obsolete industrial capacity.* A large and growing part of the nation's industrial capacity is obsolete, with more than two thirds being over ten years old.
- *Government spending.* Federal, state, and local government spending, which was 21 percent of the gross national product in 1950, is today 35 percent of the GNP—and it is rising.
- *Capital spending.* In recent years real corporate earnings—an important source of capital—have been a smaller part of the GNP than at any time in the past quarter century. As a result,

---

4 *MBA Magazine*, April 1977, p. 20.

growth in capital spending has fallen far below what is required to provide jobs for our nation's growing labor force.

■ *Stock market.* The attitudes of investors are reflected by the Dow Jones 30 Industrials Index. In mid-1977 the Dow Jones 30 was trading at about 850. The real value of the assets behind the shares in the index was about $1,440 in 1977 purchasing power. Hence, the assets of American industry are currently selling at 61 cents on the dollar—hardly an expression of investor enthusiasm.

■ *Confidence crisis.* In light of all of these factors, we should not be surprised when astute observers refer to a "confidence crisis." Businesses—even those with adequate capital—are today reluctant to make investments needed for future growth.

Strange paradox

All this has created a strange paradox. On the one hand, most Americans hope for a large gain in our citizens' economic well-being. Most people seem to recognize that this requires heavy new investment by the private sector in more modern and expanded facilities.

On the other hand, few people seem to appreciate that investors and businesses will not risk their capital unless they have confidence in the future and see an opportunity to earn a reasonable profit. Even fewer people seem to recognize that many of our nation's most baffling social problems are but a legacy of the basic problem of capital formation and that, once we surmount that challenge, we will see:

■ Unemployment receding as a national problem.
■ A higher standard of living via greater productivity.
■ More challenging and rewarding jobs.
■ Abatement of social problems and social tensions.

The government albatross on capital and job formation

The overriding factor affecting capital and job formation is government policy. But, unfortunately, there seems to be basic confusion between aims and means in this arena. For example:

On the one hand, government policy tells the American people, "Every American citizen has an inalienable right to a job with decent wages."

On the other hand, when an investor accumulates the $30,000 needed to finance a job in private industry, government policy then says, "We will penalize you by, (1) taxing your dividends twice and, (2) if you make any capital gains we'll tax that also—even though much of the gain merely reflects the impact of inflation and is not a true capital gain at all."

Other nations seem to recognize this contradiction: both West Germany and Japan tax dividends far below the U.S. rate. Additionally, West Germany has zero tax on capital gains and, for all practical purposes, Japan likewise has no capital gains tax.

To exacerbate the problem, the U.S. policy of tax free state and municipal bonds encourages the growth of government—in effect, providing a subsidy financed in large measure by taxes on industry and investors. In recent years, inflation has increased even average family incomes to such levels that many people invest in tax free municipal and state bonds rather than in the stocks and bonds of private industry.

Rethinking national priorities

There is wide agreement that many of the priorities in the laws and government policies of the nation's first century were not appropriate in the second. Are the priorities of the nation's second century adequate to meet the challenges of the third? The facts say "no."

Today, more than ever before, our nation needs public debate of the basic issues affecting capital and job formation.

This book endeavors to stimulate that debate and, with it, create public understanding. I believe that, given the facts, the American people and their leaders will see the need to change national priorities so we can meet our nation's 3rd-century challenge: capital and job formation.

January 1978   CHARLES D. KUEHNER

ACKNOWLEDGMENTS

As editor of this collection of essays on Capital and Job Formation, I wish to acknowledge my indebtedness to a number of people.

First and foremost, I would like to express my sincere appreciation to the members of the Advisory Board for helping select authorities in various fields as chapter contributors. The Advisory Board also made many suggestions with respect to the content of the several chapters, but the final product is the responsibility of the contributors themselves.

I would also like to thank G. Wallace Bates, Esq., of The Business Roundtable, Robert L. Fegley of General Electric Co., Dr. Irwin Friend of The Wharton School of the University of Pennsylvania, Joseph F. Johnston, Jr., Esq., Dr. George J. Lyons and Dr. Fred Renwick of New York University, Dr. William A. White of Harvard Business School, and Dr. Walter A. Morton of The University of Wisconsin for many insightful comments.

A number of friends in the financial community have offered many helpful suggestions. They include: Mike Armellino of Goldman, Sachs & Co., Dr. George Cleaver of White, Weld & Co., Dr. William Freund of the New York Stock Exchange, Ken Hollister of Dean Witter & Co., Iredell Iglehert of Donaldson, Lufkin and Jenrette, Jay Jones of Oppenheimer & Co., Bob La Blanc of Salomon Brothers, Dr. Jennifer Macleod of Fidelity Bank, Ann Mobley of Brown Brothers Harriman & Co., and Frank Petito of Morgan Stanley & Co.

Sincere thanks are also due to my associates at AT&T who have given me the benefit of their expertise. These include Steve Allen, Malcolm Burnside, Ed Carey, Patricia Harriss, Don Larson, Ken Militzer, Alice Roggenkamp, Pete Rosoff, Jim Tirone, Lou Winkelman, and Diane Woods.

C. D. K.

CONTRIBUTING AUTHORS

BABSON, DAVID L. (Chapter 6)
Chairman,
David L. Babson & Co.

BALDWIN, ROBERT H. B. (Chapter 8)
President,
Morgan Stanley & Co., Incorporated

BLUMENTHAL, W. MICHAEL (Chapter 22)
Secretary of the Treasury

BRENNER, JOHN A. (Chapter 3)
President,
Moody's Investors Service, Inc.

BROPHY, THEODORE F. (Chapter 12)
Chairman and Chief Executive Officer,
General Telephone & Electronics Corporation

CARLSON, EDWARD E. (Chapter 16)
Chairman of the Board,
UAL, Inc.

COREY, GORDON R. (Chapter 9)
Vice Chairman,
Commonwealth Edison Company

deBUTTS, JOHN D. (Chapter 18)
Chairman of the Board,
American Telephone and Telegraph Company

FRANCIS, DARRYL R. (Chapter 17)
President, 1966–76,
Federal Reserve Bank of St. Louis

GEORGE, W. H. KROME (Chapter 15)
Chairman and Chief Executive Officer,
Aluminum Company of America

HARRIS, LOUIS   (Chapter 5)
President,
Louis Harris and Associates, Inc.

JENKINS, GEORGE P.   (Chapter 4)
Chairman of the Board,
Metropolitan Life Insurance Company

JONES, REGINALD H.   (Chapter 1)
Chairman and Chief Executive Officer,
General Electric Company

MacNAUGHTON, DONALD S.   (Chapter 19)
Chairman and Chief Executive Officer,
Prudential Insurance Company of America

REGAN, DONALD T.   (Chapter 20)
Chairman and Chief Executive Officer,
Merrill Lynch & Co., Inc.

SHAPIRO, IRVING S.   (Chapter 14)
Chairman,
E. I. du Pont de Nemours & Co., Inc.

SIMON, WILLIAM E.   (Chapter 21)
Secretary of the Treasury, 1972–77

SPEER, EDGAR B.   (Chapter 10)
Chairman of the Board,
United States Steel Corporation

TERBORGH, GEORGE   (Chapter 2)
Consultant,
Machinery and Allied Products Institute

WALKER, CHARLS E.   (Chapter 23)
Chairman,
American Council for Capital Formation

WARNER, RAWLEIGH, JR.   (Chapter 11)
Chairman of the Board,
Mobil Corporation

WEIDENBAUM, MURRAY L.   (Chapter 7)
Director,
Center for the Study of American Business,
Washington University, St. Louis

WEYERHAEUSER, GEORGE H.   (Chapter 13)
President and Chief Executive Officer,
Weyerhaeuser Company

CONTENTS

and personal saving. Retirement and other social needs. Some non-demographic factors affecting business capital formation: *Inflation impacts. Expansion of the government sector.*

Resulting construction cutbacks. Future supply shortages. The financing problem in brief. Earnings quality. What should be done?

The domestic market for steel through 1985. Present steelmaking capability. The projected need for additional capacity. The projected capital requirements of the domestic steel industry. Additional steel production capacity. Replacement and modernization of present steel production capacity. Environmental control and OSHA equipment for existing plant facilities. Non-steel-related capital expenditures. Working capital needs and debt repayments. Financing future capital requirements.

Summary of the problem. Summary of the solution. Discussion: *U.S. energy capital requirements depend in the first instance upon U.S. economic growth policy. U.S. energy demand will grow if the U.S. economy grows. Nonpetroleum energy supplies (especially coal and nuclear) need to grow at a rapid rate. Oil supplies to grow at 2 percent per annum—huge capital required. Marshaling $244 billion (1975 dollars) in the next decade—a big challenge.* Conclusion. International postscript.

Introduction: *The composition of the U.S. telecommunications industry. The United States leads in technology. Comparison of the United States with other nations.* The projected demand for telecommunications services. The capital needs of the telecommunications industry: *Historical and future capital requirements. A highly capital-intensive industry. Other factors affecting capital needs. Investment per employee.* Problems in meeting capital needs: *External capital requirements. Competition for capital. The effect of inflation on the cost of plant and equipment. The effect of inflation on net income. The effect of inflation on interest rate. Strained debt / equity ratios. Declining interest coverage. The effect of regulation on return on equity.* The role of the telecommunications industry in the century ahead.

Introducing the forest products industry: *Investment in timber growth. Employment: Product impact is crucial.* Capital investment in the paper and paperboard mills: *The capital intensity versus jobs illusion.*

Barriers to investment in the pulp and paper industry. The escalation in investment requirements. Can the capital be obtained? Searching for a free enterprise solution. Government's responsibility. Capital investment in housing and wood products mills.

PART III   WORKING TOWARD A SOLUTION

insurance companies attract savings. The impact of public pension systems on private savings. Financial investment by the insurance industry: *Basic investment objectives. Investment activity of life insurance companies. Corporate bonds. Mortgage loans and real estate. Common stocks. Investment activity of property-casualty companies.* The insurance industry's future role.

Stock ownership in the United States and abroad. The major postwar stimuli to stock market investments. Making the individual feel welcome. Individual versus institutional market participation. The importance of the individual. Non-stock investments. Liquidity essential to make investments flow. Making the best market better. Faith in a sound economy is a major investment incentive. Alleviating tax discouragements. Economically educated citizens. Inviting greater investor participation. Contributing to the capital pool.

Government tax policies. An innovative proposal for increasing saving and investment: *Mechanisms to remove the double tax. The dividend deduction method. The stockholder credit method. The revenue implications of eliminating the double corporate tax. Recommended mechanism: A combination of dividend deductions and stockholder credits. The dividend deduction. The stockholder credit. Relief for all savers, not just stockholders. Benefits of the proposed change. The goals.*

The need to define terms. Physical capital. The growth of factor inputs. Increasing investment's share of GNP. Administration policies. The Administration program—what it will not be. The anti-inflation goal. Ensuring a greater flow of investment capital. Supporting the required growth of investment. Debt versus equity. Financial intermediaries and public securities markets.

Stabilization policy. Budget policy. Government regulation of business. Productive tax reform: An impossible dream? Impediments to productive reform. Exploding the myths. A program of information and action: *The man on the street. The press. Organized labor.* The bottom line.

PART I

Evidence of the overall problem

Chapter 1

THE NEED TO ENCOURAGE CAPITAL AND JOB FORMATION

*Reginald H. Jones**

Arnold Toynbee, in his final book, *Mankind and Mother Earth,* says that the most important invention of the human race was the invention of plant and animal husbandry. When man tamed a few plants and animals—and there's some evidence that this was really done by the women while the men were out hunting—he assured himself of a steady food supply and was able to set about the work of creating civilizations.

The crucial discovery was that by saving some of the seeds for next year's planting and by saving some of the lambs and calves to breed and sustain the flocks, the continuation and expansion of the wealth of the tribe were assured. And a shudder of fear went through any community that was forced by famine to eat its seed corn or to slaughter all the yearlings.

INDUSTRIAL SEED CORN

The same thing applies to industrial societies and business firms. Every year, some part of the total output—some seed corn—has to be saved and reinvested in the replacement, modernization, and expansion of the industrial machine. This is the process of capital formation. And nations that neglect their capital formation find themselves susceptible to scarcity, inflation, unemployment, and declining standards of living.

---

* Chairman and Chief Executive Officer, General Electric Company.

In recent years, the United States has been eating into its industrial seed corn.

This is an ironic and potentially tragic turn of events. In the century of industrialization that began after the Civil War, the United States had a social, political, and economic climate that favored savings and investment. We got the jump on other nations in the process of capital formation, and with our bountiful natural resources and growing population, we pulled out ahead of them in terms of productivity and national wealth.

In recent years, however, in our desire to "spread the good life around," we seem to have lost touch with this basic formula for success. There has been an increasing emphasis on consumption, especially in the form of government services, and a corresponding loss of incentives for savings and investment. As a consequence, our productivity advances are declining—along with our capacity to provide advances in real income and jobs for a growing labor force.

In this, the United States is not alone. One of the unfortunate side effects of economic growth is that nations are tempted to live beyond their means. This is especially true of the industrialized democracies, where governments come into power by promising more than the opposition. We've seen this process at work here in the United States, but it is almost universal among democracies, England being perhaps the most painful example. Before we examine the statistical evidence on capital formation, let's review the political process involved.

LIVING BEYOND OUR MEANS

As affluence increases, expectations rise. People demand more and still more of their economic systems. "Expectations" become "demands," and then "demands" become "entitlements." Governments respond by legislating more generous services and benefits, taking more and more out of the economy by way of either taxes or inflation. All the emphasis is on consumption rather than production, on redistribution rather than the creation of wealth. Governments grow faster than the tax base that supports them.

Capital formation—the life-giving process by which nations reinvest a proportion of what they make in future productive capacity—is forgotten in the rush to ever more comprehensive programs of social welfare. And when nations begin to eat their seed corn, to discourage savers and investors, to tax away private and corporate earnings, and to elevate the politics of envy—the results are only too predictable.

The productive private sector declines, and more and more people either go on government payrolls or join the ranks of the chronically unemployed. Demand exceeds supply, and the resulting inflation heightens class conflict in the struggle to keep ahead. Labor demands far exceed increases in productivity, and government increases its welfare programs in response to political pressures. High rates of inflation and unemployment become chronic. And the means and the incentives to break the pattern dissolve in the bitter struggle for short-term advantage.

This decline-and-fall scenario may seem to be overdone, but it is what we would see in virtually all of the industrial democracies if the film were speeded up and we could see the effects of long-term trends. Every decade sees the government sector expand and the private sector contract. Each cycle of boom-and-bust leaves our economies weaker, our ability to recover impaired, and our vulnerability to inflation and unemployment increased.

This has happened here in the United States as government expenditures—federal, state, and local—have risen inexorably, regardless of the party in power, from one tenth of GNP in 1929 to more than a third of GNP last year, and will pass 50 percent in the 1980s if present trends continue. But here again, we are not alone in this situation.

Hudson Institute Europe recently completed a study of 19 industrialized nations in Europe, North America, and the Pacific Basin, and the conclusion was this: the larger the public sector of the economy, the slower the economy's real growth. The reason is basically that government growth crowds out and destroys the incentives for productive private investment. The Hudson study and other studies suggest that the toll taken by the expanding government sector in Western industrialized countries has been massive—cutting attainable growth rates by as much as one third in the past 15 years.

As a result, the U.S. economy has drifted out of balance. The government sector is growing faster than the tax base that supports it. The consumer sector has been damaged by inflation, and its confidence has become very sensitive to changes in the price index. And the producer sector—the sector that provides the jobs and income on which everything rests—is losing its vitality because it lacks the means and the incentives for capital investment.

Unless the United States can turn this situation around and start redirecting more of its annual output into the strengthening of the producer sector, the nation faces increasing frustration of its economic and social goals. Full employment, rising income, stable prices, greater energy independence, cleanup of the environment, and a tax base for social services: every one of these goals requires increased capital formation.

What are the symptoms that would lead us to believe that the capital base of the United States is insufficient for the nation's aspirations?

CAPACITY, PRODUCTIVITY, AND JOBS

Chart 1, "Idle Plant Capacity and Unemployment," shows the relationship between jobs and capital investment in a way that must raise genuine concern. In the past, when U.S. industry was operating at or near full capacity, jobs were plentiful and unemployment was low. Now, because of the lack of capital investment, it appears that we will run out of capacity before we run out of unemployment.

It is important to note that the term *idle plant capacity* is probably a misnomer. Much of that "idle" capacity is overage, inefficient equip-

Chart 1.   Idle plant capacity and unemployment (final quarter of year)

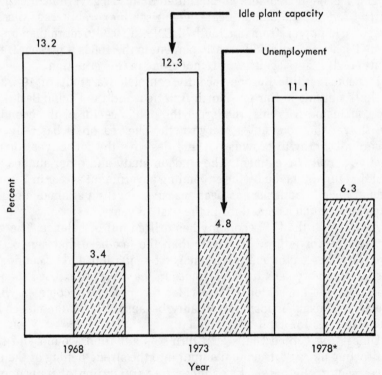

* GE forecast based on the assumption that capacity would grow at the same rate as in 1971–76 and that real GNP would grow 6 percent per year from the fourth quarter of 1976 to the fourth quarter of 1978.

Sources: Federal Reserve Board and Bureau of Labor Statistics.

ment that is used only in emergencies. Despite the so-called idle capacity, in 1968 and 1973 we had bottlenecks and shortages and industry was really operating at just about full capacity.

But note what happened to the unemployment rate. In 1968, all-out operations left 3.4 percent jobless. In 1973 that had risen to 4.8 percent. And when the economy again hits full capacity (forecasts say by the end of 1978), the unemployment rate is expected to be in excess of 6 percent.

We can no longer assume that an economy operating at full capacity will create full employment.

Chart 2.   Productivity and real wage growth (percent)

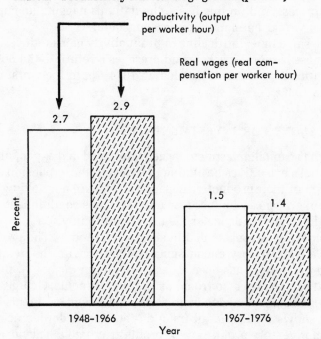

Source: U.S. Department of Labor data for the private nonfarm business sector.

Chart 2, "Productivity and Real Wage Growth," shows another disturbing consequence of the lag in capital investment. Productivity improvement has fallen almost in half during the past decade. From 1948–66, output per man-hour increased an average 2.7 percent a year. Since 1967, it has increased only 1.5 percent a year. We can only consume what we produce, and when productivity gains slow down, so do real wage gains. There is almost an exact correlation, as real wage gains declined from 2.9 percent a year in the earlier period to 1.4 percent in the past decade.

Labor must certainly be concerned about the clear relationship between declining capital investment, rising unemployment, and slower wage gains.

But the consequences move beyond labor to the entire national economy, and its capacity to produce the standards of living and the social services our citizens have come to expect. *Were it not for the productivity slowdown shown in Chart 2, today's gross national product would be $220 billion larger, and in the past ten years we would have produced over a trillion dollars more in goods and services—computed at 1977 prices.* And on this basis, the nation's nagging unemployment problems would be much more manageable.

At the same time, the decline in productivity gains reduces our competitiveness in world markets and presages a return to the bottlenecks and inflationary pressures that led, in 1974–75, to the worst recession since the 1930s.

THE REASONS FOR INVESTMENT LAG

Why has capital investment lagged both need and expectation? Why are business executives hesitating to invest in the expansion and modernization of their productive capacity? They are not holding back out of cantankerousness, but because under today's conditions they do not have either the confidence or the incentives to invest.

Consider the prospects that business faces today. The profit figures in 1976 appeared very encouraging compared with the depths of the recession, but there has been a basic, long-term decline in the real return that can be expected from business investments. George Terborgh examines this phenomenon in greater depth elsewhere in this book, but Chart 3 shows the impact of inflation-induced underdepreciation and phantom inventory profits on real profits after taxes. They declined, by 1976, to only 57.6 percent of their 1965 level. In the same period, real personal income, after taxes, increased by 38.7 percent. Business is getting a smaller and smaller share of the national income, and so lacks the means to make the needed capital investment.

Chart 4 shows how inflation has eroded the real return on investment. Adjusted aftertax profits expressed as a percentage of the *replacement* cost of the stock of plant, equipment, and inventories plummeted from 9.9 percent in 1965 to an estimated 3.7 percent in 1976 and even lower in 1974 and 1975. *This is the real return on investment, and it is simply not an incentive for further investment.*

Chart 3.   Real aftertax income (1965 = 100)

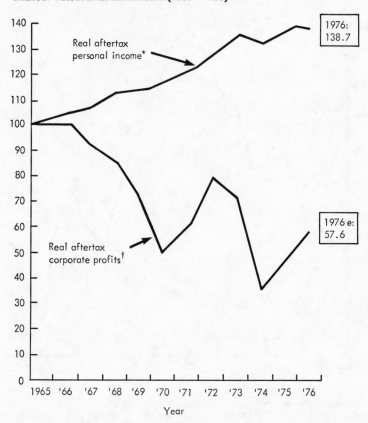

* Disposable personal income divided by the consumer price index.

† Aftertax corporate profits minus inventory profits and an allowance for underdepreciation (the difference between tax depreciation and replacement cost depreciation—double-declining balance, .75 Bulletin F service lives) divided by the consumer price index.

Sources: Commerce Department data and GE estimates for 1976 profit data.

With profitability declining and depreciation falling short of replacement costs (by as much as $23 billion in 1975, according to the Commerce Department), industry has had to turn increasingly to outside sources for its capital funds. Chart 5 shows what happened. Over the past 20 years, new equity shares have provided only 3.5 percent of the total new funds raised by nonfinancial corporations. New debt, on the other hand, has been used to meet a growing share of corporate financial needs, averaging 41 percent during the past five years com-

Chart 4. The return on investment after taxes, nonfinancial corporations*

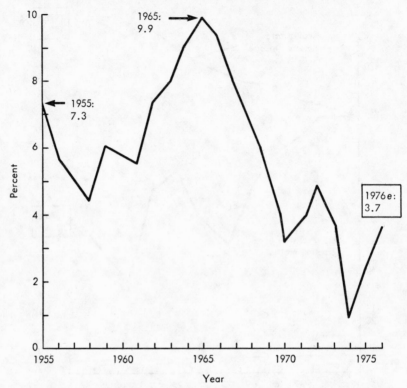

Year

* Aftertax profits, excluding inventory profits, adjusted to reflect economic depreciation (double-declining balance, .75 Bulletin F service lives) as a percent of plant, equipment, and inventories valued at replacement cost.

Source: Calculated from Commerce Department data.

pared with 33 percent during the first half of the 1960s. Why has business gone so deeply in debt?

For one thing, with profit margins declining, savers prefer to lend their money instead of risking it in equities that offer a small and uncertain return. But there is also a strong bias in the tax structure. Interest and dividends are both costs of capital—fees paid to people for the use of their savings. But interest is tax-deductible, and dividends are not. Hence the tax structure is pushing corporations toward debt financing. And the Tax Reform Act of 1976 made equity financing even more difficult by increasing the taxes on capital gains.

Moreover, the decline in real corporate profitability has had a depressing effect on the stock market.

Chart 5.   Percent of total funds raised through new equity shares and new liabilities, nonfinancial corporations (five-year moving average ending in year shown on chart)

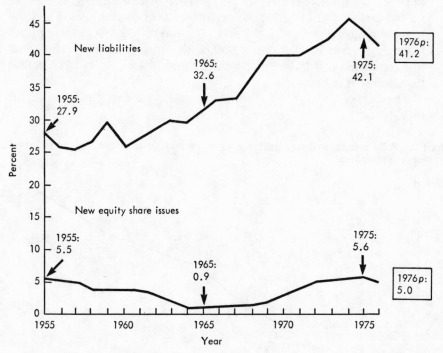

Source: Calculated from Federal Reserve data.

Chart 6.   Ratio of market value of nonfinancial corporations to replacement cost of net assets

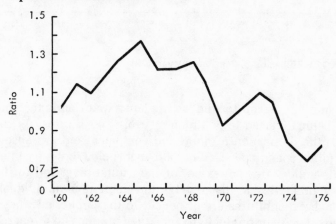

Source: Council of Economic Advisors (based on data from various sources).

Chart 6 shows that the market value of corporate assets has fallen far short of replacement costs, so that there is very little incentive to raise money for investment by the issuance of new shares. This is reflected in the volatility and poor performance of stock prices. The Dow Jones averaged close to 1,000 toward the end of 1968. Consumer prices have gone up almost 70 percent since then (by mid-1977). Thus, just to keep pace with inflation the Dow should be close to 1,700 rather than where it is today.

The market is trying to tell us something about the climate for investment!

Chart 7. Pollution control expenditures as a percentage of annual business investment in plant and equipment

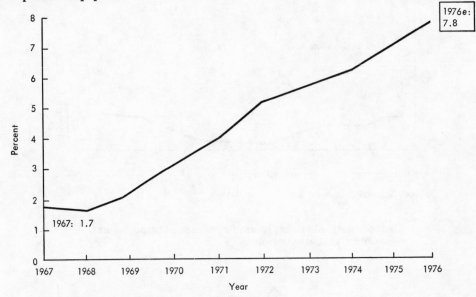

1976e: 7.8

1967: 1.7

Year

Sources: McGraw-Hill and U.S. Commerce Department.

Still another reason for the lag in plant expansion is the amount of capital being diverted to pollution control expenditures. As shown in Chart 7, the proportion of plant and equipment outlays absorbed by antipollution spending has more than quadrupled in the past ten years. And this understates the extent of the capital diversion for many of our basic industries, as discussed in the chapters on individual industries. Such expenditures are of benefit to the public, but they do not increase capacity or productivity, and they produce no direct return on investment to the companies concerned.

These are some of the basic reasons why capital investment is not coming up to expectations, and why business leaders are deeply concerned about the capacity of the U.S. economy to provide needed jobs and improvements in living standards in the years ahead.

FUTURE CAPITAL REQUIREMENTS

The most objective and authoritative study of the nation's business capital requirements was prepared in December 1975 by the Commerce Department's Bureau of Economic Analysis at the request of the president's Council of Economic Advisers. This study calculates the real volume of plant and equipment that will have to be put in place by 1980 in order to:

Create enough jobs to reduce unemployment to 5 percent.

Improve productivity and real wage gains.

Meet the requirements of environmental legislation currently on the books.

Keep the 1980 share of imported oil from rising above the 1973–74 proportion.

According to this comprehensive study, business fixed investment in the 1975–80 period will have to average 12 percent of real gross national product in order to achieve the widely accepted goals stated above. This contrasts with the historic average of 10–10½ percent of GNP.

But business fixed investment averaged 9.3 percent of real GNP in 1975 and 1976. There is much catch-up to do. Unless the figure averages considerably more than 12 percent in 1977–80, the achievement of these economic and social goals will have to be postponed beyond 1980, and the goals may not be achieved at all.

How shall we interpret these figures? It is important to distinguish between two separate economic phenomena. The first is the adequacy of savings, on a national basis, to support this level of investment. And the second is the ability of business to attract its share of total savings for risky investments.

THE ADEQUACY OF SAVINGS

Savings always end up equaling investment *after* the fact, and therefore some economists assert that there can never be a capital shortage. They tell us that our market system always provides the funds for projects that are really worth doing, and lets the rest go undone. The question, of course, is what we want to leave undone. What national objectives are we willing to forgo: full employment? environmental cleanup? greater energy independence? expansion of our basic industries? productivity improvement? restoring the cities? All of these objectives require increased business investment.

The balance of savings and investment is simply an accounting identity. It says nothing about the adequacy of investment to meet broad social goals. Moreover, the savings-investment identity must hold on an economy-wide basis. The government study of capital requirements did not take inventories and housing into account, but it is possible to make reasonable estimates of these in order to arrive at overall requirements for private investment.

Chart 8. Savings and investment as a percentage of GNP

	Historic 1965-1976	Future requirements 1977-1980
Total private investment	15.2%	18.4%
Business fixed investment	10.2	13.4
Residential construction	4.2	4.2
Inventories	0.8	0.8
Total savings	15.2	
Personal savings	5.5	?
Corporate retained earnings (less inventory profits)	2.0	?
Depreciation	8.5	?
Government budget deficits	-0.9	?
Other	0.1	

Sources: 1965–76—U.S. Department of Commerce; 1977–80—GE estimates using Council of Economic Advisers–Commerce Department study for business fixed investment. (Since real fixed investment averaged 9.3 percent of GNP in 1975 and 9.2 percent in 1976, its share of GNP would have to rise to 13.4 percent in 1977–80 in order to average 12.0 percent for 1975–80.)

On this basis, the overall private investment share of GNP would have to rise from the 15.2 percent of the past decade to a very high 18.4 percent during the 1977–80 period. Where will the savings come from to support this investment?

From individuals? Perhaps they will provide a few tenths of a percentage point more.

From government? Historically the government has been a net user and not a net producer of savings. It has run deficits, not budget surpluses, over the past ten years.

From business firms? Their contribution to overall savings depends heavily on tax law changes, such as higher investment tax credits and improvements in depreciation. Depreciation, incidentally, provides more than half of the savings in our national economy. In the presence of inflation and in the absence of improved capital recovery allowances, this critical source of savings is likely to shrink rather than rise as a share of GNP.

If savings fall short of investment, then something has to give to balance the equation. Some of our national goals will have to be postponed or sacrificed.

Even if there are somehow enough savings, will corporations be able to issue the volume of stocks and bonds necessary to finance our plant and equipment needs? Substantial light can be shed on this by putting the Commerce Department's plant and equipment requirements through a flow of funds model which also takes into account funds needed for inventories, cash, receivables, and other items.

ATTRACTING THE NECESSARY CAPITAL

Chart 9 projects the amount of capital that the nation's nonfinancial corporations will need per year in 1977–80 if business investment is to reach the required share of GNP. The chart utilizes the assumptions for real GNP growth, inflation, and profits recently outlined by the Congressional Budget Office as consistent with a return to full employment by 1980. About $341 billion a year will be required: $231 billion for structures and equipment; $16 billion for inventories; and $94 billion for financial and miscellaneous assets.

Assuming the continuation of the current (early 1977) tax laws—a 10 percent investment tax credit and historic cost depreciation—retained earnings will provide $52 billion a year and depreciation will provide $125 billion a year. *That leaves $164 billion a year to be raised through external financing.*

If we assume prudent financing and balance a dollar of new liabilities by a dollar of new equity (equity shares plus retained earnings),

**Chart 9. Uses and sources of funds:
Nonfinancial corporations—annual average,
1977–80 (billions of current dollars)**

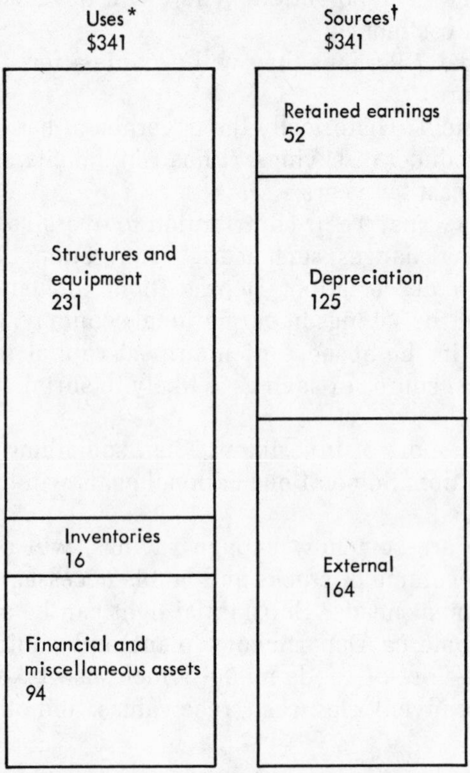

Uses* $341	Sources† $341

Uses*
$341

Structures and
equipment
231

Inventories
16

Financial and
miscellaneous assets
94

Sources†
$341

Retained earnings
52

Depreciation
125

External
164

* If business fixed investment is to average 13.4
percent of real GNP in 1977–80 to bring 1975–80
average to 12.0 percent.

† Assuming continuation of the 1975–76 corporate tax laws.

Source: GE estimates using Council of Eco-
nomic Advisers–Commerce Department study of
business fixed investment requirements and real
GNP; inflation and profits assumptions from the
Congressional Budget Office study, "Five-Year
Budget Projections: Fiscal Years 1978–82."

then corporations will have to float $56 billion a year in new equity
shares. This contrasts with the all-time record of $11.4 billion in 1971
and with the $10.1 billion raised in 1976.

From 1954 through 1967, corporations took on $1.25 of new liabil-
ities for each $1.00 of new equity. Since then, the ratio has averaged
nearly $5.00 in liabilities for each $1.00 in new equity, after phantom
inventory profits are removed. Business financial structures are al-

ready badly distorted by this plunge into debt. In the period ahead, unless there is significant change in the tax laws to permit better capital cost recovery and higher profit margins, corporations will face a very serious dilemma. Either they will have to flood the market with unprecedented volumes of new equity shares, or they will have to allow their balance sheets to deteriorate dramatically. Another conceivable alternative would be government financing of business capital requirements. But when the government becomes our source of capital, replacing voluntary savings and investment, that of course is the end of capitalism and private enterprise.

In these trying financial circumstances, business leaders will prudently restrain their investments—with all the consequences in terms of reduced economic activity, slower productivity gains, and chronic unemployment and inflation.

Yet the current Administration's targets for a balanced federal budget and full employment hinge critically on the existence of a strong, productive private sector. Strong private sector growth will come about only if steps are taken now to stimulate investment in new technology, new ventures, and new industrial plant and equipment.

IMPROVING THE CLIMATE FOR INVESTMENT

There have been many proposals for action from those who accept the seriousness of the capital formation problem—and I believe that they are in a majority among the leaders of thought and opinion. Some of these proposals have been quite utopian, looking to a drastic and revolutionary revision of our tax system. Such proposals deserve thoughtful study because we are dealing with a deep, long-term problem and cannot afford to think timidly about solutions. I hope that this book will stimulate further examination of the possibilities. But aside from the political problems involved in radical change, I think it would be wise to look before we leap. There may be unexpected side effects that would nullify the original intention, and just possibly overwhelm the world's most productive—and most intricately balanced—economic system.

To improve the climate for investment quickly—in time enough to help solve the problems facing our country in the years immediately ahead—we might take a few modest, politically practical steps.

First, we should try to restore some of the purchasing power that has been lost by both individuals and business firms in recent years.

Individual families are boosted, by inflation, into ever higher income tax brackets. The government is getting an unlegislated tax increase every year. That money should not be spent on new or expanded government programs. It should be returned to the working people who earned it, in the form of permanent individual tax cuts. There have been a number of federal tax reductions in the past three decades, under a variety of economic circumstances. In almost every case, there was only a one-year reduction of individual income tax revenues, usually less than the amount of the tax cut, and then revenues were higher than ever in the following year. This historic experience demonstrates that permanent tax reductions do in fact pay for themselves in terms of increased economic activity and higher incentives for investment.

But while permanent individual tax cuts are essential to offset the cumulative impact of past inflation and to defuse future inflation, excessive reliance on traditional Keynesian consumer-oriented programs and government spending programs will not produce a strong producer sector capable of sustained economic growth. Over time, these demand-oriented policies aggravate rather than solve our problems of inadequate capacity and productivity improvement.

Government policy must now see to it that the overall supply of savings is adequate, and also that a sufficient share of these savings is made available to the producer sector.

The most simple and direct route would be to reduce the corporate income tax rate—an approach that is at once equitable to businesses large and small, capital-intensive and labor-intensive, and in all parts of the country. Despite the political obstacles, this possibility must be addressed.

If populist pressures refuse to allow the much-needed reduction in corporate income taxes—which would result in a visible improvement in the aftertax profits of industry—then at least there should be an improvement in capital-cost recovery allowances. The effective tax rate of industry has been increased by the effects of underdepreciation. (See Chapter 2.) This overpayment of taxes should be returned to the businesses that earned it rather than provide an annual windfall for the federal government. Congress should legislate a capital-cost recovery program which will allow producers to adjust their depreciation or capital allowances to compensate for the ravages of inflation. This has already been done for inventories by allowing Lifo accounting, so why not also for capital-cost recovery?

Another step is to eliminate the bias against new equity by making dividends deductible to the corporations, just as interest is deductible today. Like the capital-cost recovery program, this would have to be phased in to minimize the immediate revenue impact; but it would have a powerful effect in stimulating our equity markets, and would bring the debt-equity ratios of American business back into a much more healthy balance.

Other changes are needed. We should have more rapid cost recovery for government-mandated pollution control expenditures. The threat of economic controls, a source of great uncertainty in investment decisions, should be convincingly removed. Regulatory bodies should concentrate on ways to accelerate, not slow down, the use of new technology. Environmental red tape and litigation, which is adding years of delay and mountains of cost to virtually all new plant construction, especially in the energy field, must be decisively reduced. Inflation—the greatest single source of business and consumer uncertainty—must be brought under control at its primary source, which is excessive government spending.

But most important of all is the will to address this challenge of capital formation. The problems that require increased business investment—unemployment, inflation, energy, the environment, international competition, cities in trouble—these problems are here now, and we cannot forever postpone the changes that will improve the climate for investment.

For too long, the nations of the West have been eating their seed corn. Now it is time to replenish our stock of capital, build up our productive resources, and take thought for the morrow.

If our leaders have the courage to ask this of the people, I am sure that the people will respond with a fervent and resounding "Yes!"

Chapter 2

DEPRECIATION POLICY AND CAPITAL FORMATION

*George Terborgh**

Capital goods live out their mortal span in an atmosphere of combat, a struggle for life as bitter, as intolerant of weakness, as the tooth and claw of biological competition. In principle, this mechanical warfare surpasses in depravity the carnage of the jungle: the beasts respect their own kind, but machines destroy their own species along with others. In principle also, mechanical combat is the more dynamic. The denizens of the jungle enjoy a limited security by reason of the stability and continuity of the species that prey upon them. Machines, on the contrary, must defend themselves in a world where new predators spring up overnight.

There is another contrast between biological and mechanical competition. In the former, death strikes suddenly, by violence; in the latter, it usually comes by degrees, through a process known as functional degradation. It is a kind of progressive larceny, by which the ever-changing competitors of an existing machine rob it of its function, forcing it bit by bit into lower grade and less valuable service, until there remains at last nothing it can do to justify further existence. In the bloodless warfare of machines, death terminates a gradual decline.

What has this to do with the subject of depreciation policy? A good deal, as we shall see. For a recognition of the phenomenon of functional degradation is essential to the determination of a rational pattern or schedule for the distribution of depreciation charges over asset lives. We may add that the failure to recognize functional degradation is responsible for a significant part of the massive underdepreciation that afflicts the U.S. economy today.

---

* Consultant, Machinery and Allied Products Institute.

A word on the sequence of the discussion, which falls into four main divisions. We first address the subject just mentioned, underdepreciation from the use of retarded write-off patterns. We consider next the even more important shortfall arising from the effect of inflation. Thereafter we explore the combined effect of both types of underdepreciation on capital formation. Finally we offer some observations on undercosting in general.

UNDERDEPRECIATION FROM RETARDED WRITE-OFFS

Since the determination of the depreciation write-off method for *book* (as distinguished from *tax*) purposes has been in the hands of the accounting profession, it is appropriate to begin by considering its views on the subject.

The accountants' solution

To the accountant, depreciation is the amortization of a prepaid cost. It is a process of *allocation*. But what is the criterion of the pattern, or time-contour, of the allocation? Here the prescription is vague. We are regaled with a string of adjectives. The system must be "orderly," "systematic," "regular," "consistent," and so on. No one can rightly question the importance of orderliness and consistency, but it is possible to devise a whole series of write-off procedures, embodying widely different patterns of time distribution, all of them satisfying these requirements. Are those procedures therefore equally acceptable? By no means.

The fact is that the customary adjectives provide no real guide to the allocation pattern. Granted that the cost must be "absorbed" or "charged" in full over the period of service, how should the write-off be distributed? How is cost "exhausted"? In what fashion does it "expire"? So far as the inherent logic of this approach is concerned, these questions find no rational answer; indeed the discussion sometimes comes perilously close to the circularity that cost expires at the rate at which it is charged off. Something more is required to provide a rational answer.

Value erosion versus cost amortization

If the accounting profession had been accustomed to thinking in terms of *value erosion* instead of *cost amortization*, we suspect that something more definite than a string of adjectives would have emerged as the criterion of the write-off pattern.

Obviously, it is not the incurment of a cost that justifies the capital-ization and subsequent depreciation of an asset; it is the existence of the value acquired through the outlay. If there is no such value, there is nothing to capitalize and depreciate; if, on the other hand, valuable assets are acquired without the incurment of cost, an allowance for their depreciation is no less appropriate for that reason. The value, not the cost, is the real measure of the amount depreciable.

In the overwhelming majority of cases, of course, cost is a practi-cally satisfactory measure of the value of assets at the time of acqui-sition, and this fact, added to the obvious availability and convenience of the measure, has made cost an almost universal depreciation base for purchased assets. This should not obscure the fact, however, that cost serves in this capacity as a convenient *equivalent* of initial value, and as a substitute for it. The amortization of cost, by the same token, is really a substitute for the amortization of value.

With the erosion-of-value approach, there *is* a guide to the alloca-tion pattern. It is the movement of capital values over the service lives of the assets concerned. In shaping the pattern by reference to this movement, we are merely applying to portions of the service life the same measure of depreciation applied to the asset life as a whole. For when cost is taken as an indication of acquisition value, the excess of cost over terminal salvage, universally accepted as the lifetime de-preciation, becomes the lifetime loss of value. *If loss of value is the appropriate measure for the entirety, it is logically appropriate for the parts.*[1]

Specific versus generalized write-offs

In suggesting this approach, we do not imply an item-by-item cal-culation. As a practical matter, it is perfectly obvious that the alloca-tion method cannot reflect changes in the value of particular assets. The decline of value in individual cases is likely to be jerky and un-even, and the periodic appraisals that would be required to trace it are out of the question. Even if they were feasible, however, we should still adhere to standard write-offs for accounting purposes.

The need for orderliness in accounting procedures may be con-ceded, and conceded gladly, without espousing the conclusion that the standard allocation method should *disregard* value movements. It is perfectly possible to have a write-off procedure that is systematic and consistent, and that nevertheless reflects in its general contour and time distribution the typical or representative pattern of declining value. *It can represent, in other words, a generalized projection of value erosion.*

What is a good pattern?

What is the typical course of value erosion over the service lives of capital assets? It should hardly be necessary to say that if we had the data to answer this question we would find different patterns for different types of assets, depending on their physical characteristics, the length of the service life, the trend of operating costs with age, the tempo of obsolescence, and other factors. A standard pattern must aim at the *average*. What should its contour be?

Here we are brought back to the observations at the beginning of this chapter. If the services of a capital asset decline in value with increasing age, it stands to reason that the most valuable services are used up first. Therefore, the erosion of capital value (the discounted amount of the remaining services) is *more rapid* in the early years than in the later years. In other words, the erosion pattern is accelerated, or front-loaded.

Space limitations preclude a theoretical analysis of this phenomenon, which we have presented elsewhere.[2] Suffice it to say that if we assume a continuous decline in service values from the starting level to zero at the end of the asset life, the erosion of capital value during the first *half* of the asset life is around *two thirds* (somewhat more for short-lived assets, somewhat less for long-lived). By the evidence of resale markets, it is even greater for freely interchangeable capital equipment, whose typical erosion at half-life (adjusted for inflation) is around *three quarters*.[3]

There are two standard depreciation methods that yield first-half write-offs in this range: the double-declining-balance method recovers about two thirds of cost over the interval; the sum-of-digits method, about three quarters. Either method is acceptable so far as we are concerned, but to avoid even the suspicion of exaggeration, we propose to deal exclusively with the more conservative double-declining-balance write-off.

Comparison with straight-line

The bulk of the depreciation charged by U.S. industry for book, or financial accounting, purposes—as distinguished from income tax accounting—is taken by the straight-line method. (A recent survey shows that more than 70 percent of large corporations use it.)[4] This is a traditional device, dating at least as far back as ancient Rome. It has only one real virtue: simplicity and ease of application. That, and that alone, is its rationale. Unfortunately, in general it understates the true erosion of value.

According to Department of Commerce estimates, nonfinancial corporations would be accruing currently about 12 percent more depreciation based on historical cost by the double-declining-balance method than by the straight-line method—assuming each method to be used *exclusively*.[5] Since in practice straight-line is not used exclusively (a minor portion of the book accrual being by accelerated methods), it is a reasonable guess that double-declining-balance would yield 10 percent over present *actuals,* an addition of $7 *billion* a year.

UNDERDEPRECIATION FROM INFLATION

This, as noted, is the underdepreciation of the nonfinancial corporate system by the use of the straight-line method rather than the double-declining-balance method, on the assumption that the asset is valued at historical cost. But underdepreciation from this cause is relatively minor compared with the shortfall of the accelerated (double-declining-balance) accrual itself by reason of *inflation.* Here we are dealing with something like $32 *billion* a year.[6]

The general problem

The impact of inflation on depreciation charges is no different in principle from its impact on other operating costs, and a word on the general problem may be in order before we consider depreciation specifically.

The basic reason for inflation adjustment is the *time difference* between (1) cost incurment and (2) cost recovery. If all costs were recovered at the time of incurment, no inflation adjustment would be required. But it is the nature of business operations that there is a lag between the two. This lag, which we may refer to as "cost lead time," varies all over the map, ranging from years (fixed assets) to months or weeks (inventories). But whatever the *duration* of the lag, the dollar shrinks over the interval, so that the dollars recovered through sales are always *smaller* in value than the dollars in which the costs were incurred.

It is obvious that the matching of *unlike* dollars yields distorted and deceptive results. Only when costs and revenues are measured in the *same* dollars can the difference between them (profit or loss) be meaningfully determined. To get such dollars on both sides of the comparison, it is necessary either to convert the dollars of one side into those of the other or to restate both in terms of some common dollar differing from either. Since the first course is clearly simpler, involving only one conversion, we shall restate depreciation costs *at their equivalent in the dollars of recovery.*[7]

The depreciation problem

Under historical-cost accounting, depreciation simply recovers the number of dollars originally committed to the asset, regardless of differences in their purchasing power. This recovery is satisfactory (given a proper write-off method) in a period of general stability in the price level, but it can be ruinously inadequate during and after a period of inflation. If a company invests 100-cent dollars and later recovers only an equal number of 50-cent dollars, it has lost half its real capital, whatever the books may show.

To protect this capital, the company must recover each year a sufficient number of *current* dollars to equal the year's capital consumption measured in *original* dollars. This number of current dollars is necessary, given the time distribution of capital consumption and the price changes that have occurred, to recover a purchasing power equal (at the time of recovery) to the amount originally invested. Superficially this looks like overdepreciation, but it is not. *It yields a result in real terms comparable with that accomplished by the recovery of original cost in a period of stable prices.*

The technique of adjusting depreciation for inflation is not particularly difficult unless a multiplicity of price indexes is employed in the conversion process. The operation requires a breakdown of the depreciable property account into year-of-origin, or "vintage," subgroups. The *historical-cost* accrual for the current period on each of these subgroups is then restated at its *current-cost* equivalent, the sum of the restated amounts being the adjusted depreciation desired.

EFFECT ON CAPITAL FORMATION

In 1976, as we have just seen, nonfinancial corporations underdepreciated their fixed assets *on their books of account* by a total of roughly $39 billion—$7 billion being attributable to a retarded write-off of historical cost, $32 billion to the effect of inflation.

What is the significance of this $39 billion underpreciation? It means, of course, that these corporations *understated* their costs and *overstated* their profits by this amount. To put it otherwise, they reported capital consumption—more precisely, the amount required to offset or restore it—as profit. This much of their alleged profit was, of course, pure illusion. It follows that the companies reporting it were kidding both themselves and the public.

What were the consequences of this Alice-in-Wonderland accounting? (1) Nonfinancial corporations paid out more in dividends than they would have if their profit had been correctly stated. (2) Their true retained earnings were *lower* than reported. (3) They underpriced their products because of the understatement of their costs.

The implications for capital formation are clear. Since *real* retained earnings have been lower than reported by the amount of underdepreciation, the corporate system has been forced to finance in the capital market an unprecedented proportion of its capacity expansion costs. The result has been rising debt ratios and impaired liquidity. Obviously, a continuance of this trend is bound to run into increased resistance as time goes on, and unless something is done to make more internal funds available, the growth of productive capacity will suffer, with grave consequences for the entire economy.

What can be done?

We referred a moment ago to the *underpricing* of corporate products, and the corresponding *overstatement* of profit, by reason of the undercosting of depreciation. It is obvious that taking full current-cost depreciation would drastically reduce reported profit margins. What can management do to restore them?

It is acknowledged that charging full current-cost depreciation may be impracticable for an individual company in a market where the competition is pricing on understated costs. The real remedy lies in the reform of policy *across the board*. If all competitors are targeting their prices on restated costs, there is a better chance that they can make the prices stick.

We have no doubt that the charging of realistic current-cost depreciation would, if generalized, expand substantially the revenue of the corporate system (the aftertax gain being roughly half of the amount added). Whether that revenue would rise (after the necessary adjustment period) by the nearly $78 billion required to restore real profit to the unadjusted level is anybody's guess, but if it *did*, the corporate system would have an aftertax cash flow larger by $39 billion than it now has.[8]

Even if this cash flow were augmented by only half or two thirds of this amount, the implications for capital formation are obvious. The availability of internal funds is a major, if not a predominant, factor in capital expenditure decisions, particularly among smaller enterprises, and an expansion of such funds cannot fail to have a stimulative effect.

Supposing tax allowability

The foregoing observations assume that income tax depreciation is unaffected by the change in book depreciation. What if it were changed also?

In 1976, the tax depreciation of nonfinancial corporations was about $92 billion, against an estimated $73 billion of book depreciation.[9] But even the tax allowance fell $20 billion short of the $112 billion estimated for the current-cost double-declining-balance accrual. If these corporations were to eliminate the $39 billion shortfall in their book depreciation by taking the full $112 billion, and if this amount were allowable for tax purposes as well, they would obviously get $20 billion more in deductions. This would enhance their aftertax cash flow by $10 billion *in addition to* whatever gains resulted from the effect of the higher costing on product prices and revenue. Whether these gains would be as large with tax allowability as with a continuance of the present system is a speculative question to which there is no good answer. The gains might be somewhat smaller. It seems likely, however, that the *combination* of these gains and the $10 billion tax saving would exceed the gains achieved in the absence of an increased tax allowance.

UNDERCOSTING IN GENERAL

Thus far we have concentrated exclusively on the undercosting of fixed-asset consumption, or depreciation. Most of this undercosting, as we have seen, is the result of inflation. Undercosting from this source is not limited to depreciation, however; it applies to *inventory consumption* (the cost of sales) as well as to the consumption of costs *not* charged to inventory, commonly referred to as "expense."

For nonfinancial corporations, the Department of Commerce estimates that in 1976 the undercosting of inventory consumption due to inflation was $15 billion. Added to the $39 billion of book underdepreciation, this gives a total undercosting of *$54 billion*. But even this total is not complete, because it leaves out of account uninventoried costs charged to expense. For nonfinancial corporations these costs run around 25–30 percent of total costs. These uninventoried costs also have a substantial average "lead time," which calls for inflation adjustment, but no one has figured out how to make the adjustment, and we shall deal therefore with the correction for fixed-asset and inventory consumption only—the $54 billion just mentioned.[10]

What does this amount to in relation to the reported profit of nonfinancial corporations? Unfortunately for our purpose, there is no comprehensive compilation of their *book* profit, but only of their *tax* profit.

On the latter basis, the Department of Commerce figure for 1976 shows an aftertax profit of $72 billion. The book counterpart of this figure was higher by at least the $19 billion difference between the tax and the book depreciation ($92 billion − $72 billion), giving $91 billion.[11] Subtracting the undercosting of $54 billion, we have a *real* profit of $37 billion.[12] This is only 41 percent of the amount reported. The rest was capital consumption masquerading as profit.

CONCLUSION

Let us add in closing that the present situation is bad not only for business, but for the nation as a whole. Despite the suspicion and disfavor that attach to "profits" in the eyes of many politicians and of a considerable part of the public, it is vital that profits be large enough not only to motivate the expansion of productive investment, but to finance a substantial part of it. It is frightening from the public policy standpoint that the reinvestment of corporate earnings, realistically measured, has become negligible.[13] If this continues it will cost the country dearly in jobs and economic well-being.

Let us add further that the weird accounting of costs and profits that now passes for orthodoxy is a problem not only for business management, but for the accounting profession, the regulatory agencies of the government, and not least, for the tax authorities. It is high time for concerted action by all concerned.

It is gratifying in this connection that the accounting profession appears at last to be grappling with the problem, though nothing definitive has issued as yet. The Securities and Exchange Commission is requiring large companies to file supplemental statements on the current-cost inventory and fixed-asset consumption. There is much activity on the subject among accounting bodies abroad, and in several countries by government commissions.

These are first steps, to be sure, but we may hope that others will follow. We may hope also, and even more fervently, that the tax authorities will not be far behind. For the evils of undercosting are compounded by the present practice of taxing capital consumption as income. No reform of costing procedures can be more than partially successful so long as this practice continues.[14]

NOTES

1. The reference here is to loss of value *in the dollars of investment*. The effect of inflation on the calculation will be considered later.
2. George Terborgh, *Realistic Depreciation Policy* (Machinery and Allied Products Institute, 1954), chap. 4.

3. Ibid., chap. 5.
4. American Institute of Certified Public Accountants, *Accounting Trends and Techniques* (New York: AICPA, 1975), p. 287.
5. The Department of Commerce declining-balance estimates assume a remaining life straight-line switch at the point of advantage.
6. Department of Commerce 1976 estimates for nonfinancial corporations place *current-cost* double-declining-balance depreciation at $112 billion, against $80 billion for the *historical-cost* accrual by the same method.
7. Reference to the "dollars of recovery" may seem to imply restatement by an index of the *general* purchasing power of money. Although we prefer this approach, others favor a multiplicity of indexes reflecting the prices of the *specific* items or groups subject to restatement. This is the approach used in the Department of Commerce depreciation conversions, and since we are using the estimates of the Department of Commerce we shall refer hereafter to "current-cost" depreciation rather than to "current-dollar" depreciation. Fortunately the overall results of the two approaches are not far different. For a discussion of the indexation issue, see *Realistic Depreciation Policy*, chap. 2.
8. If the revenue of the corporate system fell short of a full restoration, there would be a minor compensatory effect in the restraint on dividend payments resulting from the reduction in reported profit. To this extent the gain in *retained* cash flow would exceed the gain in the total.
9. The latter figure represents our adjustment of the Department of Commerce estimate for historical-cost straight-line depreciation, which is $71 billion. As noted earlier, a minor portion of book depreciation is taken by accelerated methods—hence the increase over the straight-line figure.

    The reason for the excess of tax over book depreciation is not far to seek. Although both are based on historical cost, the bulk of tax depreciation is taken by accelerated methods, the bulk of book depreciation by straight-line. Moreover, tax service lives are generally much shorter than book, owing to the use of "guideline" lives and the "asset depreciation range" system.
10. Practice differs widely with regard to the accounting treatment of depreciation, some companies charging it into cost of sales, others treating it as expense. Overall figures on the relative prevalence of the two procedures are not available. To the extent that depreciation is included in cost of sales, there is some duplication. But even if *all* of it were so charged, it would make up only 5 or 6 percent of inventory consumption, and the maximum duplication would therefore be this percentage of the inflation adjustment (in the present case, $15 billion), a relatively insignificant amount.
11. The Internal Revenue Service has made tabulations of the book profit of *all* corporations from time to time, but the results vary so erratically in relation to tax profit that they are questionable.
12. It is interesting to note that this reckoning comes close to the $26 billion derived from the restatement of tax accounting profit. See George Terborgh, *Inflation and Profits* (Machinery and Allied Products Institute, 1976).
13. Of the estimated $37 billion of real profit earned by nonfinancial corporations in 1976, $32 billion was paid out as dividends, leaving a real reinvestment of $5 billion.
14. See George Terborgh, *Inflation and the Taxation of Business Income* (Machinery and Allied Products Institute, 1976).

Chapter 3

THE NEED TO STRENGTHEN CORPORATE CREDIT

*John A. Brenner**

The need to expand plant and to add to, and improve, equipment has over the years been one of the main reasons for steadily growing corporate debt. The upward trend in corporate borrowing has taken a worrisome turn due to a combination of ever-greater purchases of physical assets and a concomitant slower growth of internally generated funds. Over the past decade, it has become increasingly apparent that American corporations are growing less able to meet their capital requirements from retained earnings and other internally generated funds. This deficiency of funds soared from $1.1 billion as recently as 1964 to $57 billion in 1974. A notable exception, a surplus of $7.6 billion, was recorded in 1975, primarily because of a recession-related cutback in capital spending. However, in 1976, a resumption of capital spending resulted in a deficiency of funds amounting to $15.8 billion.

One result of these developments was a dramatic climb of net corporate debt to a total of $1.4 trillion during the decade through 1976. Net corporate debt, which comprises total debt other than that owed to affiliates, grew at an average annual rate of 10.9 percent over that period. At the same time, the nation's output of goods and services advanced at a rate of only 6.4 percent.

In view of these trends and the likely continuance of inflation-induced increases in replacement costs of plant and equipment, total net corporate debt will probably continue to accumulate. An absence of new tax incentives or of laws designed to encourage the buildup of additional equity should further increase the dependence on debt.

Corporations, therefore, must be able to obtain long-term financing

---

* President, Moody's Investors Service, Inc.

Chart 1. Corporate financing needs

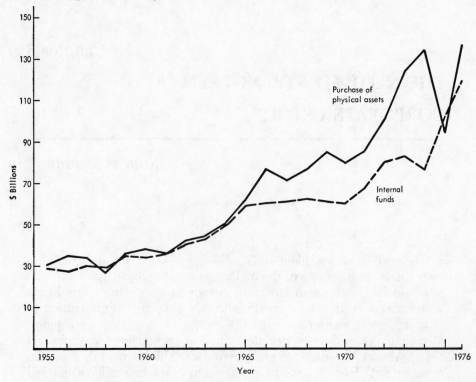

Source: Board of Governors of the Federal Reserve System, *Flow of Funds Accounts*, August 1973, pp. 16–17; February 1977, pp. 8–9; May 1977, p. 11.

in order to modernize and expand plant facilities. To do this they must maintain credit structures capable of supporting their debt-service requirements. When the demand for funds exceeds the supply, interest rates rise. At such times, borrowers with strong financial credentials have access to the capital markets, whereas weaker credit risks have to pay significantly more for borrowed funds and may even find it economically unfeasible to borrow, as has happened in recent years.

Among the major components of a strong financial structure are a company's cash flow and its equity base, that is, retained earnings, common capitalization, and surplus. Financially strong companies are able to maintain a balance between debt and equity by reinvesting earnings and, occasionally, by selling common or preferred stock. However, inflation as well as a lack of business and investor confidence causes

Chart 2.   Corporate debt

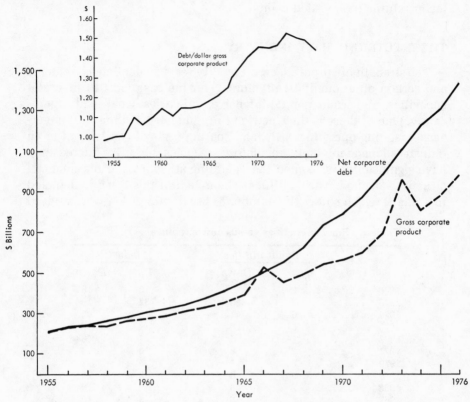

Source: United States Department of Commerce, *Survey of Current Business*, vol. 56, no. 1, part 2 (January 1976), pp. 24–25; vol. 57, no. 8 [August 1977], pp. 11–12.

occasional weakness in the equity markets. Thus, in recent years companies have been hesitant to sell stock and, in far too many cases, have turned to the debt market.

In the bond rating process, rating agencies scrutinize a number of key financial measurements.[1] Total long-term debt as a percentage of total capitalization is a key measure of the degree of financial leverage. Should debt build up faster than the equity base, debt leverage is increased and the strength of a company's credit weakens. Accumulating debt forces a larger portion of earnings to be allocated to debt service. At the same time, pre-tax coverage of interest charges may deteriorate.[2] There has, in fact, been just such a deterioration in the strength of key financial measurements of the capital-intensive industries as a result of the accumulation of debt, higher interest rates, and lower returns on invested capital.[3]

THE ELECTRIC UTILITY INDUSTRY

The strength of corporate credit quality rests on debt measurements and certain other qualitative factors. Over the past decade, the credit capacities of certain capital-intensive industries weakened significantly. One of these is the electric utility industry. Falling debt coverage, escalating operating costs, and soaring costs of capital—all in an industry dependent upon regulatory agencies for price increases—have significantly weakened the operating statistics and the financial structures of the electric utilities. The extent of this trend is depicted in Table 1, which shows the number of bond ratings that were revised

Table 1. Bond upgradings versus downgradings

	Public utilities		Industrials	
	Up	Down	Up	Down
1976	2	10	12	18
1975	7	16	32	19
1974	6	41	13	22
1973	5	3	14	19
1972	1	5	17	8
1971	2	6	10	14
1970	6	7	5	11
1969	5	8	12	8
1968	2	6	12	8
1967	5	0	3	10
Total	41	102	130	137

Source: "Issuer Statistics on Rating Changes," mimeographed paper (New York: Moody's Investors Service, Inc., 1967–76).

by Moody's during the past ten years. The table shows that Moody's lowered 102 ratings in the public utility sector, whereas it raised only 41. In 1974 and 1975, Moody's lowered ratings on the bonds of 43 electric utility companies, or about 25 percent of all the electric utilities it rated.

In many cases, electric company earnings have been eroded by restrictive regulation. In those situations, the companies have undertaken capital spending far in excess of their available internally generated funds in order to meet service demands. The restrictions that have prevented the utilities from raising prices to reflect their higher expenses, have led to a shortage of cash relative to construction outlays.[4] This is evidenced by the historical ratio of retained cash flow as

Chart 3. Electric utilities' construction expenditures and financings (includes refundings)

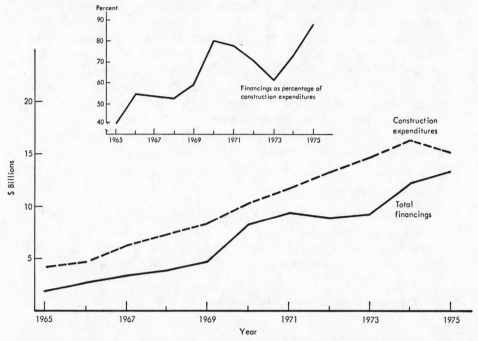

Sources: Edison Electric Institute, Inc., *Statistical Year Book of the Electric Utilities Industry* (annual); Ebasco Services, Inc., *Analysis of Public Utility Financing* (annual).

a percentage of construction expenditures.[5] After climbing sharply to 60 percent in 1963, this ratio declined steadily to less than 25 percent in 1971. Some improvement has occurred since, but it has been far from adequate. The trend clearly shows the need for more realistic regulation which would permit the generation of an increase in internal cash flow required to meet spending objectives.

As the percentage of capital additions funded internally has decreased, the utilities have had to increase their use of external debt. The rapid increase in dollar outlays for construction expenditures has been primarily the result of inflation, new requirements for pollution control equipment, and the greater costs of new types of generating plants. Chart 3 shows the relationship between construction expenditures and external financings of investor-owned electric utilities over the last decade. It is obvious that relatively low internal cash generation is at the heart of this industry's problem.

Over the past decade, reliance on outstanding financing (including refundings) for construction surged dramatically, from 40 percent to

88 percent of total expenditures. Although the dollar amount of corporate long-term borrowing increased, it decreased as a percentage of total external financings. This was mainly because utility companies were able to obtain funds by selling equity and issuing short-term debt. The more frequent use of the equity market as a source of capital has been a favorable development. However, a number of companies were obliged to sell new common stock below book value in endeavoring to restore an adequate debt-to-equity relationship. External financing requirements are expected to remain relatively high, since internally generated funds seem likely to continue to be inadequate to finance capital programs.

The cost of borrowing

External financing, particularly via long-term debt, has been an increasingly expensive way for the utility industry to raise money. The cost of borrowing rose rapidly in the past ten years, as is clearly shown by Moody's Composite Average of Yields on Newly Issued Public Util-

Chart 4. Electric utilities' coverage of interest charges

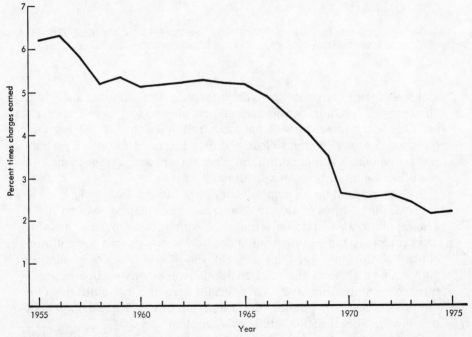

Source: "Selected Statistics on Moody's 24 Electric Utilities," *Moody's Public Utility Manual,* 1976 ed. (New York: Moody's Investors Service, Inc., 1976), Special Features Section, pp. a12–13.

ity Bonds,[6] which was just 5.59 percent in 1966 and peaked at 9.81 percent in 1975. Needless to say, the compounded effect of having to borrow more funds at higher interest costs had an adverse impact on income. In the absence of appropriate rate relief from regulatory agencies, this resulted in a steady deterioration of key operating measurements. A significant statistic that highlights this trend is the coverage of interest expense. As depicted in Chart 4, the interest coverage of Moody's 24 electric utilities, which was 6.34 times in 1955, narrowed steadily to 2.75 times by 1976.

This precipitous decline was a major consideration in the numerous downgradings of utility company bonds in recent years. Further indications of weaker measurements have been a long-term decline in pre-tax return on invested capital and in retained cash flow as a percentage of debt.

It should be clearly understood that bond ratings are not based solely on financial measurements and are not tied to specific statistical guidelines. Financial measurements present a quantitative picture of the financial strength of a company. The correlation between bond ratings and debt measurements varies from company to company, depending on the results of a detailed analysis of absolute and relative risks. The need to improve the credit status of the utility companies is manifest. The ability of these companies to generate substantially more funds is essential if their equity bases are to be strengthened and their debt measurements reinforced. Recognizing the clear-cut public interest in a financially viable utility industry, the U.S. Supreme Court emphasized that

> ... it is important that there be enough revenues not only for operating expenses but also for capital costs of the business. These include service on the debt and dividends on the stock. . . . By that standard the return to the equity owner should be commensurate with risks on investments in other enterprises having corresponding risks. That return, moreover, should be sufficient to assure confidence in the financial integrity of the enterprise, so as to maintain its credit and to attract capital.[7]

Future requirements

According to one estimate, the electric utilities will have to spend about $750 billion over the next 15 years merely to accommodate the power needs of our economy, assuming a 3 ½ percent average annual growth in GNP and an inflation rate of around 4 percent or 5 percent a year. Dependence on the capital markets will continue, and that will keep long-term debt at high levels. And the already substantial debt

38

service requirements will increase should older, lower coupon debt be refunded at higher interest rates. Table 2 illustrates the refunding vol-

Table 2.   Debt refundings for total utility industry ($000)

Year	Principal amount as of 12/31/75	Actual interest require- ments	Potential interest require- ments at 8 percent	Interest cost differ- ential
1976	$ 1,521,561	$ 84,916	$ 121,725	$ 36,809
1977	1,672,863	80,833	133,829	52,809
1978	1,566,088	71,439	125,287	53,834
1979	2,818,053	175,975	225,444	49,462
1980	2,171,261	128,088	173,701	45,613
1981	2,548,100	186,920	203,848	16,928
1982	4,519,700	322,650	361,576	38,926
1983	3,521,200	260,812	281,696	20,884
1984	2,745,800	146,107	219,664	73,557
1985	2,782,100	178,745	222,568	43,823
Total	$25,866,726	$1,636,485	$2,069,338	$432,832

Source: *Electric Utility Bond and Preferred Stock Rating*, pamphlet (New York: Moody's Investors Service, Inc., 1976), p. 9.

ume over the next ten years of publicly held debt rated Ba or higher outstanding at the end of 1975. For the purpose of estimating interest cost requirements, an 8 percent interest rate has been assumed.

The actual interest requirement figures are based on outstanding debt without refunding. The interest cost differential figures illustrate the increased debt-service requirement as older debt is refunded at the assumed rate. Unless operating revenues improve relative to the expected rise in interest expenses, there will eventually be further downward pressure on the coverage ratios, which, as we have already seen, have shrunk substantially over the past 20 years.

The sale of equity

A favorable development during the past decade or so has been the ability and willingness of the electric utilities to sell additional equity. In 1965, sales of preferred and common stock totaled about $300 million. This figure has increased steadily since then, particularly during the 1970s, and in 1976 it jumped to $5.5 billion.

Sales of preferred and common stock as a percentage of total financings rose from 19.1 percent in 1965 to 41.5 percent in 1975. Electric utility companies sold a record $3.8 billion of new common stock in 1976, and they are expected to sell about $3.5 billion worth in 1977.

The resulting improvement in the industry equity ratio—to 35.5 percent from a low of 34.3 percent in 1974—is, of course, a credit-strengthening factor. Notwithstanding this improvement, the absolute dollar amount of debt is expected to continue its upward trend, given the immense future capital requirements of the electric utility industry. From a bond rating standpoint, higher rates of return must be allowed if the erosion of earnings protection is to be halted and the quality of debt maintained.

THE CAPITAL-INTENSIVE INDUSTRIALS

At this point, let us turn from the regulated sector and examine the credit strength of corporations in the nonregulated industrial sector. Emphasized here are four major capital-intensive industries: steel, forest products, chemicals, and petroleum. Although the manufacturing processes and the products of these industries are admittedly different, all four industries must make impressive capital outlays simply to maintain effective operations. Corporations have been subject to some of the same economic influences as the electric utility industry. In the past 20 years these industries have steadily increased capital spending as their capital formation objectives grew. What is more, in recent years these industries have had their capital programs swollen by outlays for pollution control equipment as they have attempted to comply with environmental regulations. Corporate retained cash flow has been insufficient to meet these very substantial capital requirements. Consequently, long-term debt has been used more and more as a source of external financing. This trend became particularly evident in the last decade when severe inflation boosted both the replacement cost of plant and equipment and working capital requirements.

One effect on corporate capital structures in all four industries has been an increase of long-term debt as a percentage of total capitalization. And as with the electric utilities, there has been a significant increase in the cost of long-term debt. As measured by Moody's Composite Average of Yields on Newly Issued Industrial Bonds, the average yield on new industrial debt was 5.51 percent in 1966. Ten years later, in 1975, the figure had risen to 9.21 percent.[8] The increased resort to long-term borrowings plus the higher cost of those borrowed funds led to a general deterioration of interest charge coverage in the capital-intensive industries.

This higher leverage stands in sharp contrast to the post-war period of unusually high liquidity and low debt levels. This provided considerable excess debt capacity, enabling borrowings to go on without impinging on debt ratings. Now, with much of that capacity reduced, a continuation of the trend may place certain ratings in tenuous positions—particularly for those companies whose competitive positions have been adversely affected.

Financial trends

In Charts 5 and 6, we can see the composite trend of long-term debt as coverage of interest charges and a percentage of total capitalization for 20 capital-intensive industrial companies.[9] The most rapid escalation to higher debt levels took place in the last ten years, as the need for capital funds increased in step with the multiplying costs for new

Chart 5.   Composite industrials' coverage of interest charges

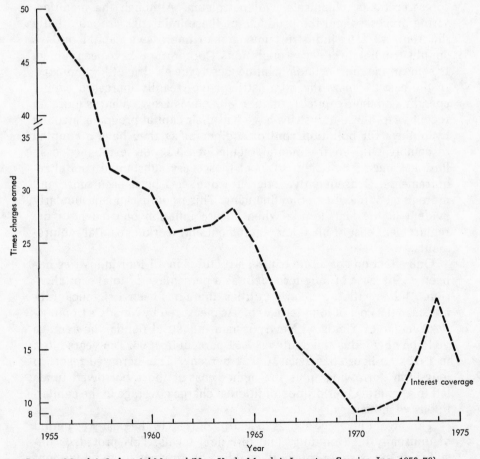

Source: *Moody's Industrial Manual* (New York: Moody's Investors Service, Inc., 1956–76).

Chart 6.   Composite industrials' long-term debt as a percentage of total capitalization

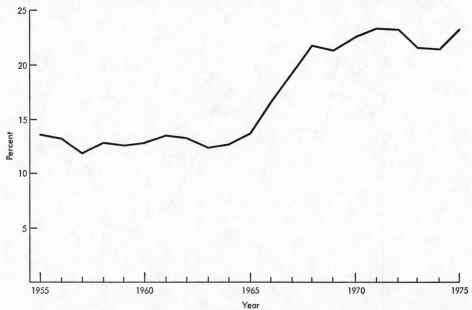

Source: *Moody's Industrial Manual* (New York: Moody's Investors Service Inc., 1956–76).

plant.[10] Except for a moderate rebound in the 1970s, interest coverage has declined steadily for the past 20 years, closely paralleling the increases in debt and in the cost of borrowed funds. As a result of the accumulation of debt, retained cash flow relative to long-term debt has trended downward, as shown in Chart 7.

The composite trend, as the charts illustrate, depicts the long-term overall direction that the capital-intensive industries have taken. However, individual trends have varied as diverse factors influenced debt measurements and asset strengths of particular industries. This becomes evident when one examines the long-term trends of key financial measurements in each industry.

The most severe deterioration in financial measurements has taken place in the forest products and steel industries; the chemicals industry has suffered a relatively moderate decline; and the petroleum industry has actually been able to improve its return on invested capital in recent years. But all four industries show a secular decline in retained cash flow support of long-term debt and coverage of interest charges, and a rise in debt as a percentage of total capitalization.

These trends have been tied to the greater use of external financing to raise capital. The dollar figures for capital additions have been ris-

Chart 7. Composite industrials' retained cash flow as a percentage of long-term debt

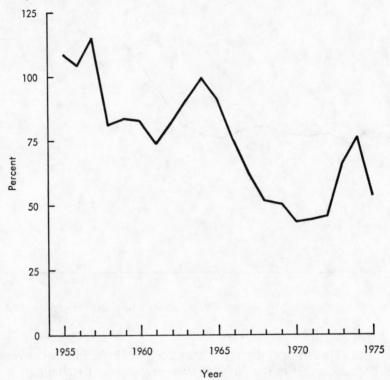

Source: *Moody's Industrial Manual* (New York: Moody's Investors Service, Inc., 1956–76).

ing for 20 years for all but the steel industry, in which such spending has fluctuated. With the exception of the petroleum industry, product price increases have generally failed to offset higher costs for new plant and equipment. This trend has led to a serious drop in the return on newly invested capital, and until that changes there will continue to be a lack of incentive for major corporate expansion.

Evaluation of credit strength

Despite the foregoing statistical trends in the four industries under examination, over the past ten years more bond ratings were raised than were lowered in all but the steel industry. This can be traced to the evaluation process, which must take into account a constantly evolving economy. In the past ten years or more, a higher level of debt reduced the excess debt capacity of the past. Considering the basic earning power and the asset bases of the major corporations in these areas, the ensuing accumulations of debt have been deemed acceptable. In view of the very low levels from which it started, this has been particularly true for those low-cost producers that are able to pass cost increases along to the consumer and still hold strong, competitive market positions. However, producers with less financial and market strength that have fully utilized their debt capacities are likely to suffer a deterioration of creditworthiness if they keep adding to their long-term debt. Many have little leeway for more debt given current returns.

The composition of the asset base and current position are major qualitative considerations in the rating process. For example, the value of the petroleum industry's oil and gas reserves has increased substantially, and the vast timber holdings of the forest products industry are the only major natural resource that is regenerative. The true value of these assets, which are carried on the balance sheets at historic cost, tend to be understated in financial statements. Other qualitative factors, such as competitive position and the indispensability of the product line, must also be considered. Hence, when evaluating corporations whose qualitative attributes are essential to their long-term viability, it would not be appropriate to make a judgment strictly on the basis of statistics. Thus, despite negative trends, the quality of the debt of many companies, when viewed within the universe of outstanding ratings, has held up well. In some cases, it actually improved in recent years, particularly for those companies that were able to strengthen their competitive positions, and restructured their balance sheets.

CONCLUSION

At present, many capital-intensive companies continue to have good debt ratings. But future capital needs loom very large. Consequently, a continued buildup of long-term debt without a reinforcement of the equity base would undermine the credit strength of these companies. Higher returns on invested capital which would allow healthier cash flows are a prerequisite for stronger capital structures.

The achievement of that desirable goal will depend on more than effective corporate management. Success or failure will also be determined by factors outside the immediate corporate sphere. The government's direct influence on business has been and will continue to be a key element affecting the operating environment of corporations. Changes in government policy appear to be mandatory if some companies are to generate returns sufficient for effective capital and job formation without excessive use of funded debt.

The elimination of double taxation on corporate dividends would certainly encourage more equity financing, as would the elimination, or at least the diminution, of ultimately self-defeating taxes on capital gains. If we as a nation are truly intent upon capital and job formation, then it is time to reflect this purpose in our tax policies. Otherwise continued debt leveraging will surely weaken the credit standing of our corporations. To the extent that this occurs, bond ratings will have to be reevaluated.

The expansion of productive capacity to keep pace with the demands of the nation's growing economy is a goal common to the entire business community. To achieve that expansion, substantial capital outlays will be required on an ongoing basis. It is likely that funds from the capital markets will continue to finance a large portion of our country's corporate spending programs. Given the anticipated needs of business and the ever-changing economic environment, the strengthing of corporate credit must be recognized as an essential national economic goal.

NOTES

1. Moody's rating scale consists of nine rating categories: Aaa, Aa, A, Baa, Ba, B, Caa, Ca and C. Issues rated Aaa and Aa are considered high grade. A and Baa issues are classified medium grade. Issues that are rated Baa or higher are considered investment grade, whereas Ba and B ratings are reserved for speculative issues. Issues in the Caa to C range generally have a high probability of default on interest and principal payments or may already be in default.
2. Interest coverage is derived from earnings before interest and income taxes, net of minority interests and equity in earnings of unconsolidated subsidiaries, divided by interest charges on debt.
3. The pretax return on total capital is pretax income divided by total capitalization. For purposes of consistency, capitalization includes total long-term debt and equity, excluding minority interests, deferred income taxes, and short-term debt.
4. The financial measurements employed were derived from a composite of Moody's 24 Electric Utilities, consisting of the following companies of varying sizes and geographic areas:

Baltimore Gas & Electric Co.	Detroit Edison Co.
Boston Edison Co.	Florida Power Corp.
Carolina Power & Light Co.	Houston Lighting & Power Co.
Central Hudson Gas & Electric Corp.	Idaho Power Co.
Central Maine Power Co.	Indianapolis Power & Light Co.
Cincinnati Gas & Electric Co.	Northeast Utilities
Cleveland Electric Illuminating Co.	Pacific Gas & Electric Co.
Commonwealth Edison Co.	Pennsylvania Power & Light Co.
Consolidated Edison Co. (N.Y.)	Philadelphia Electric Co.
Dayton Power & Light Co.	Public Service Co. of Colorado
Delmarva Power & Light Co.	Southern California Edison Co.
	Tampa Electric
	Utah Power & Light Co.

The bond rating categories represented in this group range from Baa to Aaa.

5. Retained cash flow consists of earnings from continuing operations plus depreciation, depletion, and amortization, less dividends paid.

6. "Moody's Composite Average of Yields on Newly Issued Public Utility Bonds," *Moody's Public Utility Manual,* 1976 ed. (New York: Moody's Investors Service, Inc., 1976), Special Features Section, p. a3.

7. *FPC* v. *Hope Natural Gas Co., 320 U.S. 590,603 (1944).*

8. "Moody's Composite Average on Newly Issued Industrial Bonds," *Moody's Industrial Manual,* 1976 ed., vol. 1 (New York: Moody's Investors Service, Inc., 1976), Special Features Section, p. a34.

9. For the industrial sector, a set of composite debt measurement statistics was compiled from groups of five major corporations in each industry as follows:

Steel	*Forest Products*
U.S. Steel Corp.	Weyerhaeuser Co.
National Steel Corp.	International Paper Co.
Bethlehem Steel Corp.	Crown Zellerbach Corp.
Inland Steel Co.	Kimberly-Clark Corp.
Republic Steel Corp.	Mead Corp.

Chemicals	*Petroleum*
du Pont (E. I.) de Nemours & Co.	Exxon Corp.
Union Carbide Corp.	Shell Oil Co.
Monsanto Co.	Standard Oil Co. (Indiana)
Allied Chemical Corp.	Texaco Inc.
Hercules, Inc.	Gulf Oil Corp.

10. Prior to the mid-1960s, du Pont, Hercules, International Paper, and Weyerhaeuser had no long-term debt, as their capital requirements were basically funded internally.

Chapter 4

THE IMPACT OF POPULATION TRENDS ON CAPITAL FORMATION AND SAVING

*George P. Jenkins**

PAST PATTERNS OF POPULATION GROWTH

Over the long run, demographic and economic forces are highly interactive with each other. The size and the age composition of the population influence the quantities and the types of goods and services demanded by consumers. This demand in turn affects the nature and the amount of investment business will undertake. The size and the age composition of the population influence the volume of saving that takes place in the economy. Hence, it impacts the amount of investment that can be supported.

The U.S. economy affects population trends mainly through inducing fluctuations in the birthrate. To some extent, it operates through improvements in the life expectancy of U.S. citizens. One obvious example of the effects of economic conditions upon the birthrate is the sharp decline that took place during the Great Depression. This development strongly influenced subsequent population forecasts.

In September 1946 the U.S. Bureau of the Census issued a series of estimates of the U.S. population by age to the year 2000. The report stated: ". . . the population of the U.S. will reach a peak of about 165 million in 1990 and will then begin a gradual decline."[1] In actuality the U.S. population reached 213,450,000 in 1975, and current projections expect it to rise to 234 million by 1985.

As the Census Bureau forecast of 30 years or so ago was being re-

---

* Chairman of the Board, Metropolitan Life Insurance Company.

leased, a phenomenon was just beginning to take place that would radically change any conclusions that might have been drawn from its projections. This phenomenon was later characterized as the postwar "baby boom." This boom caused, and is still causing, the most dramatic changes ever wrought by a demographic factor in our society and economy. Births rose from almost 2.9 million in 1945 to 3.9 million in the following year. They gradually increased to a level of around 4.3 million in the early 1960s, as shown in Chart 1. A population wave of this magnitude passing through the various life-cycle stages has profound impact on the size and shape of the national economy. So large was this group of youngsters that it has had an impact on the social attitudes and customs of the entire society.

Since the peak in the early 1960s, the number of births has declined in spite of an increase in the number of families. This reflects more family planning and the social acceptance of many couples' decision to have fewer children or none at all. Further, with the increasing job opportunities for women many people are electing to postpone mar-

Chart 1. Total U.S. births, 1930–1985

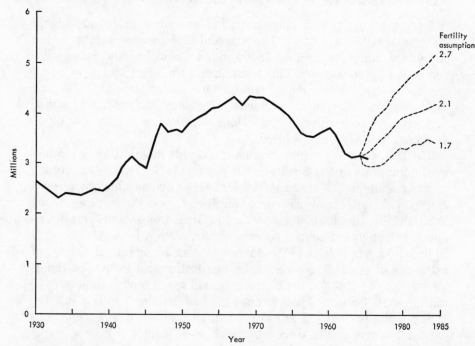

Sources: Data for calendar years 1930–75 from U.S. Department of Commerce, Bureau of the Census, "Current Population Reports," Series P25, no. 632; projections for years beginning July 1, 1975 from U.S. Department of Commerce, Bureau of the Census, "Current Population Reports," Series P25, no. 613.

riage or are simply not getting married. This latter development is best illustrated by viewing the projected composition of household formations over the next ten years. While primary family households are expected to increase almost 18 percent, households headed by primary individuals are projected to increase 35 percent. Such developments as later marriages and fewer children lead many demographers to predict an increase in the number of births simply because of the rising number of women of childbearing age in the population. In fact, there is a distinct possibility that the post–World War II baby boom will touch off its own baby boom.

FUTURE POPULATION TRENDS

Births are obviously hazardous to forecast, but expectations concerning the age mix of the adult population are not. These people have already been born, and their flow through the various age brackets can be predicted with a high degree of accuracy. In the decade ending in 1985, the nation should record an increase of approximately 21 million people, or a gain of nearly 10 percent. In and of itself, this gain points up the need for increased capital formation.

At present, the population wave stemming from the postwar baby boom brackets the ages from 10–29 years. The tremendous expansion in the labor force over the last several years has been due in large part

Table 1.   U.S. population by age group, 1975–1985

Age	Number of persons (thousands)			Percent change		
	1975	1980	1985	1975–1980	1980–1985	1975–1985
Under 5	15,910	17,259	19,785	8.5	14.6	24.4
5– 9	17,330	16,139	17,501	−6.9	8.4	1.0
10–14	20,402	17,804	16,605	−12.7	−6.7	−18.6
15–19	21,003	20,589	18,000	−2.0	−12.6	−14.3
20–24	19,226	20,908	20,496	8.7	−2.0	6.6
25–29	16,919	18,933	20,572	11.9	8.7	21.6
30–34	13,987	17,224	19,274	23.1	11.9	37.8
35–39	11,625	14,027	17,249	20.7	23.0	48.4
40–44	11,195	11,675	14,083	4.3	20.6	25.8
45–49	11,786	11,014	11,497	−6.6	4.4	−2.5
50–54	11,972	11,626	10,881	−2.9	−6.4	−9.1
55–59	10,531	11,303	10,898	7.3	−2.8	4.3
60–64	9,238	9,744	10,477	5.5	7.5	13.4
65 and over	22,330	24,523	26,659	9.8	8.7	19.4
All ages	213,450	222,769	234,068	4.4	5.1	9.7

Sources: Percent change figures calculated by Business Economics Department, Metropolitan Life Insurance Company, from data contained in U.S. Department of Commerce, Bureau of the Census, "Current Population Reports," series P25, no. 601, Series II projections.

to the number of persons reaching the job entry level age of 16. The economy has been hard pressed to absorb the surge of new workers at rates compatible with formerly acceptable unemployment levels.

The magnitude of the impact of the baby boom "coming of age" is best illustrated by noting changes in the size of some key age groups, shown in Table 1. Between 1975 and 1985, the 25–29 age group will swell 22 percent, and the 30–34 age group will grow by 38 percent. The 35–39 age group will increase a staggering 48 percent, and the 40–44 age group will gain 26 percent.

The proportion of persons in the 45–64 age group, a key age range for saving and investing, will actually shrink from more than 20 percent of the population to less than 19 percent over the 1975–85 period. Individuals over age 65 will increase 4.3 million by 1985 and will constitute almost 11½ percent of the total population.

THE DEPENDENCY RATIO

In general, the higher the dependency ratio, that is, the greater the number of nonworking people who must be supported by the working

Chart 2.   Trends in dependency ratios (under 20 years and over 65 as percent of 20–64 age group)

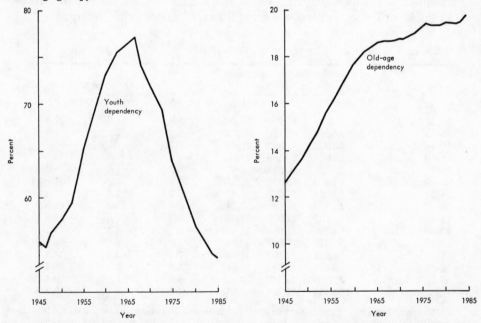

Sources: Calculated by Business Economics Department, Metropolitan Life Insurance Company, from data in the table B-26, p. 217, of *Economic Report of the President,* January 1977. Estimates for 1977–81 based upon U.S. Department of Commerce, Bureau of the Census, "Current Population Reports," series P25, no. 601, Series II projections.

population, the more difficult it is for an economy to maintain a high saving ratio. One useful approach to measuring dependency is shown in Chart 2. This indicates the past and projected ratios of the population under 20 and 65 and over to the prime working age group—namely the population 20–64.

The chart shows that the youth dependency ratio peaked in 1966 and is expected to continue trending downward. This ratio is somewhat difficult to predict, since it is dependent upon assumptions regarding the birthrate, which has varied significantly over time. Nevertheless, over the next ten years the probability is great that the needs of youth will not constitute an important source of investment demand. Pressures for new education facilities, for example, are expected to be minimal and to stem mainly from replacement requirements and needs arising from migration patterns.

The old-age dependency ratio is expected to continue trending upward. The aged already constitute an important voting group, and further increases in their number should intensify pressures to increase payments for their retirement, health care, and housing needs. Because of their great importance, retirement and other social needs will be discussed in greater detail in a subsequent section.

THE RELATIONSHIP OF POPULATION TO THE WORK FORCE

Not all of those under 20 and over 65 are "dependent" in any sense of the word. Likewise, not all individuals in the 20–64 age group are participants in the labor force. In fact, the official definition of the labor force includes only those persons 16 and over who are employed or are actively seeking work.

In general, a rising participation rate for women has more than offset the downdrift in the rate for men, and this pattern may be expected to continue. Thus, the overall labor force participation rate will continue to rise to new high levels and will reach more than 63 percent in 1985. *Translating these rates into labor force data and then making allowances for unemployment indicates that the economy will have to provide about 15 million net new jobs between now and 1985—including almost 10 million in the current five-year period.*

Based upon the experience of the past decade and expressed in today's prices, the incremental investment cost of adding one new job while maintaining the existing labor force is roughly $100,000 per worker. Thus, between now and 1985 the private economy will have to invest $1.5 trillion if adequate work facilities and jobs are to be available for our expanding labor force. If future inflation is allowed for, the amount, of course, will be considerably greater.

Any shift in the mix between labor and capital inputs in favor of labor would not prove advantageous in terms of economic growth and well-being. It is the buildup in the investment base which permits the productivity growth necessary to support the dependent segments of the population while still allowing the working groups to enjoy rising standards of living.

POPULATION MOBILITY

Another factor affecting capital needs is population mobility. The highest mobility rates are found among young adults, reflecting such life-cycle changes as the completion of education, entrance into the labor force, and marriage. Between 1970 and 1975, over 41 percent of all persons 5 years old and over moved, but the rate for persons 25–29 years of age was 72 percent over the same five-year period. Since the number in this age group will grow almost 22 percent by 1985, it is reasonable to expect that migration activity will continue at a high level. This will undoubtedly have a major impact on the demand for capital investment.

The migration of the population from the northeastern and north central states to the South and West, and the movement of the population from the large central cities to the suburbs and medium-sized communities, is well documented, as shown by Chart 3.

Population mobility increases private capital needs for new housing, new work facilities, and new utility and communications networks. It also increases the capital investment needs of state and local communities for expanded educational, health, and administrative facilities; additional water, sewerage, and waste systems; and more roads and other transportation facilities.

Another important consideration is the plight of areas suffering out-migration. Most of their facilities are already in place and cannot be readily reduced to reflect population shifts. The result is that real fixed costs, excluding inflation, remain relatively constant. Hence, the tax burdens of the population remaining in such areas must rise accordingly. This often discourages new needed investment, and it often encourages deferred maintenance outlays to hold down the rate of tax increases. Accordingly, it accelerates the deterioration of the existing capital stock. This process cannot continue indefinitely, of course, and it has the potential to become one of the major economic and social concerns of the 1980s.

Chart 3.   Net migration for regions, 1965–1970 and 1970–1975

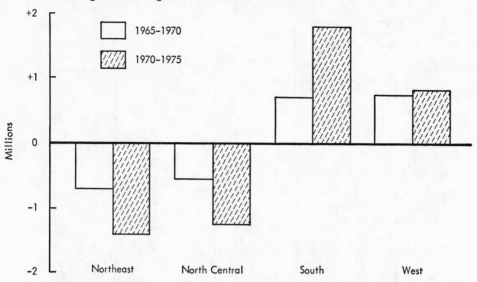

Source: U.S. Department of Commerce, Bureau of the Census, "Current Population Reports," series P20, no. 285.

HOUSEHOLDS AND HOUSING NEEDS

The heavy demand for housing that emerged in the early 1970s is closely related to the surge in new households that occurred during the same period. Household formations averaged slightly under 1.2 million annually in the five years ending March 1, 1970, but then averaged more than 1.5 million annually over the next five years.

Growth in the number of husband-wife households was accompanied by a rapid rise in households with female heads and in primary individual households. Further rapid expansion in the last two categories is expected to continue, with growth in household formation between 1975 and 1980 about matching that of the previous five years and with the 1980–85 period averaging slightly higher, as shown in Chart 4.

Current housing activity still reflects the adverse effects of the 1973–75 recession. It also reflects the extremely rapid inflation of 1974–75, including rising fuel and other operating costs. These developments have priced some households out of the single-family home market. They have also eroded the purchasing power of savings intended for down payments on homes and have adversely affected rates of return on multifamily housing investment. However, as real per-

54

Chart 4. Increase in U.S. households

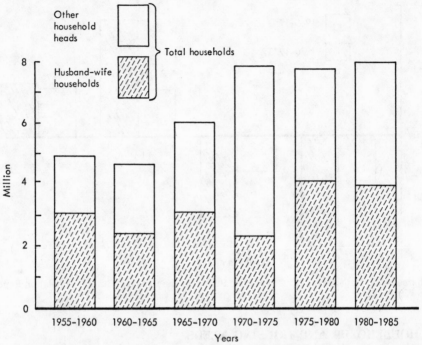

Sources: Plotted by Business Economics Department, Metropolitan Life Insurance Company, from data contained in U.S. Department of Commerce, Bureau of the Census, "Current Population Reports," series P25, no. 607, and P20, no. 282.

sonal income improves along with rising consumer and investor confidence, demographic forces should reassert themselves more strongly. These forces, together with adjustments for demolitions and casualty losses, should push housing starts back up over the 2 million mark by 1980. In all likelihood, housing starts will average above that level through 1985.

DEMOGRAPHIC FACTORS AND PERSONAL SAVING

The amount of investment that can actually take place is determined by the volume of real saving that occurs in the economy—that is, by the willingness on the part of the various economic sectors to forgo current consumption. Significantly, *the age distribution of households during the next ten years will clearly be adversely weighted with regard to those age groups with a high propensity to save.*

More specifically, household heads in the 45–64 age group, that is, the largest saving age group, will increase by only 470,000 over the next ten years, compared to an increase of 6.4 million in the 25–44 age bracket. The latter group has a higher propensity to consume. Its members are forming families and raising children. They are large purchasers of homes and consumer durables. These people will be seeking vast amounts of consumer and mortgage debt.

Savings attitudes also seem different for this generation. There have been significant increases in the number of people who favor greater government involvement in such areas as improving the availability and quality of medical care, providing for children's college education, accumulating funds for retirement, providing for dependents in the event of an unexpected death, and purchase of living quarters.[2] It is thus not surprising that today fewer married people consider it important to save regularly.[3]

Years ago, with no Social Security, no prepaid medical care, no unemployment compensation, no welfare, and so on, Americans tended to save for emergencies. Today, with government seeking to care for all human needs, there is a sharp drop in the incentive to save. In addition, *those over 65 will be growing more rapidly than the total population, and this segment of the population tends to draw down personal savings accumulated in the past. Moreover, this tendency is accelerated during periods of rapid inflation.*

RETIREMENT AND OTHER SOCIAL NEEDS

As already mentioned, demographic forces such as the rising old-age dependency ratio and the absolute increase in those aged 65 and over, will be exerting upward pressures on the benefits to be paid for retirement and related needs. The mix between public and private efforts to provide these benefits has significant implications for future saving and investment flows in the economy. More specifically, Social Security is essentially a pay-as-you-go transfer system, with taxes approximating the benefits paid. However, the private system is a funding system generating saving for capital and job formation. Both Social Security and private retirement plans serve an important purpose, but an appropriate balance between the two is essential. It is obvious that if private pension plans are vitiated by a rapidly rising Social Security system, both capital and job formation will be hampered.

Social Security benefits and the taxes collected from business and individuals to support these benefits have grown dramatically in recent years. The maturation and expansion of the Social Security system to include new coverages have contributed to the rise. In 1950 only 37 percent of all people over 65 were receiving Social Security benefits. By 1960 this proportion had increased to 72 percent, and it now stands at 92 percent. In absolute terms, about 21 million people aged 65 and over receive retirement benefits, as do another 12 million retired or disabled workers, survivors of deceased workers, and dependents of retired or disabled workers under age 65.

At present, Social Security benefits must be assessed in the context of all payments relating to social insurance and public assistance, as shown in Table 2. The total of all such transfer payments equaled

Table 2. Social insurance, public assistance, and related payments

	Amount ($ billions)	Percent of personal income
1950	9	4.1
1955	16	5.0
1960	27	6.8
1965	38	7.2
1970	75	9.4
1976	180	13.1

Sources: Compiled from data in table M–39, p. 73, of the *Social Security Bulletin*, vol. 40, no. 1 (January 1977). Estimate for 1976 made by Business Economics Department, Metropolitan Life Insurance Company. See also note 4.

about $180 billion in 1976, or more than 13 percent of personal income. This contrasts sharply with $27 billion and 6.8 percent in 1960.[4]

After such rapid growth, it seems appropriate that the nation reappraise the whole social welfare system. It seems socially desirable to consider such questions as the optimum relative size of these transfer payments and the appropriate mix between private and public efforts at meeting social insurance and public assistance needs. Above all else, we should consider the long-run implication of the growth in the social welfare system for the incentives to work and save.

SOME NONDEMOGRAPHIC FACTORS AFFECTING BUSINESS CAPITAL FORMATION

Coincident with demographic forces tending to accelerate investment demand and suppress saving, there are other economic forces which have similar impacts. On the investment side, for example, in addition to meeting the usual expansionary demands and providing work facilities for the expanding labor force, other considerations have been pushing business capital spending up in recent years. These include:

1. The need to modernize and replace outmoded facilities.
2. Improvements in overall productivity.
3. Strengthening our competitiveness in international markets.
4. Increased stress upon pollution control.
5. Higher investment for worker safety.
6. Stepped-up investment for energy needs.

More than a tenth of all business fixed investment and about one sixth of all manufacturing facilities are technologically outmoded. *To replace all of these obsolete facilities would require almost a quarter of a trillion dollars, or about 1½ times all business capital outlays made in 1976!*

Improved worker safety and the elimination of air, water, and waste pollution stemming from industrial activities are desirable social goals. But investments for these purposes do not directly contribute to increased productivity. Hence, they serve to raise capital output requirements. Roughly 2½ cents of every investment dollar is now related to employee safety and health, and in recent years roughly 7 cents out of every investment dollar has been related to pollution control. The cost of bringing all U.S. business facilities in compliance with present pollution control standards is estimated to be in excess of $30 billion.

Finally, the long-developing energy problem has been very dramatically highlighted since the formation of the OPEC cartel, and its importance has been even more fully appreciated as a result of the severe winter of 1976–77. This can only mean increased investment spending not only by our energy-supplying industries, but by all other industries as well. Our energy-supplying industries must find, develop, and make available new, less readily accessible, and therefore more expensive, sources of energy. Fuel storage facilities must be greatly expanded. As fuel prices adjust more closely to economic realities, higher capital outlays by other industries may be anticipated as these industries seek to achieve more efficient use of fuels.

Inflation impacts

On the saving side of the capital formation equation, inflation is probably the most serious problem. Prices may be expected to increase by about 6 percent annually over the next five years and could be close to that rate out to 1985. Inflation tends to raise the proportion of asset prices that must be raised externally, and under our existing tax structure it shifts saving from the private to the government sectors. The progressive personal income tax structure is one illustration of this process.

Perhaps less obvious, but very important for business capital formation, is the effect of inflation upon the quality of profits. This can be illustrated by the experience of 1972–76. It is estimated that corporate depreciation allowances as reported for tax purposes and based upon historical costs ran almost $200 billion below actual replacement cost. Moreover, inventory "profits" totaled another $91 billion over the 1972–76 period. Thus, due to inflation, profits were overstated by roughly $290 billion, or an average of $58 billion per year. *This gap between real and reported profits, however, is taxed at the full corporate income tax rate, which, for a viable corporation, results in the need for periodic injections of external funds to merely maintain existing business investment.*

Expansion of the government sector

As indicated earlier, an important consideration affecting capital formation is the long-term expansion of the role of government. When total government outlays, rather than just purchases of goods and services, are related to gross national product, the increasing share of government in the economy is clearly evident. Total federal outlays rose from 18.9 percent of GNP in 1957–61 to 21.9 percent in 1972–76, and state and local outlays rose from 9.8 percent to 14.4 percent. All government outlays combined jumped from 27.4 percent of gross national product in 1957–61 to 33 percent in the five-year period ending in 1976.

The effect of these trends has been a substantial increase in the government sector's demand for funds in the money and capital markets. These trends have increased taxes on the private sector. The net result has been a drain on the productive private sector's ability to generate an adequate volume of saving and investment.

SUMMARY AND CONCLUSION

It is clear that over the next decade demographic forces will stimulate strong demands for investment but that, at the same time, they will be a drag on efforts to provide adequate saving to match those demands.

In addition, special nondemographic factors, such as energy, pollution control, and worker safety, will raise capital output requirements. When viewed from the saving side of the capital formation equation, inflation and expansion of the government sector—if allowed to continue—will have similar adverse impacts. Detailed flow of funds analyses indicate that the capital shortage gap may total $150 to $200 billion during the five years ending in 1981. Unfortunately, there is no indication that this situation will improve by the mid-80s.

Under these conditions, market forces should be allowed to determine the most efficient allocation of saving and investment flows. All of this suggests that present tax policies and government regulations need to be rigorously reexamined to eliminate roadblocks to capital and job formation. Failure to recognize this need and to act promptly will hamper the nation's ability to meet its twin challenges of capital and job formation.

NOTES

1. U.S. Department of Commerce, Bureau of the Census, *Population—Special Reports Series,* P46, no. 7 (September 15, 1946), p. 1.
2. See *MAP—Monitoring Attitudes of the Public* (Washington, D.C.: Institute of Life Insurance, 1976), pp. 112–13.
3. See *Youth 1976: Finance-Related Attitudes* (Washington, D.C.: American Council of Life Insurance, 1977), p. 14.
4. See *Social Security Bulletin,* vol. 40, no. 1 (January 1977), table M–39, p. 73. Estimate for 1976 made by Business Economics Department, Metropolitan Life Insurance Company. Includes government transfer payments to beneficiaries under OASDHI, railroad retirement, public employee retirement, unemployment insurance, MDTA training allowances, trade adjustment assistance, "black lung," and veterans' pensions and compensation programs; cash and medical payments under workers' compensation and temporary disability insurance; and court-awarded benefits for work injuries sustained by railroad, maritime, and other workers under federal employer liability acts. Also includes government transfer payments to recipients of direct relief under programs of old-age assistance, aid to families with dependent children, aid to the blind, aid to the permanently and totally disabled, and general assistance. Excludes payments made in behalf of recipient to suppliers of medical care (vendor payments). Beginning 1961, includes bonus value of food stamps. Beginning 1974, includes supplemental security income payments.

Chapter 5

PUBLIC KNOWLEDGE AND ATTITUDES TOWARD BUSINESS

Louis Harris*

In the United States, the debate between free enterprise and socialism is 30 or 40 years out-of-date. The realities of economic and political life are vastly different than they were, and the American people are no longer sympathetic with business leaders who claim to dedicate their lives to keeping the country from going socialist or with liberals who are obsessed with ending the reign of unbridled free enterprise.

Basically, the American people are deeply committed to pluralism. They support a system that allows individuals, organizations, and institutions to follow diverse pursuits in an essentially free society. Obviously, when one individual, group, or institution reaches a point where it threatens the freedoms and rights of others, then ground rules must be written to allow those threatened to preserve their options to operate freely. Essentially, people are convinced that we have a mixed society, where business and government live side by side in relative independence, and this is the way they prefer it.

BUSINESS AND GOVERNMENT: REBUILDING PUBLIC CONFIDENCE

Thus, surveys have consistently shown that by an 84–9 percent margin, the public is opposed to "a federal government takeover of business." This result has not changed over the past ten years, and it is unlikely to change drastically in the near future. When the Penn Central Railroad went bankrupt, a cross section of the public was asked whether it wanted to see the federal government take over the running

---

* President, Louis Harris and Associates, Inc.

of the railroad. By 53–34 percent, a majority of the public opposed such a takeover. When people were pressed for a reason, they gave one dominant answer: "As badly run as the Penn Central might have been to end up in this plight, if the government took over, it would be even worse run."

Ongoing surveys since 1966 have shown that business leadership has sunk lower and lower in public esteem. The percentage of people expressing high confidence in "those running major corporations" went down from 55 to 16 percent in the decade between 1966 and 1976. Yet when people were asked which they felt was a greater threat to the country in the next decade, only 10 percent of a nationwide cross section said "big business," 15 percent said "big labor," 32 percent said "big government," and 33 percent volunteered "all three." The inescapable conclusion is that though people may have grave doubts about the stewardship of American business, they hold equal doubts about two major adversaries of business—big government and big labor. Public confidence in the executive branch of government has declined from 41 percent to 11 percent over a ten-year period.

However, it would be foolhardy for business to see the weakness of public confidence in government as a protection for itself. In the early days of his Administration, President Carter raised confidence in the White House up to 31 percent from the low 11 percent it reached under Presidents Nixon and Ford. Confidence in business has only risen from 16 percent to 20 percent. So it is entirely possible that a new president can bring back confidence in government while business continues to languish in the low confidence of the American people. In that case, business could be in for very rough sledding if it hopes to cling to some vaguely defined status quo or to revert to some even fonder but vaguer version of a status quo ante.

Recently, the Harris firm asked a basic question which we have been asking the American people for a number of years. A cross section of 1,540 adults nationwide was given this question: "I want to ask you about various activities some companies are involved in. For each, tell me if that is something you think most big companies are involved in in a major way, a minor way, or not at all. (READ LIST AND RECORD BELOW)."

Even a cursory examination of the results in Table 1 reveals that on only 6 out of 15 items is big business credited by a majority of the public with deep involvement in these key and important areas. And these items deal mainly with the technological, know-how capabilities of the business establishment rather than with direct contributions to the general society in which business lives and operates. Only one item, "providing steady work for employees," stands out as a real so-

Table 1.   Extent of big business involvement in key areas

	Major way	Minor way	Not at all	Not sure
Major business involvement:				
Extensive research and development of new and better products	73%	18%	2%	7%
Using the most modern equipment and technology	73	18	2	7
Providing steady work for employees	67	23	4	6
Concern about their reputation standing on their products and services	64	27	4	5
Hiring, developing, and retaining the best management team	58	26	4	12
Finding the money to expand the business to provide more jobs	52	31	6	11
Caring about product safety	47	40	7	6
Turning out high-quality products and services	45	41	7	7
Minor business involvement:				
Paying good wages and salaries	41	44	8	7
Providing career opportunities for minorities	37	42	9	12
Helping the well-being of the community where located	36	43	13	8
Giving women a real chance to hold down important jobs	31	47	12	10
Giving customers the best value for the money	30	50	14	6
Giving employees high job satisfaction for working there	28	47	14	11
Working for better government	28	39	18	15

cial asset of big business. And in a period where unemployment has lingered on at high levels, this is not an inconsiderable attribute. Another item, "turning out high-quality products and services," does yield a plurality who feel that big business has a major involvement. However, the number who saw a major business concern for product quality fell from 52 to 45 percent between 1966 and 1977, indicating that business might well be slipping in this pivotal bottom line dimension.

The areas where business is credited with no more than "minor" involvement all imply a deep criticism of how big business handles the human dimension. There is widespread feeling that big business is not providing career opportunities for minorities, not really contributing to the communities where it is located, not giving women much of a chance to hold down really important jobs, not giving customers good value for the money, not giving employees high job satisfaction, and not working for better government.

From these and other extensive data, it can be concluded that three major criticisms of American business exist today:

■ The American people feel that business has little concern with the human dimensions of doing business, whether among consumers or employees, and that it does not care enough about the quality performance of products and services.

■ The American people also feel that business shows a lack of understanding about the emerging quality of life issues in society: product safety, employee safety, employment of women and minorities, conservation of energy, concern in handling product complaints, and air and water pollution control. To these might be added a concern for finding jobs for the unemployed and for helping to curb inflation.

■ There is also a continuing and unabating criticism that business is more concerned with making profits at the expense of the public than in identifying its own well-being with that of its customers, its employees, and the public as a whole.

PROFITS: BOTTOM LINE PERFORMANCE AND THE PUBLIC INTEREST

The profits area is a classic case study of just how poorly business has communicated what its main business is and should be. Most Americans think that business profits are too high. And little wonder that they do, for when people were asked to estimate the aftertax profits of most of business, the mean profits level came out at an estimated 34 percent (versus an actual 5 to 8 percent, depending on the year).

When those questioned were asked to volunteer what they thought were the main uses to which most American companies put their profits, a substantial 29 percent suggested the following: "pay higher salaries to top executives," "get rich, personal gain," "bribery, political payoffs," or "luxury, high living." Nearly one in every three people in this country is convinced that the primary use of corporation profits is to line the pockets of the top executives. When people were asked what American business profits should be used for, every one of the above uses promptly disappeared from the list.

At the same time, the identical people who answered these previous questions were asked the following question: "Now let me read you a number of things companies do with the money they earn. For each, tell me if, in your opinion, that is a justified use for the profits that companies make or not. (READ LIST, RECORDING BELOW FOR EACH ITEM)."

Table 2. Whether specific uses of company profits are justified

	Justified	Not justified	Not sure
Provide money to pay for new machinery and equipment, to produce better products	95%	2%	3%
Provide a pension plan for the retirement security of the company's employees	95	2	3
Provide the money to expand the company, to create more jobs	95	2	3
Expand research and development to turn out new and better quality products	95	2	3
Put in improvements for air and water pollution control	94	2	4
Make contributions to education and good causes in the community	89	4	7
Pay workers in the company higher wages and salaries	85	6	9
Pay stockholders a dividend in return for their investing in the company's stock	85	7	8
Show a good growth in earnings so the price of the stock will go up, thus making it a good investment for the stockholders to put their money into	72	15	13
Raise new money to improve and maintain their bond ratings and stock prices	61	18	21
Pay higher profit sharing and bonuses to executives to keep able people with the company and to attract well-qualified executives	60	27	13

In the aggregate, the profits of most modern corporations go almost exclusively to the purposes stated in Table 2. There are, of course, other items, such as debt service, acquisitions, and other corporate activity, which are also candidates for the utilization of corporate profits. But nearly everyone would agree that most profits of American companies go to the uses stated.

The significance of the results is far-reaching indeed. *It is obvious that the ways most corporations use most of their profits are, in the end, highly justifiable to the rank and file of Americans.* In fact, other questioning reveals that sizable majorities feel that there would be a real loss to the economy and to the country if profits were not regularly generated to provide for these very same purposes.

Why, then, is there all this fuss about profits, if the facts show clearly that the American people heavily support the uses to which profits are usually put?

It is this writer's belief that much of the blame for the criticism that business regularly gets on the question of profits lies with the business establishment itself. For at least one generation now, chief executives have emerged in major corporations who behave as though they hope to go their graves with inscriptions on their tombstones which would read, "Here lies Mr. X, who for ten years presided as the chief executive officer of the XYZ Corporation. During those ten years, his average aftertax incremental increase in corporate earnings achieved came to 14 percent per annum. May he now rest in peace."

As a director in a major Wall Street investment firm, the writer can state with some real knowledge that in a very important way, Wall Street misled a whole generation of chief executive and chief financial officers. It convinced them that they would be judged *solely* on the basis of the bottom line performance. Increase your profits every year, and you have it made. Unfortunately, this prevailing view of chief executive officers has become contagious and the disease has spread to the public, which has concluded, in turn, that all business wants to do is to make bigger and bigger profits, often off the back of the poor, beleaguered consumer. It is no happenstance that when people were asked to choose from a list of 23 adjectives and phrases the six which "best describe big business," the top runners were: "massive," "impersonal," "well-known," "greedy," "stifles competition," and "shrewd." By the same token, the top six from the same list that *least* describe big business were: "warm," "honest," "backward," "generous," "inefficient," and "trust."

The notion that profits are an end in themselves has become an obsession with far too many top executives in business. But what is golden with top business leaders is almost a dirty word to most of the public. And the reason is obvious: *the fact that profits must be generated in order to flow through to other and highly positive uses has largely been lost on the consciousness of the American people.*

If business had more awareness about communications, it would spell out precisely *what its profits are used for, how relatively little it retains,* and *how much it utilizes for economic and social purposes that people are bound to approve.* The classic case in modern times, of course, is that of the oil companies, whose reputations were severely damaged when they reported record earnings following the oil embargo period of 1973. Few industries have as large capital needs as the oil companies. And few can show such a direct and obvious benefit from their use of capital: expansion of existing energy resources. On the face of it, it would seem obvious that the oil companies could justify relatively high profits—if they only spelled out how much of their profits have to go into exploration and the development of new energy sources. Just about the same time, unfortunately, revelations were made about a spate of illegal political campaign contributions both in the United States and abroad, some of them by major oil companies. The public made an immediate connection between high profits, on the one hand, and sizable and illegal campaign contributions, on the other. And in the process, confidence in business generally, and in oil companies in particular, sank to all-time lows among the public.

ANTITRUST: HOW FAR IS THE PUBLIC WILLING TO GO?

As shown in Table 3, there are three other "negative activities" of business. These were not reported in Table 1 of this chapter, which only listed positive operations of companies.

Table 3.   Extent of big business involvement in negative activities

	Major way	Minor way	Not at all	Not sure
Trying to influence government to improve the company's position	68%	18%	3%	11%
Getting together and fixing prices	59	22	6	13
Making illegal contributions to political campaigns	57	26	4	13

If these three negative activities were added to the earlier list, they would emerge as numbers 3, 5, and 7 in importance in terms of concentration of effort by big business. Taken together, this means that people are prepared to believe that business spends a sizable amount of time on dubious and self-serving activities, even if the public recognizes the right of business to lobby.

Given this high degree of skepticism and suspicion about American business, one would expect that most people would look forward eagerly to slapping business down with antitrust suits on a scale never before witnessed in this country. Yet this is hardly the case. By only a halfhearted plurality, 49 percent to 32 percent, people think that the antitrust laws do "more good than harm" rather than "more harm than good."

An in-depth examination of what the public feels it might lose or gain if antitrust laws were eliminated is revealing, both because it demonstrates a lack of deep commitment by the people to the antitrust concept and because it shows the essentially pragmatic quality of public thinking about business.

Table 4 reflects the results obtained when a cross section of the public was asked: "If eliminating the antitrust laws in this country meant (READ LIST), would you favor or oppose eliminating those antitrust laws?"

Here, under one umbrella, we can see how the American people can

Table 4. Attitudes toward antitrust laws if their elimination has certain consequences

	Favor elimination of antitrust	Oppose elimination	Not sure
If elimination of antitrust laws meant:			
Costs of production could be lowered through greater efficiencies, and price rises could be slowed down	61%	25%	14%
More efficient products and services would result to the consumer by avoiding costly duplication	57	27	16
Better products could be produced by a sharing of research and development costs	57	29	14
Money would be used more efficiently to expand industry	53	29	18
Companies would expand rapidly, but would pay attention to antipollution concerns	51	29	20
Even though companies might be bigger, government could better regulate industry and could demand that industry meet the public's needs better	47	33	20
Several government regulatory agencies would have to make sure companies were working together to serve the public interest	39	41	20
Companies in the same industry could get together and set prices, subject to review by the federal government	29	55	16
Bargaining with labor unions would take place more on a national than a local basis	23	54	23
In some industries it would be found to be more efficient to have only a few big companies instead of a lot of small ones	22	60	18
Competition in many industries would be sharply reduced	21	62	17
Smaller, less efficient companies would go out of business and be bought up by bigger ones	15	70	15

range from a 61 to 25 percent majority favoring elimination of the anti-trust statutes to a 70 to 15 percent majority favoring their retention. One might infer, therefore, that the public is fickle and unstable in its opinions on this matter. But a careful reading of the responses would show otherwise.

People tend to sympathize with the idea of eliminating antitrust activity when they feel that this would lead to greater efficiency in production and expansion, better products and services, better utilization of capital, and a possible slowdown of the rate of inflation. Now one might argue that all or none of these eventualities can follow from the elimination of antitrust laws. But the fact is that the American people would seriously entertain their elimination if such pragmatic benefits were to result. However, the moment it could be inferred that the elimination of antitrust laws might mean price-fixing, national rather than local collective bargaining, and an inevitable decline in competition and the disappearance of most small business, then the public supports antitrust as at least one source of protection.

In fact, it is probably fair to say that if laws were kept on the statute books that provided very tough penalties for collusion in restraint of trade or for price-fixing, then public opinion in this country could be persuaded to go along with virtual elimination of the whole structure of antitrust legislation. At a minimum, this exercise is significant because it does point up the rather ambivalent commitment of the public to the antitrust course as the ultimate way to keep business in line.

THE QUALITY OF LIFE: NEW DEMANDS, NEW REWARDS FOR BUSINESS

If the American people are in no mood to nationalize business and are not enamored of the antitrust process, is there another approach under which they could be guaranteed that American business would be more in harmony with the growing quality-of-life goals that appear to be emerging in the last quarter of the 20th century?

There is every likelihood that we are going to enter a new era in public demands upon business. Saved for the moment by a public aversion to big government that is even greater than the public's aversion to business, and certainly by a public aversion to a takeover of business by government, business is likely to be confronted with the demand that its tax structure be geared to how well it performs in fulfilling national quality-of-life objectives.

Table 5 indicates widespread public acceptance of a system of business operation in which direct rewards and penalties for business are geared to the primary quality-of-life objectives of the society.

Table 5. Suggestions for changing the tax system through quality-of-life improvements

	Favor	Oppose	Not sure
Companies that are bad polluters of the air and water have to pay higher taxes, and those companies cleaning up air and water pollution pay lower taxes	78%	13%	9%
Companies wasting energy are taxed more, and those conserving energy are taxed less	76	15	9
Companies not taking proper safety precautions in their products are taxed more, and those taking real safety precautions in their products are taxed less	75	17	8
Companies not taking proper safety precautions for their employees are taxed more, and those making working conditions for their employees safer are taxed less	74	17	9
Companies ignoring product complaints are taxed more, and those correcting product faults when complaints are made are taxed less	66	22	12
Companies that do not try to upgrade the skills of minority workers are taxed more, and those training minority workers to do more skilled jobs are taxed less	57	28	15
Companies that do not try to upgrade the skills of women are taxed more, and those training women for better positions are taxed less	56	29	15
Assuming no difference in the price of products, companies putting out higher quality products are taxed less and those putting out lower quality products are taxed more	56	31	13

A very strong implication of these findings is that the public does not necessarily want a direct governmental solution to many of its quality-of-life problems. To the contrary, it would opt strongly for having the government use the taxation instrument as a device for guiding the private sector toward certain goals. In fact, it is no over-statement to conclude that the public not only wants business to face up to its quality-of-life demands, but also to become a major vehicle for realizing them. At the same time, if business could be made to connect directly with these mainstream aspirations, which are likely to increase in the years ahead, it is clear that the reputation of business and the public's confidence in business would rise accordingly.

CONCLUSION

For many years, it was assumed by both the most ardent advocates and the most ardent critics of business that the dominant motivation of people in this country was rooted in basic economic considerations. The motive of economic self-interest has been the basis of much of the thinking of both the leaders and the critics of business. But in the present period, a time in which people are being made to understand that resources are finite not infinite, nonmaterial aspirations are rising in importance, as perhaps never before in our history. It would be ironic indeed if, in the end, American business were to find its salvation in its ability to fulfill these nonmaterial aspirations.

Chapter 6

INFLATION, CROWDING OUT, AND OTHER DETERRENTS TO CAPITAL AND JOB FORMATION

David L. Babson*

Inflation has been going on for so many years that everyone thinks it is as certain as death and taxes. Consumers, workers, business leaders, and retirees all now expect prices and wages to mount ever higher and higher. This expectation is being routinely factored into economic decisions and contractual arrangements, thus helping to keep the inflation wheel spinning.

The wheel cannot be brought to a halt until the nature of inflation is better understood by more people. *Unfortunately, the current problem has no precedent in U.S. economic history.*

In earlier times, inflation stemmed primarily from the financing of wars. The ensuing price spirals were mostly washed out as the free market economy readjusted to normal peacetime activities. Few people are aware that the wholesale price index of all U.S. commodities in 1946 was only 20 percent higher than a comparable index for 1796, when George Washington was president. For most of those 150 years, this nation experienced relatively little inflation except for the self-correcting wartime spirals.

A NEW PATTERN

A wholly new pattern has emerged over the past three decades. Wages and prices advance inexorably—in peace as well as in war, in recessions as well as in booms, under Republican as well as Demo-

---

* Chairman, David L. Babson & Co.

Chart 1. The vanishing American dollar (1946 = 100 cents)

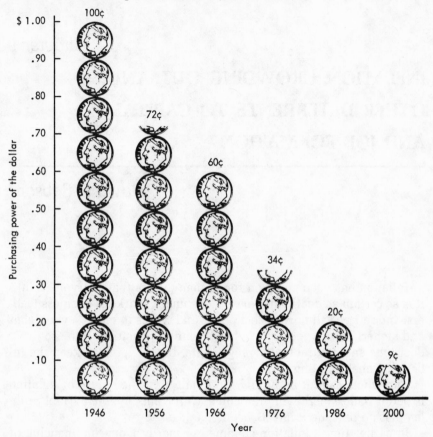

Source: U.S. Department of Labor consumer price index.

cratic administrations. The basic interplay of supply and demand is no longer able to check the rising cost of living. *Instead, inflation has turned into a chronic and self-perpetuating force.*

The dollar has shrunk for 21 years in a row and in 36 of the past 38 years. Its buying power has dropped from 100 cents in 1946—the first full year of peace after World War II—to only 34 cents last year. And as Chart 1 shows, it will be worth less than a dime by the end of the century if inflation continues at the 5.8 percent pace of the past ten years.

When the value of a currency drops 90 percent within the life span of the average citizen, it is a dangerous development for any society. History tells us that when people lose confidence in the soundness of their currency, profound social and political changes can ensue. The French Revolution and Napoleon are one example; the rise of Nazism is another.

We do not even have to look way back into history to see the damage a severe inflation can inflict. The once mighty British economy and the pound sterling are both under siege. In the past quarter century, Britain has slipped from second place to fifth place as an industrial nation. Many other countries where inflation is rampant are also experiencing a decline in living standards and growing social unrest.

PROGRESSIVE SPEEDUP

One of the most disturbing trends in the United States is that each new wave of inflation has been rolling up higher—and staying up higher—on the beach. Recessions, though painful, could once be counted on to slow the rise in the cost of living. But their dampening effect has been steadily diminishing. The progressive speedup of the inflation rate in each recent recession and in each first year of economic recovery may be seen in Table 1.

Table 1.   The progressive speedup of inflation

	Annual rate of increase in consumer price index	
Recession period	During recession period	In first 12 months of economic recovery
November 1973–March 1975	+11.0%	+6.1%
December 1969–November 1970	+ 5.4	+3.5
April 1960–February 1961	+ 1.9	+0.9
August 1957–April 1958	+ 3.2	+0.2
July 1953–May 1954	+ 0.3	−0.6

Source: U.S. Department of Labor.

During the 1973–75 recession, the consumer price index increased at an average annual rate of 11 percent—the steepest climb in history not directly related to war. This rapid pace stemmed partly from temporary factors—commodity shortages, crop failures, and the quadrupling of OPEC oil prices. After the recession ended, the inflation rate dropped in half, to 6 percent.

But even a trend of 6 percent is without precedent during a normal economic recovery. Unfortunately, the long-term forces behind inflation have not been lessened by the worst recession in four decades and are more powerful today than ever before.

What are these long-term forces? In recent years inflation has been blamed on one scapegoat after another—steel price hikes, Russian grain purchases, oil sheikhs, bad weather. Yet these are marginal factors that do not lie at the heart of the problem. A list of the basic, ongoing forces of inflation would have to include:

- *First,* the disproportionate growth of government spending. In each of the past three decades, it has expanded 40–60 percent more than the tax-supporting private economy.
- *Second,* the stepped-up rate of pay increases. There has been a wide gap between the trend of compensation and the trend of productivity.
- *Third,* the spreading morass of government regulation. It impairs efficiency, raises costs, and stifles incentives.
- *Fourth,* the pro-consumption, anti-investment bias of tax policies. This discourages savings and the creation of capital needed to expand the number of jobs, boost productivity, and increase the supply of goods and services.

All four of these factors underlying inflation stem from social and political roots. *Most Americans simply do not understand how the economic system works.* And through the political process they continually place more demands on the economy than it has the capacity to deliver.

HUGE NEW SOCIAL PROGRAMS

In the mid-1960s, President Johnson and Congress launched huge new social programs simultaneously with a war. From 1965 to 1973, a total of $135 billion was spent to finance the war in Southeast Asia. Over this same span, annual federal outlays on transfer payments and grants-in-aid to state and local governments tripled from $39 billion to $127 billion. Spending for this purpose above the 1965 base level came to an eight-year total of $320 billion—or 2½ times the cost of Vietnam.

The war spending—which peaked at $29 billion in fiscal 1969—virtually disappeared in the early 1970s. In contrast, the social welfare spending has continued to soar. In the past four fiscal years alone, federal transfer payments and grants-in-aid have nearly doubled to $240 billion. They have been responsible for two thirds of the increase in the federal budget.

Some of the six-fold growth in social welfare spending over the past dozen years reflects the rising costs of supporting the disabled, the aged, and the handicapped. But the lion's share of the gain stems from the huge expansion in the number and types of benefits. In the early

1960s, the federal government was running about 200 separate aid programs. Today, there are over 1,000 of them, bearing upon almost every aspect of daily life.

REDISTRIBUTION OF INCOME

The rapid pace at which the redistribution of income is proceeding raises some big economic issues. *How much further can society go in shifting the economy's resources from the producers to the nonproducers—from those who are pulling the wagon to those who are riding in it? How much longer before the wagon creaks to a halt?*

As laws are continually—and often hastily—passed to ease hardship and redistribute income, more and more members of society are being supported through taxes on the producer sector. Although precise figures are not available, it can be conservatively estimated that one out of every three adults in the 20–64 age group is either on a government payroll or receives regular public assistance. The number of people in this category has expanded by about 60 percent in the past decade—nearly seven times as much as the population has grown.

The growing load being placed on the productive, tax-supporting

Chart 2. The mounting public sector as a percentage of the private economy

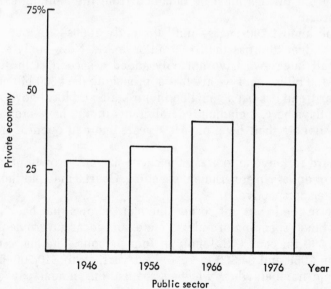

Public sector = total outlays of federal, state, and local governments.
Private economy = gross national product less the public sector.
Source: U.S. Department of Commerce.

side of the economy can only weaken private initiatives. Incentives to work and to produce are reduced *both* for those from whom income is taken and for those to whom it is given. Meanwhile, the public sector looms bigger and bigger in the economy. The trend is shown in Chart 2. Two decades ago, total government spending—federal, state, and local combined—was 33 percent as large as the private sector. A decade ago, it was 40 percent as big. It is now up to 52 percent, and it promises to gain even more ground in the years ahead.

UNDERWRITING BIGGER GOVERNMENT

As long as government continues to grow faster than the economy which supports it, the trend can be financed in only two ways. First, the effective overall tax rate levied on incomes must be raised higher and higher; and/or second, more public debt must be continuously issued. Both of these means of underwriting bigger government are inflationary.

The first alternative—a faster rise in taxes than in incomes—serves to increase the cost of living. This, in turn, encourages unions to demand compensating wage boosts, business managers to seek offsetting price increases, landlords to boost rents, and so forth. The second alternative will overinflate the nation's money supply because big new Treasury borrowings must be obtained from the banking system or from abroad.

It took almost 200 years—until the early 1960s—for our nation's federal budget to cross the $100 billion mark. Now—only a decade and a half later—we have not only added a second, a third, and a fourth $100 billion, but we are fast approaching the $500 billion mark. A similar trend has been going on in our state and local governments. Total outlays here, including federal grants-in-aid, have crossed $250 billion—double their level of just 7 years ago and quadruple that of 14 years ago.

It's hard for anyone to grasp the sheer size and growth of all these billions of dollars in government spending. Chart 3 may put the picture into better perspective.

Down in the lower left corner, the chart shows that back in 1946, the combined spending of federal, state, and local governments averaged $1,300 for each U.S. family of four persons. The figure reached $2,500 in 1956 and $4,300 in 1966. Last year, it hit $10,700. That's a pretty big number when weighed against the annual pay of most workers.

Chart 3 also extrapolates the trend at the average annual rate of in-

Chart 3.   Total government outlays for each family of four (federal, state, and local)

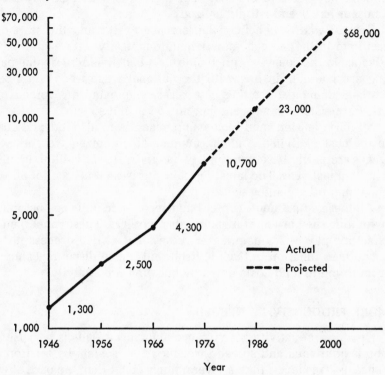

Source: U.S. Department of Labor.

crease during the past quarter century. On this basis, public spending per family of four will reach $23,000 in 10 years and $68,000 in less than 25 years.

PUBLIC SPENDING ACCELERATES

Some people might think the trend is certain to slow down. Actually,.the average yearly rise over the past decade has been even faster than that of the past 25 years, on which the extrapolation is based. At this more recent rate of increase, annual public spending would climb to $28,000 per family in another decade and to $105,000 by the end of the century.

Government spending is now less likely than ever to moderate below its historic 9 percent yearly pace because of a new factor that entered the picture in 1974. Congress linked over half of all federal transfer payments to the cost of living. Thus, we might say that the dinosaur has been institutionalized.

Social Security benefits—the largest transfer and the second biggest item in the budget—now rise automatically with each 3 percent advance in the consumer price index. As benefits increase, the payroll tax also goes up, in line with the national wage trend. As a result, workers demand offsetting pay raises, employers are forced to lift prices, the CPI advances another notch . . . and so on.

Military pensions and food stamp benefits are also indexed directly to the cost of living. And the number of unionized workers whose wages are partly based on the CPI has risen from 2 million in 1965 to 6 million last year. The latest figure comprises 60 percent of all workers in major bargaining units.

All these adjustments protect some economic units against inflation by putting the burden of higher costs on others. These must then seek offsetting pay raises or price increases. The whole process not only encourages inflation to feed on itself, but it also discourages industry from trying to hold costs down by boosting productivity.

MORE PRODUCTIVITY NEEDED

Greater productivity is a vital economic need. This is because inflation is nourished and spread throughout the system by a chronic advance in wage levels that is several times faster than the pace at which the output of the average worker can be increased through more efficiency.

Since inflation speeded up in the mid-1960s, the average worker's pay in the private economy has risen at an accelerated pace of 7.5 percent a year. Meanwhile, the overall rate of improvement in productivity (as measured by output per man-hour) has slowed to only 1.8 percent a year. As a result, unit labor costs (that is, pay increases in excess of productivity gains) have climbed at an average pace of 5.7 percent. Table 2 shows the trend of these three key factors for the three decades since World War II.

The American people—and their political leaders—do not seem to understand that all wage hikes which are not offset by higher productivity must be recouped through price increases. Otherwise, the economy's private sector would go bankrupt. So there has been a close correlation over the years between the trend of unit labor costs and the advance in the consumer price index. It can be seen in the lower section of Table 2 that the average annual rise of 5.7 percent in unit

Table 2. Compensation, productivity, and inflation (average annual increases)

	Private business sector			Increase in consumer price index
	Increase in compensation −	Productivity increase =	Gain in unit labor costs	
1976	8.2%	4.4%	3.6%	5.8%
1975	9.7	2.1	7.4	9.1
1974	9.3	−3.4	13.2	11.0
1973	8.2	2.0	6.2	6.2
1972	5.6	2.9	2.7	3.3
1971	6.7	3.2	3.2	4.3
1970	7.1	0.8	6.4	5.9
1969	7.0	0.4	6.6	5.4
1968	7.6	3.3	4.1	4.2
1967	5.6	2.2	3.3	2.9
1966	7.1	3.3	3.6	2.9
1966–76	7.5%	1.8%	5.7%	5.8%
1956–66	4.9	3.4	1.5	1.8
1947–56	5.9	3.3	2.5	2.2

Source: U.S. Department of Labor.

labor costs over the past decade is nearly identical with the 5.8 percent yearly increase in the CPI.

Based on recent three-year labor settlements, the average worker's pay is likely to rise by 8–9 percent annually over the next few years. The record also indicates that the growth in productivity will probably not exceed 2.5 percent a year at best. The difference—a projected rise of 5.5 percent to 6.5 percent in unit labor costs—can be looked upon as a floor under the U.S. inflation rate. Faster productivity growth would make a big difference.

ROADBLOCKS TO PRODUCTIVITY

One reason for the slowdown in productivity is the fact that over half of all the new jobs created since the mid-1960s have been in (1) state and local government and (2) such labor-intensive services as tourism, building maintenance, hospitals, private education, and the legal, engineering, and other professional fields. These two areas have simply not made any measurable improvement in productivity. Because of higher taxes and rising costs, many U.S. industrial firms are no longer able to compete in world markets—or domestic markets. Layoffs and increased unemployment reflect this development.

A second roadblock to greater efficiency has been the proliferation of government regulation in all spheres of business activity. Some 75,000 people are now employed by the federal government alone in regulatory functions. The six largest agencies have close control over 10 percent of U.S. commerce, while a host of others reaches virtually every company in one way or another.

According to some estimates, U.S. industry spends over 130 million man-hours and nearly $20 billion a year just to keep up with the paperwork. The government spends another $18 billion a year to print, mail, and store this material. Much of this effort is sheer duplication and waste.

Some regulation in some fields is necessary. But the decrees issued by regulators—in such complex and interrelated areas as energy, pollution control, occupational safety, equal employment opportunity, and transportation—frequently ignore fundamental economic realities. As a result, businesses are often burdened with added unnecessary costs and reduced efficiency, product shortages sometimes come into being, and consumers end up paying higher prices than they otherwise would. The Office of Management and Budget has estimated that government regulation—directly and indirectly—costs each American family an average of $2,000 a year.

U.S. TAX LAW BIAS

A third factor holding down productivity is the built-in bias of our tax laws. The U.S. public sector obtains more of its revenues from taxes on income and wealth and less of its revenues from taxes on consumption than does any other major industrial country in the Free World.

As one illustration, corporate dividends are taxed twice—when they are earned and again after they are paid to shareholders. Also, capital gains are taxed more heavily in the United States than in most other countries. Under the Tax Reform Act of 1976, they are now subject in some cases to nearly the same tax rate as ordinary income. Assume that you purchased a share of stock for $100 in 1960 and that you sold it for $195 in 1976. You made no *real* capital gain. Because of the 95 percent inflation in that period, you are merely "getting your bait back." But under existing laws, you would pay taxes of up to $46 on your "phantom profits."

Rules such as these discourage people from wanting to save and invest in the nation's productive assets. It is no wonder that the number of individual shareowners in the United States has been dropping by about a million a year during the 1970s.

The nation's tax laws work against investment at the corporate level. The rate of capital recovery allowed under U.S. depreciation rules is well under those of most other countries. The United States permits a 55 percent write-off in the first three years of equipment life, versus 100 percent in Canada, 64 percent in Japan, 90 percent in France, 96 percent in Sweden, and 100 percent in the United Kingdom.

THE RATE OF INVESTMENT HURT

As a result of all these factors, the United States devotes less of its economic activity to investment than does any other large nation, including the United Kingdom. And less investment means fewer additions and improvements to the nation's productive assets, which supply the goods and services that are consumed. Table 3 relates in-

Table 3.   **Investment versus growth in productivity and output**

	Investment as a percentage of GNP, 1966–1975	Average annual increase, 1965–1975	
		Output per man-hour	Real GNP
Japan	33.7%	8.7%	8.7%
France	25.4	4.7	4.7
Germany	24.4	5.2	3.2
Canada	22.6	3.6	4.5
Italy	20.4	5.1	3.8
United Kingdom	18.6	3.0	2.0
United States	16.8	1.6	2.5

Sources: International Monetary Fund; U.S. Department of Labor; *International Economic Report of the President,* 1976.

vestment to economic growth and productivity improvement in seven countries.

The table shows that Japan, which leads the pack in investment, has increased its productivity and its constant-dollar gross national product faster than any other nation. In contrast, the United Kingdom and the United States—with the lowest investment rates—bring up the rear in both economic growth and productivity gains.

Over the next decade, the U.S. economy faces two enormous tasks:

■ *First,* it must provide some 18 million more jobs to make room for new workers and reduce the present ranks of the unemployed. This amounts to a 25 percent step-up in job formation over the previous ten years.

■ *Second,* it must generate the enormous sums of capital needed to create those jobs, find the energy required for expansion, and meet the nation's antipollution goals.

TWO CORNERSTONES FOR JOBS AND CAPITAL

If these are the major economic priorities, then slowing inflation significantly must be the overriding goal. The inflation of recent years has undermined the general level of public confidence and weakened the nation's profit structure. These are the two cornerstones on which both jobs and capital must be built.

Nothing would do more to restore the confidence that people need to save and invest and that business leaders need to add new plants and hire more workers than a slowdown in the rate of inflation. According to national polls, a majority of Americans now place inflation first among the country's problems.

Less inflation would also help restore the required profitability of large segments of U.S. industry. This would enable these sectors to increase employment and productivity. Though often subject to public scorn, profits are the economy's lifeblood. They are the means of allocating resources within the private sector; they encourage research and the development of products and services; they provide and attract capital investment; and they guide the flow of these funds into productive use. In the process, more jobs are created, incomes are boosted, and spending is stimulated. All of this enables the public's standard of living to rise.

Inflation hurts profitability and investment. Most directly, it affects a company buying equipment and materials in much the same way that it affects a consumer buying food, clothing, and shelter. For instance, a new 1,000-daily-ton linerboard mill costs around $185 million to build today—three times as much as in the mid-1960s.

Yet the big rise in the cost of capital goods is not fully recognized under present accounting procedures, since these base depreciation charges on original costs. As a result, U.S. industry is not charging income with the entire cost of replacing its assets and inventories as they are used up or become obsolete.

Last year, *stated* corporate profits totaled $92 billion—up 96 percent from the 1966 level. However, when adjusted by the Commerce Department to reflect today's inflated costs, they were only $63 billion—only 30 percent higher than in 1966. And in the same time period, the actual value of corporate fixed plant and inventories had increased by almost 170 percent.

The difference between stated and *real* profits in 1976 came to $29 billion. In effect, this amount represents capital that has been used up in the course of business and must be replaced in the future. Yet under present laws it is taxed as if it were current income—thus depleting existing capital and increasing industry's need for investment funds.

THE RISING DEBT LOAD

In recent years, most companies have had to rely more and more heavily on external borrowing in order to finance their expansion. The ratio of debt to equity in the capital structure of manufacturing companies as a whole has climbed from 32 percent in 1966 to nearly 45 percent last year. Then, too, as inflation has accelerated, lenders have demanded greater rates of interest to make up for their loss in purchasing power. For corporate borrowers, this has meant higher interest rates applied to higher equipment costs—a double whammy that has helped hold down the rate of capital investment.

Plant and equipment spending has been the most depressed part of

Chart 4. Average federal deficit, by four-year periods (including off-budget federal entities)

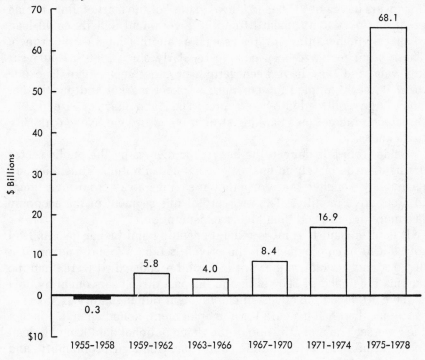

Source: *Economic Report of the President*, 1977.

the economy during the 1975–77 recovery. When this key sector picks up, the competition for capital is certain to intensify as the federal government continues to finance its growing deficits.

Chart 4 traces the growth of the average annual federal deficit by successive four-year periods. Since the mid-1960s, the average deficit has zoomed from $4 billion to $64 billion.

It is obvious that the federal deficit is expanding much faster than the economy as a whole. The deficit in fiscal 1976 reached 4.6 percent of gross national product—by far the highest share since World War II.

CROWDING OUT

The huge Treasury and agency borrowings, together with the continual new debt offerings of state and local governments, accounted for 48 percent of the total funds raised in U.S. credit markets in 1975 and for 34 percent in 1976. During the previous decade, the government share averaged 18 percent.

Since the total credit supply has continued to expand, most private borrowers have not yet been "crowded out" of the market. But at some point, the persistent upward trend in government deficits could lead to sharply higher interest rates as well as another huge credit crunch. These crunches have been coming regularly since 1966 in four-year intervals, and they have been getting progressively worse. The one in 1970 nearly toppled the commercial paper market and put the nation's largest railroad into bankruptcy. The last money squeeze in 1974 threatened the nation's banking structure and brought New York City to its knees.

Aside from this danger, the heavy borrowings by the public sector are being used largely to finance current consumption. Thus, they are channeling a higher share of national savings away from investment in productive facilities. The recovery of this segment of the economy is a more urgent need than higher consumption.

It is often said that more federal spending and bigger deficits lead to reduced unemployment in the private sector. We have never seen any empirical evidence that this is a valid premise. If it were, then the cumulative deficit of $200 billion in the past three years ought by now to have produced the lowest unemployment rate in history.

Rather than being a cure for unemployment, deficit spending is just the reverse. The monetization of the rising national debt can only lead to more inflation, lower public confidence, reduced profitability, and more limited job opportunities.

As the government continually spends beyond its income, more and more demands are placed on the economy for goods and services. At the same time, the supply side—the private sector—encompasses less and less of the economy. As a result, inflationary pressures grow.

The nation is currently experiencing an inflation rate well above what was considered intolerable only five or six years ago. Is it now possible to live with a rate of 6 percent, or 7 percent, or 8 percent?

The answer is no. Already inflation has done serious harm to the American economy as a whole and to the well-being of every American. And its impact is cumulative—the longer it lasts, the more it undermines the public's confidence.

SLOWER ECONOMIC GROWTH

Since inflation speeded up in the mid-1960s, the U.S. economy has grown much less rapidly than before. In the past decade, real GNP has grown at an average annual rate of only 2.5 percent, versus 4 percent during the first two decades after World War II. Industrial production has increased by only 3 percent a year, compared with 5 percent in the earlier period.

Chart 5. Productivity in the private business economy

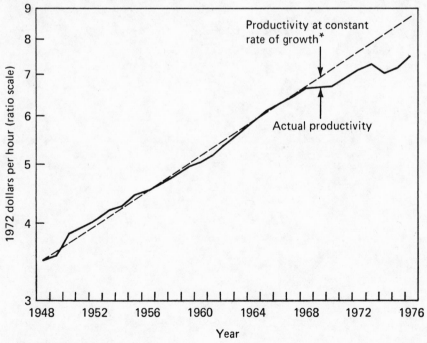

* Growth rate of 3.3 percent per year.
Source: U.S. Department of Labor.

The key to the nation's economic growth is productivity—the amount of goods or services generated by each man-hour worked. No matter how the pie is sliced, the average person's consumption cannot in the long run exceed the average person's production. So output per man-hour is a good proxy for the trend of the national standard of living. Chart 5 shows how far we have fallen behind in the past decade.

The main determinant of how much workers can produce is the value and efficiency of their tools—that is, the capital investment behind them. As long as the inflation rate remains high, the growth in the supply of capital will be impaired.

MAJOR POLICY CHANGES NEEDED

So if the private sector is to provide enough jobs and a rising standard of living, inflation has to be contained. The regulatory process and the tax system both need a major change—less emphasis on consumption and more on investment. But, above all else, the public sector must not be permitted to continue usurping a rising share of the nation's income.

Chapter 7

THE DEBATE OVER SAVING, INVESTMENT, AND CAPITAL SHORTAGES

*Murray L. Weidenbaum**

Most of the public and professional discussions on saving, investment, and capital shortages center on variations of one or more of the following three propositions:

1. Saving always equals investment, so no problem can ever arise.
2. Saving will equal investment in the United States in the years ahead, so there is no need to worry now.
3. In any event, we should not be concerned about capital and capitalists, but about workers and consumers.

The first two propositions are generally debated in professional circles, while the third is aimed at a less sophisticated audience. Let us deal with the third proposition first, and then turn the bulk of our attention to the first two.

WHY WORRY ABOUT SAVING AND INVESTMENT?

It should be recognized that it *is* difficult to arouse public interest in the question of the adequacy of investment capital in the United States in the years ahead. To many citizens, any discussion of capital immediately conjures up visions of greedy bankers, wealthy coupon clippers, and—to use what is to many a pejorative word—capitalists.

* Director, Center for the Study of American Business, Washington University, St. Louis.

Nevertheless, capital plays a pivotal role in providing the basis for the future standard of living of the population. Capital is basic for increasing productivity and thus providing an opportunity for the society to dampen down inflationary pressures while simultaneously providing rising real incomes.

Educators at times find it amusing when some of their students discover Maoist economists writing about the need to hold down consumption in the Chinese economy in order to free up the capital resources needed to invest in the future growth of that economy. "Why, they are not even a capitalist society," these students will note in wonderment. Then the thought will sink in—sometimes with a little faculty assistance—that a rising stock of capital is necessary for any growing society, capitalist (that is, private enterprise or market-oriented) or other. It is really a basic matter of how much we want to eat, drink, and be merry today—and how much we want to set aside for the future. Boiled down to its fundamentals, assuring an adequate flow of saving and investment is little more than demonstrating a proper concern for the future.[1]

EQUATING SAVING AND INVESTMENT

Some economists, as well as others, seem to be offended by studies that show—for some future year—a yawning gap between the amount of saving that will be available and the amount of investment that will be desired. They note, quite properly, that they are dealing with an accounting identity.[2] A capital shortage can never appear in the traditional national income (gross national product) accounts as a discrepancy between saving and investment. Such economic statistics can only show the amount of saving and investment which actually occurs, not the amount socially desirable. Unlike many of the speeches based on it, the often-cited study by the New York Stock Exchange does clearly and properly distinguish between (1) the gap between forecast saving and estimated investment requirements and (2) the equality—at some level—of the actual saving and investment that will take place.[3]

The equality between actual saving and actual investment is similar to the equality, on business balance sheets, of assets and liabilities (including net worth). Yet at the company level, the simple accounting identity is not permitted to inhibit serious analysis. It is universally understood that the Assets = Liabilities relationship is true for both bankrupt concerns and corporations with Aaa credit ratings. Similarly, Saving = Investment both in the case of a rapidly growing national economy and of a stagnant or even declining economy. There are serious questions to be considered. At what level does the balancing of saving and investment take place? What investment needs are rationed (or "crowded out") in the process? What types of investments are actually funded? What impacts are likely on productivity, living standards, and similar indicators of economic performance?

The equilibrium between saving and investment does not seem to be taking place as effortlessly as might be inferred from the critics. An examination of that burgeoning but almost universally ignored category of economic policy, the government credit programs, is pertinent. Surely, the rapid expansion in the size and scope of these federal financial intermediaries is symptomatic of growing dissatisfaction with the operation of the saving and investment process.

Chart 1. The federal government's share of the credit market

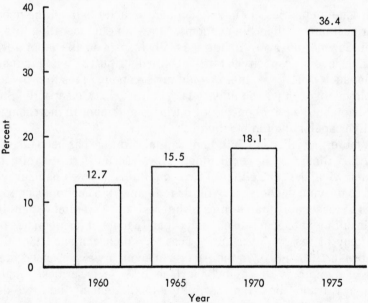

Sources: Federal Reserve; U.S. Treasury Department.

As shown by Chart 1, fifteen years ago about one tenth of the flow of private saving was directed to investment via the use of the government's credit power. At present, the ratio fluctuates around one third.[4] The rapid growth of "off balance sheet" federal financing is shown in Table 1.

As Henry Wallich has pointed out, capital inadequacy can show up in various forms. First, it can manifest itself in bottleneck situations,

Table 1. The impact of the federal government on credit markets (fiscal years; $ billions)

	1960	1965	1970	1975
A. Federal borrowing (budget financing)	$ 2.2	$ 4.0	$ 3.8	$ 50.9
B. Federally assisted borrowing (outside of budget)	3.3	6.8	12.6	13.9
C. Total (A + B)	5.5	10.8	16.4	64.8
D. Total funds advanced in credit markets	$43.4	$69.6	$90.5	$177.9
E. Federal portion (C ÷ D)	12.7%	15.5%	18.1%	36.4%

Sources: Federal Reserve; U.S. Treasury Department.

with some industries not having enough capacity to meet the needs of their customers when the economy as a whole is operating at a high level. Second, an overall shortage with respect to the labor force is possible, even if capacity is fairly evenly distributed among industries. Under such conditions, there would not be enough jobs to provide full employment even when industry is operating close to capacity. Should that happen, the joint concern of business and labor in increasing productive capacity would be obvious.[5]

A more specialized definition of capital shortage has been developed by Allen Sinai and Roger Brinner. They use the term to refer to an economy which meets either of two conditions: (1) the financial system fails to provide the necessary funds to finance the economy's expenditures at reasonably stable rates of interest; or (2) capital expenditures are insufficient to generate enough capacity to meet the demands of the economy at reasonably stable prices.[6] Wallich contends that during periods in 1973 and 1974, the American economy experienced the two sets of symptoms of capital shortage that he describes. Sinai and Brinner warn us about the possibility of experiencing their two definitions of capital shortages within the next few years.

It is generally the newer and smaller businesses rather than government or the larger and better established companies that get crowded out of credit markets during periods of financial stringency. That should be of concern to all who favor a competitive economy. The available data are striking. Of the $6.4 billion of bonds issued by the companies listed in the Fortune 500 in 1974, $5.1 billion was raised by the top 100 and $1.3 billion by the next 400. The top 100 companies reported 28 bond issues in 1974, and the bottom 100 only 1.[7]

In a sense, capital will always be scarce to the extent that more could be employed to advantage if it were somehow available. The question of capital adequacy can sensibly be addressed only in terms of the level of capital formation desired to attain the economic goals of the society—full employment, rising living standards, domestic energy independence, and so forth.

WILL SAVING EQUAL INVESTMENT?

Some analysts contend that saving flows will be adequate to the investment financing task in the decade ahead, provided only that the federal government learns to operate at a surplus for an extended period of time.[8]

To back that up, they cite several public and private forecasts which show that by 1980 or some other future year, the federal government may be operating at a surplus, thus adding to the availability of private capital funds. For example, the January 1978 budget estimates that on a full-employment basis, revenues would exceed outlays by a margin of $24 billion in 1982.[9]

Such statistical exercises can be very useful for policy purposes, provided that the user is aware of their limitations. *The key to understanding these, as well as any other long-term forecasts, is to look at the underlying assumptions. That is critical in this case. The key assumption, which may not always be apparent to the users of these forecasts, is that no further change will be made in the expenditure programs or the revenue structure of the federal government.*

THE GROWTH OF FEDERAL SPENDING

This is plainly unrealistic. If there is anything that can be forecast with confidence, it is that over the years Congress will pass laws increasing the scope of existing programs and instituting new spending programs. Likely candidates are not hard to find, ranging from incentives to explore and develop new domestic energy sources to a national health insurance program.

This is not an attack on the projections per se, but on their use. The projections are not intended to be forecasts of reality. Rather, they indicate the amount of discretion that is available to increase outlays and/or cut taxes within the existing budget structure. In the future, as in the past, the public's appetite for new government services and benefits is likely to outrun its willingness to pay for this largess in the form of higher taxes. Thus, the federal government is likely to run

Table 2.   Range of assumptions on policy in major capital forecasts

Author and time period covered	Assumptions	Projected total private saving rate (percent of GNP)	Projected investment needs (percent of GNP)	Conclusions
Bosworth, Duesenberry, and Carron (1973–80)	No net new federal programs; grants and transfers continue to grow to fund existing programs. Monetary policy easier (interest rates lower) than in 1974. Tax revenues rise as real output and prices increase. Government expected to generate a net surplus of $13 billion in 1980.	15.2	15.6	Capital shortage can be averted if government achieves projected surplus. "We can afford the future, but just barely."
Benjamin M. Friedman (1977–81)	Modest new government spending, programs; transfers grow faster than GNP. Budget balanced by tax reductions during inflationary periods when revenues rise rapidly. Budget balanced in 1977 and all subsequent years in study. Monetary policy relatively tight.	15.7	15.8	Foresees no problem in nonfinancial corporate sector; but expects sector's reliance on external funds to be greater. Believes residential share of output will decline.
Sinai and Brinner (1975–85)	Government expenditures increase, but decline relative to GNP. Transfer payments increase according to law. Monetary policy is largely accommodating; interest rates higher than in past decade, but this reflects influence of inflation and strong credit demands. Large deficits are projected through 1970s; smaller deficits in 1980s.	16.4	15.3	Shortages unlikely, especially in late 1970s. Financing becomes more difficult in 1980s. Rising ratios of short-term to long-term debt and debt/equity rise, leading to some decreases in investment.

Table 2 (continued)

Author and time period covered	Assumptions	Projected total private saving rate (percent of GNP)	Projected investment needs (percent of GNP)	Conclusions
New York Stock Exchange (1974–85)	Assumes $3.5 billion annual deficit. No change in tax policy. Makes no mention of monetary policy.	14.6	16.4	Serious capital shortage likely to occur. Cumulative capital shortage could exceed $650 billion under some circumstances.
Bureau of Economic Analysis, U.S. Department of Commerce (1975–80)	Slower growth in government expenditures; tax incentives developed to encourage investment. Deficit is reduced to avoid preempting investment. Monetary policy is expansionary when deficit is small.	—	—*	Under assumptions of study, no shortage is likely to occur.

* Business fixed investment is estimated to rise from 10.4 percent of GNP in 1965–70 to 12.0 percent in 1975–80 because of environmental legislation and the effect of domestic energy independence.

Source: Murray L. Weidenbaum and James McGowen, "Capital Formation and Public Policy," Electric Perspectives, 1976, no. 5.

deficits and, on balance, to be not a supplier but an important user of investment funds in the years ahead. Continuing large budget deficits are not inevitable, of course. Yet it must be realized that budget surpluses would be a marked change from recent experience. That would require drastically revised public attitudes toward government spending and taxation.

As might be expected, individual analysts differ in their specific estimates of future saving and investment flows. Nevertheless, there are many visible factors which, given current public policies, should make it difficult for saving to equal investment at a satisfactorily high level.

FORCES DEPRESSING SAVING

On the supply side, several basic factors will be dampening the potential for generating saving in the years ahead. In absolute terms, of course, there will be large increases in the funds available for investment. Important forces, however, will be exercising a depressing effect on the growth rate of saving.

The changing age distribution of the population. Consumers, who are a basic source of saving in the economy, will be experiencing some adverse factors. The changing age distribution of the U.S. population suggests that, if past saving patterns are maintained, the personal saving rate (although not the absolute amount) could decline over the coming decade.

The saving rates of different age groups. The anticipated trends in the low-saving age groups are quite different from those in the high-saving age brackets. That does not require much forecasting ability because these are people who are already born and living in the United States. The prospects are very unfavorable. The number of Americans in the high-spending, low-saving age brackets (20–34) will be rising substantially, from 46 million in 1972 to 60 million in 1982. These are the young people who borrow heavily, particularly to finance and furnish new homes. Most of the people who shift from renting to buying a home are under 35. In contrast, the high-saving age brackets (40–54) will show a decline in absolute numbers, from 36 million in 1972 to 34 million in 1982.[10]

The liberalization of Social Security. Another factor dampening the private saving rate is the repeated liberalization of Social Security and other government welfare programs. This relationship has been noted by several scholars, liberal and conservative. Recent studies show that the provision of public pensions substantially depresses the rate of private saving.[11] With the Social Security system operating at best on a pay-as-you-go basis, there is no offsetting government saving. Should the system begin to operate at a deficit, there would be government dissaving, that is, increased "crowding out" in the nation's capital markets.

The overstatement of corporate profits. Inflation has resulted in substantial overstatements of real business profits (a basic source of corporate saving), especially as a result of inadequate depreciation allowances and transient inventory profits. Real corporate profits (adjusted for these factors) declined by over 40 percent in the past decade, from $37.0 billion in 1965 to $20.6 billion in 1974. As long as inflation continues and traditional accounting methods are employed, this problem will persist. Consequently, business is being forced to use virtually all of its saving from depreciation allowances and retained earnings simply to maintain existing capacity.[12]

FORCES INCREASING DEMAND

On the demand side, in contrast, there will be many rising needs for capital investment, to meet both new priorities, such as reliance on domestic energy, and the requirements directly imposed on business by government.

Pollution control spending. Both public and private projections show that rapidly rising annual dollar outlays for new pollution control facilities will be required to meet existing legal requirements, as shown in Table 3. About 5 percent of industrial plant and equipment investment is expected to be devoted to these purposes.

Table 3.   The increase in mandated investments in pollution control (in billions of 1973 dollars)

Category	1973	1982	Cumulative, 1973–1982
Air pollution	$1.2	$7.2	$47.6
Water pollution	0.5	1.5	14.2
Noise	0.1	1.2	7.4
Radiation	—	—	0.3
Total	$1.8	$9.9	$69.5

Source: U.S. Council on Environmental Quality.

OSHA outlays. Government-mandated industrial safety and noise abatement outlays will be significant, with estimates ranging to $40 billion or more during the coming five-year period.[13] These government-mandated investment requirements help to explain the anomaly of a declining return on capital, which is supposed to be a characteristic of a capital surplus economy. It is evident that the typical firm realizes little if any return on these involuntary outlays. Thus a larger than average return is required on the capital investments that are devoted to production.

Rising capital-output ratios. A more basic concern has been the tendency for the ratio of capital stock to output to rise during the past decade. This reversed the trend of the preceding period, during which capital efficency was improving. A recent report of the nonpartisan Congressional Budget Office states the matter very clearly: "Certainly growth in the capital stock of the economy plays an important role in increasing labor productivity, and per capita living standards are unlikely to rise without increasing productivity or output per worker. Thus, the recent weakness in investment and in productivity is a matter of some concern."[14]

THE ROLE OF PUBLIC POLICY

Before considering possible changes in public policy, it is important to understand the impact of existing policies. If any doubt remains about the bias in the tax system in favor of consumption and against saving, it can be resolved quickly with a simple and straightforward example. Take the case of three factory workers, Mr. A, Mr. B, and Mr. C. They are the same in age, have the same work experience and the same size families, and earn the same wages. To keep it simple, also assume that each rents the house he lives in.

- Mr. A is the saver—each week he deposits a portion of his paycheck into his savings account.
- Mr. B regularly spends what he earns, no more and no less.
- Mr. C is the big spender. Not only does he spend everything he earns, but he borrows to the hilt, buying as much on credit as he can.

Which of the three pays the most income tax, and which pays the least?

Clearly, Mr. A, the saver, will have the highest tax bill, paying taxes on his wages as well as on the interest he earns on his savings account. Mr. C winds up with the lowest tax bill, as he receives a tax deduction from the the interest he pays on his borrowings. Mr. B's tax bill will be in between that of Mr. A and Mr. C.

Actual practice, of course, includes many variations in the tax treatment of financial transactions. Yet, as a general principle, it does seem that, for the average citizen, the existing personal income tax structure favors consumption over saving. In addition, many government spending programs operate with a similar effect.

Assume that Mr. A, Mr. B, and Mr. C all get laid off at the same time and that none of them obtain a new job.

- Mr. C, the big spender, will be the first one to be eligible for welfare, food stamps, and medicare.
- Mr. B, who spends all he earns, will be next.
- Mr. A, the big saver, will be the last to qualify for federal assistance. Unlike the good Lord, federal government policy does not seem to help those who help themselves!

FINANCING THE NATION'S FUTURE

What can be done to provide greater encouragement to saving and investment?

Reducing federal deficits. The first and perhaps most important idea that comes to mind is essentially a negative one. The federal government should stop being such a large dissaver. That is, it should eliminate or at least reduce the massive extent to which it currently competes with the private sector for the relatively limited supply of investment capital. As the economy continues to recover from its recession lows, the rising pace of business activity will yield increasing flows of federal revenues. Unless Congress increases government spending at that same rapid rate, the result will be a substantial reduction in the federal deficit in the years ahead. The result is not a foregone conclusion. The advocates of economy will have to exert sufficient political pressures to offset the proponents of greater government spending.

Off-budget spending. There is a related need, which is far more technical, and hence for which there is little public support or even understanding—the need to curtail the various off-budget agencies. These are mere subterfuges whereby normal federal expenditures do not show up in the budget. Because these expenditures are not subject to the scrutiny of the budgetary process, they are expanding at a far more rapid rate than the budget. In fiscal 1972, they totaled $249 million. In the fiscal 1978 budget, they are estimated at over $9 billion. That is $9 billion that the U.S. government has to borrow above and beyond the official budget deficit. Should the proposals for an off-budget Energy Independence Authority or an off-budget national health insurance program be adopted, the size of this category would more than triple.

Table 4. Expansion in outlays of off-budget federal agencies (fiscal years; $ billions)

Agency	Amount excluded from the budget			
	1970	1972	1975	1978
Export-Import Bank	0	$0.2	$1.4	*
Postal Service	0	0	0.8	$2.5
Rural Electrification Administration	0	0	0.5	0
Housing for the Elderly or Handicapped Fund	0	0	0.1	0.7
Environmental Financing Authority	0	0	0.2	0
Rural Telephone Bank	0	0	0.1	0.1
Federal Financing Bank	0	0	6.4	5.9
Total	0	$0.2	$9.5	$9.2

* Outlays are now included in the budget totals; $1.0 billion planned spending would raise the total from $9.2 billion to $10.2 billion.

Source: Compiled from various federal budget documents.

More realistic government controls. A third useful contribution that the federal government can make to ensure capital adequacy in the years ahead is in the area of government controls over business. An increasing number of regulatory agencies impose investment requirements on business firms, requirements which do not generate more productive capacity but are intended to meet various social priorities. These social requirements should not be eliminated, but they should be subject to the rigors of a benefit/cost test. These expensive federal regulatory requirements should only be continued if it can be demonstrated that their value or benefit to the society exceeds the costs that they impose on the public.

True tax reform. Let us turn now to the more positive possibilities for encouraging saving and investment. There are important and useful lessons to be learned from the past. The more specific the focus of a federal tax incentive, the more likely it is that inefficiencies and other unwanted side effects are going to result. What is needed is true tax reform of general applicability. For a growing number of economists, both liberal and conservative, the most economically sensible and efficient approach to increasing private saving is to reduce the corporate income tax. That action would have a number of desirable effects. Clearly, a lower corporate income tax rate would increase aftertax corporate profits. That should also increase the amount of business "saving" in the form of retained earnings. But not all of the tax reduction is likely to be saved. Some of the added profits would be disbursed in the form of higher dividends, and individual disposable income and personal saving would therefore rise. To some extent, the tax saving may also be shifted—forward to consumers in the form of lower prices or more slowly rising prices, and backward to labor in the form of higher wages, salaries, and fringe benefits. The precise distribution of these resultant benefits would depend on the operation of market forces.

A lower corporate income tax rate would reduce the indirect but pervasive role of the tax collector in internal business decision making. It would tend to promote more efficient use of resources to the extent that fewer low-priority business expenses would be incurred merely because they were tax-deductible. It would soften the double taxation of corporate income, that is, the taxes on corporate earnings which are then taxed again as dividends received by shareowners. A lower corporate income tax would also reduce the current bias in the tax system toward debt financing—because interest paid on debt is deductible from taxable income, and in most cases dividends on equity capital are not. Rising debt/equity ratios and declining interest coverages on corporate balance sheets clearly demonstrate the importance of permitting a greater reliance on equity rather than on debt financing in the future.

Corporate income taxes.   The present corporate income tax contains some of the more regressive elements in the tax system. This may be especially true for the portion of the corporate tax that reduces the income that would otherwise be available to such "capitalist" shareholders as philanthropic institutions, foundations, universities, and employee pension funds. A tax at the personal level, in contrast, can differentiate among various categories of people on some rational basis.[15]

But unlike the negative suggestions made earlier, tax cuts would increase the federal deficit and thus increase the amount of government borrowing that competes with private investment demands. The positive impacts on production and employment of a cut in corporate income taxes would generate "feedback" effects that would result in some compensating increases in federal revenues.

Professor Charles McLure of Rice University states, on the basis of his examination of the public finance literature, that a separate tax on corporation income cannot be justified under commonly accepted canons of taxation.[16] Nevertheless, it has seemed easier in the past to get far less efficient special interest legislation into law than to achieve a general reduction in corporate tax rates. If the naive advocates of closing tax "loopholes" have their way, Congress may be enacting legislation further reducing the incentive and ability of the private sector to save and invest.

Capital gains taxes. It is ironic that the pressures to increase capital gains taxation, are far stronger in the United States than in other industrialized nations, although our tax burden on such gains is already so much higher. In Japan, France, the Netherlands, and West Germany, for example, capital gains are generally exempt from income tax. It should also be recognized that a large portion of "capital gains" is not gains at all. Rather, it reflects higher asset prices caused by inflation.

Depreciation-capital recovery. If Congress does take specific action in the corporate tax area, it should give favorable consideration to converting depreciation allowances to a true capital recovery system. This could be done by shifting the depreciation base from historical cost to current replacement cost. Such forward-looking action would help to halt the decline of real saving in the business sector of the private economy.

The depreciation practices of other leading industrialized nations are in general far more liberal than those of the United States. Even including the effect of the investment credit and the use of the more liberal asset depreciation range (ADR), only about 23.5 percent of a new investment in machinery and equipment can be written off in the first year under our federal tax system. In contrast, France allows 31.3 percent; Japan allows 37.1 percent; Canada, 50.0 percent; and the United Kingdom, a full 100 percent.[17]

Encouraging individual saving and investing. Encouragement to individual or consumer saving could be accomplished through excluding from gross income all or a portion of interest on deposits in savings institutions. Some legislative proposals would provide a partial percent tax credit for funds deposited into a savings account or used to purchase the stock or bonds of a domestic corporation. Others would eliminate double taxation of common stock dividends.[18] These proposals would begin to move the federal tax structure away from taxing saving and investment so heavily and toward placing more of the burden on consumption. The timing of their enactment will be influenced strongly by the overall state of the federal budget and by competing demands on the public purse.

CONCLUSION

Unless the nation acts on many fronts to encourage private saving and to dampen government competition for investment funds—by voting a lower tax burden on saving, by reducing deficit spending, and by reforming regulation—the underlying demand for capital may outrun the supply of saving required to finance it.

As Secretary of the Treasury W. Michael Blumenthal states, "If we are to move toward a full employment economy over the balance of this decade, investment in productive capacity will have to absorb a higher proportion of our national output. We will have to achieve a better balance in distributing the results of economic growth between current consumption and investing for even greater future growth."[19]

In practice, available saving will be allocated one way or another among the various categories of investment requirements. But a high average level of interest rates is likely to be the balancing factor, and numerous weaker demanders of capital—notably small and new business, local governments, and individuals—will be elbowed out of financial markets and thus will obtain smaller real shares of the nation's resources. Hence, gearing public policy to encouraging an adequate flow of saving and investment does indeed show a proper concern for the future of our nation and deep compassion for its people.

NOTES

1. For more detailed analysis, see Murray L. Weidenbaum, *Saving, Investment, and Capital Shortages*, publication no. 8, Center for the Study of American Business, Washington University, St. Louis, February 1976; and Murray L. Weidenbaum and James McGowen, "Capital Formation and Public Policy," *Electric Perspectives*, 1976, no. 5, pp. 24–29.
2. See Robert Eisner, "Capital Shortage: Myth and Reality," *American Economic Review*, February 1977, pp. 110–15.
3. New York Stock Exchange, *The Capital Needs and Savings Potential of the U.S. Economy* (New York, 1974).
4. Murray L. Weidenbaum, *An Economic Analysis of the Federal Government's Credit Programs*, working paper no. 18, Center for the Study of American Business, Washington University, St. Louis, January 1977.
5. Henry C. Wallich, "Is There a Capital Shortage?" *Challenge*, September/October 1975, pp. 30–36.
6. Allen Sinai and Roger E. Brinner, *The Capital Shortage* (Lexington, Mass.: Data Resources, Inc., 1975).
7. Henry Kaufman and Richard I. Johannesen, Jr., *The Cost of Money for Corporate Finance* (New York: Salomon Brothers, 1975).
8. Barry Bosworth, James S. Duesenberry, and Andrew S. Carron, *Capital Needs in the Seventies* (Washington, D.C.: Brookings Institution, 1975).
9. *Budget of the United States Government for the Fiscal Year 1978* (Washington, D.C.: Government Printing Office, 1977).
10. Josephine M. McElhone and Henry J. Cassidy, "Mortgage Lending: Its Changing Economic and Demographic Environment," *Federal Home Loan Bank Board Journal*, July 1974, p. 11.
11. Martin Feldstein, *Social Security and Private Savings* (Cambridge, Mass.: Harvard Institute of Economic Research, 1974); and Robert Eisner, "Business Investment Preferences," *George Washington Law Review*, March 1974, p. 495.
12. George Terborgh, "Corporate Saving and the Capital Shortage," *Capital Goods Review*, September 1975, pp. 1–4.
13. Murray L. Weidenbaum, *Business, Government, and the Public* (Englewood Cliffs, N.J.: Prentice-Hall, 1977).

14. U.S. Congressional Budget Office, *Sustaining a Balanced Expansion* (Washington, D.C.: Government Printing Office, 1976).
15. C. Lowell Harriss, "Tax Equity and the Need for Capital," *National Tax Journal,* September 1975, pp. 292–300.
16. Charles E. McLure, Jr., "Integration of the Personal and Corporate Income Taxes," *Harvard Law Review,* January 1975, pp. 532–82.
17. Gary P. Gillum, "Capital Gains," *Business Review of the Federal Reserve Bank of Philadelphia,* September 1973, p. 5.
18. U.S. Department of the Treasury, *Blueprints for Basic Reforms* (Washington, D.C.: Government Printing Office, 1977).
19. W. Michael Blumenthal, "The Government's Role in the Capital Formation Process," *Department of the Treasury News,* March 3, 1977, p. 3.

Chapter 8

THE CRUCIAL MATTER OF BUSINESS AND INVESTOR CONFIDENCE

*Robert H. B. Baldwin**

Many people have recently expressed concern about the ability of the U.S. economy to meet national objectives requiring fixed-capital formation during the coming decade. New plant and equipment will be essential for creating jobs, for retarding inflation, for increasing the nation's international competitiveness, for enhancing environmental protection and improvement, for meeting stricter standards of worker and product safety, and for achieving energy independence. Yet investment must be financed, and the focus of much of the recent concern has been on the U.S. financial markets. Will saving be adequate to finance a rate of capital formation in the United States which will be consistent with achieving these all-important national goals? Will financing be available on a cost basis which will make it sensible for business to go ahead with new productive facilities?

It is alarming to consider the number of ways in which U.S. capital formation, which is so vital to the nation's economic health, is increasingly being frustrated. The warning signs on the horizon—and closer than that—are clear; but almost inevitably, only a crisis situation can force a courageous political decision on economic issues. Politicians are never quick to make the hard decisions that economic problems demand, and the problem of capital formation is no exception to this general rule.

Nevertheless, politicians merely respond to the predominant public opinion. *The root problem for capital formation in the United States, therefore, is that there is so little public understanding of how invest-*

---

* President, Morgan Stanley & Co., Incorporated.

ment in productive plant and equipment affects the lives and jobs of every citizen.

PUBLIC UNDERSTANDING

There is some reason to be a bit more optimistic about public understanding of this problem than there was a year or two ago. If the continuing natural gas crisis has a silver lining, that silver lining may be that the natural gas crisis has caused the print and broadcast media to take a closer look at how our economic machine really functions.

Two brief examples from well-known publications may illustrate the grounds for cautious optimism. First, near the peak of the 1976–77 winter natural gas crisis, *Newsweek* said the following:

> The administration, shaking its fist at fate, has asked Congress for power to allocate natural gas and temporarily suspend price ceilings on it. This request is a timely reminder that government often is the disease for which it pretends to be the cure. Under the proposed legislation, government will ration a commodity it has helped to make scarce.[1]

Second, at about the same time the *New York Times* said this:

> The market for fuel produced and sold within a single state—and thus out of reach of federal regulators—has captured a major portion of newly discovered supplies. Why sell gas to an interstate pipeline at the regulated rate, $1.42 per thousand cubic feet, when local utilities in Texas will pay $2.10? It is conceivable, even probable, that gas fields subject to Federal Power Commission controls have not been developed in recent years, the gas companies anticipating the collapse of regulation. To put it another way, if the companies had been in a hurry to sell at regulated prices, they would now owe their stockholders an explanation.[2]

Two aspects of these excerpts are important. First, they are written with a good deal more sophistication about, and understanding of, business, free markets, and the roots of our energy problems than many people in business have come to expect. Second, they appeared in national publications. (It is especially heartening to see this sort of writing in the *Times*, whose editorial page, many in business agree, has not always been sympathetic to the viewpoints of business, but which has recently taken a more understanding position.)

ENERGY, CAPITAL INVESTMENT, JOBS, AND PRODUCTIVITY

There is a certain urgency to the current situation. The United States is now coming out of the second worst recession in half a century, and the economy is still stuttering. Before a full recovery emerges, at least two things must occur: the nation must come to grips with its energy problems, and it must lay the groundwork for a much higher level of capital investment, which is essential for more jobs. For either of these developments to come about, it is necessary first to have a quantum jump in public understanding of the interrelationships among the various elements of the economy. Before the public will support policies designed to promote greater saving, it must see how capital formation can increase both employment and productivity and can help contain the rate of inflation.

With respect to the public's consciousness of these problems, business is faced with a plus and a minus in getting its message across. The minus is the discouragingly low level of common understanding of how this economy's free enterprise system works. The plus is that, at least according to opinion surveys conducted during the election campaign, most Americans now assign top priority to economic objectives; in other words, they are ready to listen.

If the public listens, understands, and gets a feeling for the urgency of the current situation, some of the nation's political leaders may feel the heat, and there may be some improvement. Many business leaders are now looking hopefully in the direction of the national media—especially to television—for signs that "business solutions" to some of our current national problems are going to get a clear presentation and a fair hearing.

THE BACKGROUND OF THE SPECIFIC PROBLEMS

To understand the specific problems confronting capital investment, it is necessary to examine the background against which they are occurring.

First, the climate which prevails now is very different from the one that existed during the last real boom period of the 1960s. This altered environment is, to a large extent, going to determine how readily investment capital is made available.

In the 1950s and 1960s, decision-makers and investors alike wore rose-colored glasses. Corporations added capacity to protect market share, believing that the growth of the economy would pull them out of any temporary overproduction. All they had to do was ride out the cycle. A booming economy cures all ills.

Since then the economy has slipped down the other side of the boom-bust curve, and today it is somewhere along the way up the next one. But the market jitters linger.

INVESTOR CONFIDENCE

Investor confidence has been badly bruised by a number of factors, including the following:

1. Stocks have undergone what amounts to a five-year bear market, during which returns on equity investments were extremely low by any standard.

2. The memory of double-digit inflation is not easily shaken off, nor is the fear of its return. Even relatively unsophisticated investors are watching the wholesale commodity price index with the sort of rapt attention once reserved only for the Dow Jones industrial average.

3. The markets have witnessed a whole series of investment debacles: New York City's problems, along with those of other municipalities; three major bank failures; the difficulties of real estate investment trusts; the Penn-Central bankruptcy.

4. The threat of prolonged and costly strikes in major industries is another cause for concern. Investors have seen what a four-week strike did to the rubber industry and to the price of automobile tires.

The list goes on and on.

There is little wonder, then, that investors still have a strong taste of caution in their mouths. And this caution has, in turn, been augmented by a basic lack of confidence in developments at the macroeconomic level. When President Carter announced his $30 billion tax package in early 1977, the market underwent one of the most rapid declines in recent history.

Why? People are still scared about their jobs and their savings—that is, about security. Easy money of the type the Carter Administration was then prescribing is in theory supposed to mean lower interest rates—at least for the short run. But investors sensed the seeds of more inflation and sold. This comes under the heading of what academics have called "expectational economics," a field of study which explains why people don't act quite the way they should under some macroeconomic theories.

It is impossible, at least right now, to program human considerations into a national economic model—people have been scarred by the severe 1973–75 recession, and they are acting differently from what historical statistics would suggest.

This psychology of caution carries over to the stock markets in particular, with chaotic and somewhat bizarre results. Institutions, which account for over 70 percent of the trading volume on the New York Stock Exchange, are getting a double dose of caution today: first, from the overall economic considerations just enumerated, and second, from the Employee Retirement Income Security Act. ERISA has made "prudence" the order of the day for managers of funds coming under this law and, by extension, for most managers of other institutional funds. With all these uncertainties, especially the prospect of a resurgence of inflation, money managers cannot be faulted for being cautious with their capital. It is unnecessary to dwell on the fact that a skittish, skeptical market environment makes capital-raising a precarious undertaking. But it is useful to emphasize that the investment climate is only one of—and perhaps the least of—the difficulties that the economy is facing.

UNKNOWNS IN THE INVESTMENT EQUATION

Two other unknowns in the investment equation remain. Where will the funds come from? And will it, once all the factors are weighed, be a rational business decision for many firms to launch new capital projects?

First, what are the possible sources of funds?

The generation of internal funds through aftertax profits and depreciation allowances has traditionally been the greatest single source of funds for capital investment. In recent years, however, as shown in Chart 1, profit rates have fallen substantially relative to the compensation of employees.

In the early 1960s, corporate profits, adjusted for inventory profits and capital consumption, were about 17 percent of employee compensation. In contrast, during the 1975–76 period corporate profits had dropped to about 10½ percent of employee compensation.

Research done by Professor William Nordhaus[3] of Yale, who has recently been appointed to the Council of Economic Advisers, indicates that it is still too early to tell whether the decline in the overall profit rate is a permanent shift or simply a response to the unusually depressed economic conditions of the first half of the 1970s. One point is clear, however: profitability will have to be improved before businesses can look to internal funds to play the same role in capital formation that they have played in the past.

While conditions in the credit and equity markets have tended to improve over the last 9–12 months, there are still a number of factors deterring firms from going to those markets for investment capital.

Chart 1.   Corporate profits as a percentage of employee compensation, 1960–1976

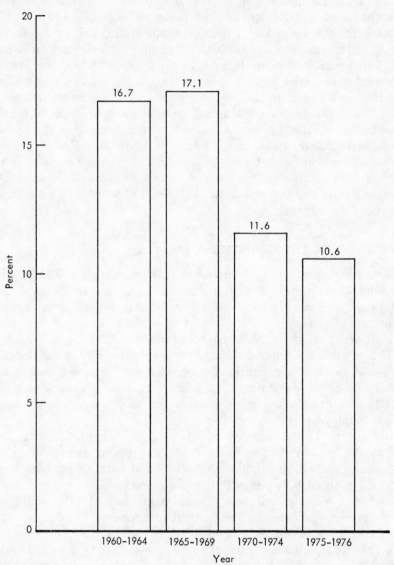

Source: U.S. Department of Commerce, *Business Conditions Digest*, February 1977, p. 48.

THE DEBT BURDEN

A great number of corporations are still overleveraged as a result of the debt binge of the 1960s. Their debt/equity ratios and long-term-debt/short-term-debt ratios remain out of line. The market is reluctant to extend further credit to these corporations without an interest premium, and the companies themselves, fearful of lowering their bond ratings, are hanging back.

As Chart 2 shows, in dollars of constant purchasing power, the Dow Jones 30 industrials have been in a "downdraft" since the late 1960s.

Chart 2.   Dow Jones 30 industrials index, 1960–1976 (in dollars of 1976 purchasing power)

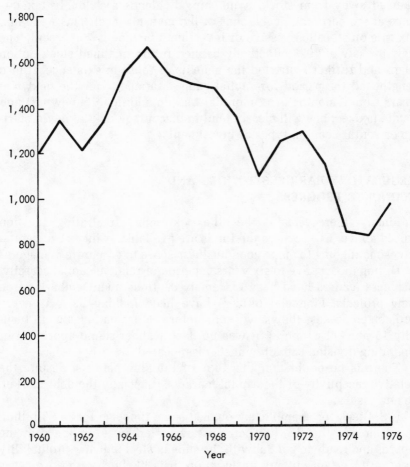

Sources: Dow Jones and Company; *Wall Street Journal; Economic Report of the President,* January 1977, p. 241.

Currently, in the wake of the prolonged bear market and galloping inflation, price-earnings ratios are too low for many companies even to consider an equity offering.

Equity offerings are, therefore, open mainly to top-tier firms, a situation tied to a very great extent to investor concerns about recurring inflation and depressed profitability, as noted above.

TAX BARRIERS TO JOBS AND ECONOMIC PROGRESS

No discussion of the situation in the equity markets, however brief, can avoid focusing on the tax barriers erected against equity investment. Congress has arranged it so that most investor incentives are skewed away from stock ownership: dividends are doubly taxed— once at the corporate level, once at the investor level. The maximum tax rate on so-called passive or investment income is 70 percent. The new tax law of 1976 effectively banned future qualified stock option plans and further restricted the benefits of those in existence. It also lengthened the period for capital gains treatment over the next two years from 6 months to 12 months. And, in addition, its new gift and estate tax sections will clearly tend to discourage risk-taking in start-up or venture capital types of investments.

REGULATORY BARRIERS TO JOBS AND
ECONOMIC PROGRESS

Finally, there remains the other, extremely frustrating question raised above: Even where the funds are available, is increased capital investment going to make good business sense to corporate managers?

During the last five to six years, a period of relative capital scarcity, business leaders have been extremely cautious about embarking on new projects. Financial officers have been looking hard at every project, and unless they saw a satisfactory return on investment (usually 15 percent or more), it was no deal. Rubber-stamp approvals of operating division capital budgets disappeared.

There is no doubt that this type of thinking persists, despite the relative receptivity of the capital markets, especially the debt market, to new issues.

U.S. Steel, for example, announced some time ago that a $3 billion "greenfield"—that is, 100 percent new—plant was on the drawing boards and ready to go. But with the slide in steel industry profitability and an uncertain outlook on inflation, it is likely that the project is going to stay on the drawing boards until a satisfactory return is in prospect. And, of course, the jobs to build it and the jobs to run it will also remain on the drawing boards.

What especially alarms business leaders is that they see an increasing number of barriers to earning a satisfactory return on capital investment projects.

First, any new investment is going to be expensive. Since 1960, when the word *inflation* was hardly in anyone's vocabulary, capital goods prices have risen more rapidly and more consistently than any other major component of the U.S. price structure, as shown in Chart 3.

Next, add to capital goods prices some of the nonproductive costs that are being imposed on capital projects, such as costly, time-con-

Chart 3.   Cost of plant and equipment, 1960–1976 (1960 = 100)

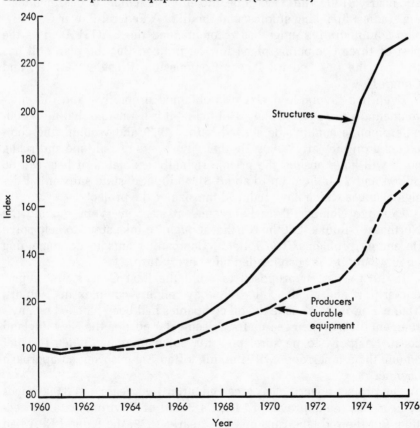

Source: *Economic Report of the President*, January 1977, p. 190.

suming planning and approval processes and superprecise, prohibi-
tively expensive environmental protection standards. The proposed
U.S. Steel plant noted above is a case in point. Even if the financial
hurdles are cleared, it will be at least two years from the date a go-
ahead decision is made until the first shovelful of earth can be dug to
begin construction. And this is true, apparently, in all 50 states.

Other examples are useful, too.

Example Number One is particularly appropriate while the recent
natural gas shortages are fresh in people's minds. The Canadian-
Arctic gas pipeline is potentially one of the quickest partial fixes to
the gas shortage. It will be able to supply about 5 percent of the U.S.
daily consumption, bringing gas from the North Slope of Alaska and
the Mackenzie Delta to mid-America and eastern Canada.

Planning for this project has been under way for over four years,
and nearly $130 million has gone into environmental studies, engineer-
ing studies, financing studies, and the like. A Federal Power Commission administrative judge has recommended the CAGSL Plan as the
best of three competing plans for the project. But the plan still has
to clear the full Federal Power Commission, President Carter, and
Congress.

Even if a favorable decision is obtained promptly—and the envi-
ronmentalists are promising a stiff fight—it is estimated that the 4,000-
mile pipeline couldn't be started before 1979 and wouldn't be completed until the early 1980s. By then, five years of red tape and rising
costs will have pushed the price, originally estimated at between $6
billion and $7 billion, up to about $11 billion, despite substantial design changes which have reduced the size of the project.

Example Number Two: Everyone—at least everyone outside the
Northeast—thinks that the Northeast ought to take steps to help solve
its energy problems. The Pittston Company wants to do something
about it, but it has been headed off at every turn.

In 1973, Pittston proposed to build the East Coast's first super-
tanker port and a 250,000-barrel-a-day refinery complex in Eastport,
Maine. For over a decade the oil companies had been blocked by envi-
ronmentalists in their search for a deepwater port on the New England
coast. Eastport, to be sure, presents some unique problems—chief
among them a narrow, swift-running, often fog-enshrouded approach
channel.

The project nevertheless received, after two years and 8,000 pages
of hearings, the approval of Maine's Board of Environmental Protection. But the red tape runs on. As of early 1977, the federal EPA had
yet to reach a decision. The Corps of Engineers was squabbling with
the Coast Guard over the Coast Guard's report on the channel's navi-

gability. This seemed likely to set the project back another six to nine months.

In four years Pittston has spent about $3 million on the project while the estimated cost of the refinery complex itself has jumped from $350 million to $650 million.

What's at stake besides badly needed oil for New England? About 1,100 permanent jobs and 2,000 construction jobs in one of the most chronically depressed areas of the country.

Example Number Three: Dow Chemical Company has shown what can happen when the red tape runs too long. Two years ago Dow embarked on a project to build a $500 million petrochemical complex on the Sacramento River. But in January 1977, after spending $6 million on land and $4 million on planning, Dow threw in the towel. The reason? Environmental red tape—65 permits were necessary from 12 local, state, and federal agencies to get permission to begin construction.

By the time it gave up, Dow had only been able to obtain one minor permit and three agreements with the California Fish and Game Department. The key permits had either been denied or were being withheld pending the final approval of two environmental reports.

The cost? About 1,000 construction jobs, 1,000 permanent jobs, and a $15 million annual payroll at a time when California's unemployment had hit 9.1 percent. Dow, it is interesting to note, recently announced that it is going to build an $800 million petrochemical plant in Saudi Arabia.

It is safe to say that business has reached a point where it accepts and agrees with the general goals of the EPA and environmental groups, but there are very hard, practical limits to how far down the environmental path we can travel.

Business is going to have to balk at excesses, and it is right to do so. For example, most paper industry executives would agree to a goal of, say, 95 percent pure effluent. But when that figure gets up to about 98 percent, the reply has to be, "Sorry, but that extra 3 percent is too expensive; it prices us out of the project." The same is true of auto and coke oven emission standards.

The frustration and costs don't end after planning and installation, either. Once environmental systems are in place, they are costly to run and to maintain. If they become too fancy, the rate of return may not be high enough to support the project.

ROADBLOCKS TO PROFITABILITY

The beginning of this discussion noted the need to lay the groundwork for a much higher level of capital investment. What that implies on the practical level is removing some of the roadblocks to profitability that have been erected. The message is clear: priorities must be set. Does this nation want to put its economy on a sound basis, or does it want to continue adding expenses which will price business out of much of the capital investment that the country needs in order to increase employment and to help keep the inflation rate within bounds?

The ability of the credit markets to finance business capital formation is, of course, hardly independent of public policy. The weakness of the credit markets of most other economies, in comparison with those in the United States, is in no small way due to the cumulation of years of policy actions which, in country after country, ultimately proved counterproductive. The United States now has the best capital market mechanisms in the world. But if it is to maintain them, those who are responsible for pulling economic levers in Washington must proceed with caution. Investor confidence is a delicate flower, and its restoration, always a slow, deliberate process, should be a principal goal of Congress and the Administration.

What is needed are clear signals from Washington. Investors will respond, albeit slowly at first, to positive investment stimuli and to constructive long-range government policies. The alternative may be further shortages in investment funds in the years ahead. In other words, if those at the levers in Washington should feel compelled to tinker, let their tinkering be aimed at spurring saving and capital investment, not hindering it.

CONCLUSION

In closing, it is useful to return to the fundamental questions raised at the outset. Will saving in the United States be adequate to finance a rate of capital formation consistent with achieving the important national objectives which require new plant and equipment? Will financing be available on a cost basis which will make it sensible for business to go ahead with plans for new productive investments?

The answers to these questions will depend in part on purely economic developments over which no one has any control; but they will also depend on the policy decisions made at every level of federal, state, and local government in the United States. And given this nation's democratic form of government, those policy decisions will in turn depend on the pressure of public opinion. *Will the public in general have the foresight to see its own self-interest in promoting capital formation? Will people see the advantage of saving and investing now so as to achieve important goals later? The answers still lie in the balance. The responsibility of business, in addition to its physical activ-*

ities of production and distribution, must also include undertaking the difficult task of promoting public understanding of the economic problems and choices confronting the United States in the years ahead.

NOTES

1. *Newsweek,* February 7, 1977, p. 80.
2. *New York Times,* February 1, 1977, p. 28.
3. *Brookings Papers on Economic Activity,* no. 1 (1974), pp. 169–208.

PART II

Evidence from specific industries

Chapter 9

THE CAPITAL PROBLEMS OF THE U.S. ELECTRIC POWER INDUSTRY

Gordon R. Corey*

The U.S. electric power industry is composed of a wide variety of institutions. Nearly 80 percent of the industry's plant investment is concentrated in about 400 investor-owned firms. The remainder includes five large federal generating systems and over 3,000 municipal electric systems, public utility districts, rural electric cooperatives, and other small distribution entities.

Investor-owned electric power firms are regulated as public utilities and as such are required to supply all comers with adequate service at reasonable rates and without discrimination. In fact, most managers of electric power supply firms, public or private, are typically required by law to meet their customers' expanding requirements. Since the prices they can charge are often held below the long-run marginal cost of doing so, many today are finding it difficult to obtain enough investment capital to ensure the long-run adequacy of future electric power supplies.

LARGE CAPITAL INVESTMENTS

About $200 billion is now invested in the U.S. electric power industry (book value). Some $400 billion more will be spent on new plant construction from 1976 through 1985.[1] Approximately $180 billion of the present investment is in the form of plant and equipment, which represents approximately 20 percent of all domestic industrial and utility plant investment, more than that of any other U.S. industry.[2]

---

* Vice Chairman, Commonwealth Edison Company.

122

Chart 1.   Total business plant investment ($ billions)

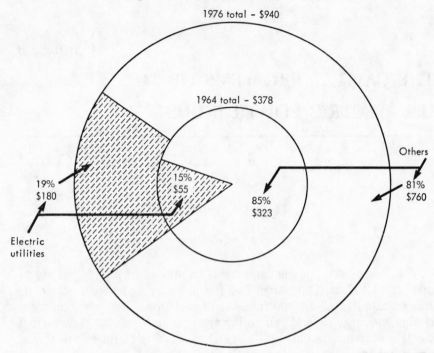

The figures represent the approximate year-end book value (partially estimated) of plant investment (including nuclear fuel in the case of electric utilities) after deducting depreciation reserves. The 1976 figures were derived from data for earlier years by projecting past trends.

Sources: Edison Electric Institute, *Statistical Yearbook of the Electric Utility Industry for 1975*; U.S. Department of Commerce, *Statistical Abstract of the United States*, 1974 ed.

Electric utility investment per worker now exceeds half a million dollars on a replacement cost basis, and electric power is the most capital-intensive of all U.S. industries, with $3.25 invested for each dollar of annual sales. During most of the postwar period such electric investment averaged more than $4 per dollar of annual sales. While the investment to sales ratio dropped below $4 about two years ago, the decline resulted from the effect of higher fuel prices on electric rates rather than a reduction in investment, which actually increased $50 billion in the three years between 1973 and year-end 1976. Increases in fuel costs during the two years following the oil embargo boosted the fuel expense portion of the average electric revenue dollar nearly 50 percent, from 23 cents in 1973 to 33 cents in 1975.

Chart 2.   U.S. electric power industry investment in business assets per worker (investor-owned sector), 1960–1976

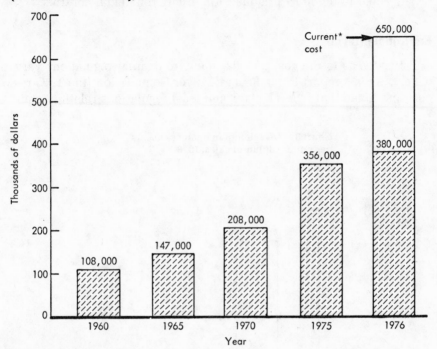

* Replacement cost basis.

The data shown represent year-end values after deducting depreciation reserves. The replacement cost data for 1976 have been similarly reduced by depreciation reserves adjusted to a replacement cost basis.

Source: Edison Electric Institute, *Statistical Yearbook of the Electric Utility Industry for 1975*, and prior editions.

FUTURE CONSTRUCTION EXPENDITURES

The industry's contemplated annual spending rate of $40 billion is nearly treble the $14 billion a year rate of the past decade.

This increase reflects a combination of factors. First, construction cost escalation is projected at an annual rate of 8 percent. Second, a growing proportion of the nation's future energy supply is expected to be in the form of electric power. Third, nearly all of this increase in electric power will be provided by nuclear and coal-fired generation which require more capital than oil- and gas-fired generation. Fourth,

124

the electric power industry, being large and visible, will continue to be subjected to the most pristine form of environmental controls.

Environmental costs

Estimates as to the cost of today's environmental regulations vary widely. A 1974 report to the Federal Power Commission (the TAC report) predicted that federal, state, and local regulations relating to air

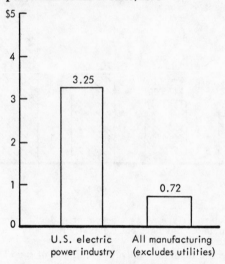

Chart 3. Investment in business assets per annual dollar of sales, 1976

The data shown represents the ratio of 1976 year-end book values of assets, after deducting depreciation reserves, to 1976 sales.

Sources: Edison Electric Institute, *Statistical Yearbook for the Electric Utility Industry for 1975;* Federal Trade Commission, *Quarterly Financial Report of Manufacturing, Mining, and Trade Corporations,* 1976.

and water quality would result in increased construction expenditures by the electric power industry of between $30 and $60 billion over the next 15 years. The average of these predictions, or $45 billion, represents roughly 7 percent of the $650 billion electric utility construction expenditures estimated for the same period.[3] However, even the high-side $60 billion estimate may in fact be low. It does not fully reflect the cost of several important elements involved in meeting environmental requirements.

Flue-gas desulfurization, coal gasification, and fuel desulfurization technologies are still in their infancy. It is difficult to predict, therefore, what they will ultimately cost. The report to the FPC referred to above used high-side estimates of $89 to $112 a kilowatt (1972 dollars) for flue-gas scrubbers which are now costing substantially more than that.[4]

Chart 4.   U.S. electric power industry spending for new plant and equipment, 1966–1985

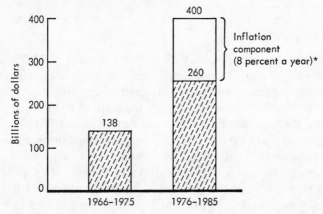

* The inflation component represents only the effect of increases above 1975 cost levels. Compared with average cost levels for the 1966–75 period, the inflation component of the next decade's construction expenditures would be substantially greater than that shown and might come close to equaling the entire projected rise of $262 billion in such expenditures.

Source: Backup material for the report of the Technical Advisory Committee on Finance to the Federal Power Commission, *The Financial Outlook for the Electric Power Industry*, December 1974.

Moreover, the cost of such readily identifiable equipment as scrubbers and cooling towers does not represent the total cost of environmental cleanup. There will be important continuing day-to-day expenses of operating complex cleanup facilities, disposing of solid sulfur wastes, and providing cleaner fuels—none of which are reflected in the $30 billion or $60 billion capital cost estimates. For example, the use of high-priced low-sulfur coal (from Montana and Wyoming) for Chicago-area generation cost Commonwealth Edison's ratepayers an additional $90 million last year, compared with formerly-used Illinois coal. This suggests that the low-sulfur fuel requirement is probably adding at least $2 billion—probably more—to the nation's annual electricity bill, since Commonwealth represents only about 3 percent of the U.S. electric power industry.

Finally, there is the whole matter of the added expenditures which may be required to meet environmental regulations if the conversion of oil- and gas-burning generating facilities to coal becomes widespread. The effect of this is difficult to assess, but it could cost another $20 billion, if only a portion of existing facilities were converted.

Anticipated growth

After reviewing a wide array of projections, the 1974 TAC report to the Federal Power Commission accepted an annual electric load growth rate of 6½ percent for the last half of the 1970s and 6 percent for the early 1980s.[5] These projections may prove to be too low, especially in the 1980s, if significant substitutions of electricity for gas and oil occur. On the other hand, plausible arguments can be made for future growth rates in the area of 5 percent a year, in view of the opportunities for conservation, and some have put future load growth possibilities as low as 3 percent per annum.[6] However, actual 1976 growth in electricity usage was 6½ percent for the United States as a whole, and the 6 to 6½ percent growth projections used in the TAC report still appear reasonable, given the countervailing effects of conservation and energy substitution.

New money needs

Only about 40 percent of the U.S. electric power industry's $400 billion construction program for 1976 through 1985 will be financed with internally generated funds. At least 60 percent, or $250 billion, must be paid for with new money, in contrast with the situation just a decade ago, when the proportions were approximately the reverse—60 percent internal cash generation and 40 percent external financing.

Reduced internal cash generation

Reinvestment of funds provided from operations is the most important way in which U.S. industry finances plant modernization and expansion. This provides additional jobs as well as additional goods and services.

During the early 1960s, $13 ½ billion a year, or nearly 60 percent of the electric power industry's construction funds, were provided internally, with only about 40 percent, or $9 ½ billion a year, raised externally. By contrast, during the first half of the 1970s the electric power industry had to go to the money market for two thirds of its construction funds, raising only one third of such funds internally.

In 1976, external financing dropped to 62 percent of construction expenditures, apparently due to construction cancellations and delays. However, a resurgence of growth may well cause the proportion of outside financing to rise again.

FUND-RAISING PROBLEMS

The electric power industry's fund-raising problems have always been substantial. Recently, however, these problems have been exacerbated by deteriorating credit.

Beginning in the mid-1960s, sharply increased construction cost inflation halted the long postwar declines in electric plant construction costs and resulted in a sharp rise in outside financing, particularly debt. At the same time, interest rates began to rise. The combination of the two resulted in a steady decline in fixed charge coverages commencing in the mid-1960s, which cut average before-tax coverage ratios for the industry as a whole roughly in half between 1965 and 1973. In 1965, the average ratio of earnings available to pay income taxes and fixed charges to the amount of such fixed charges was approximately 5 ½ for the investor-owned sector of the U.S. electric power industry. By 1973, the figure had dropped to less than three.

Then, late in 1973, the Arab oil embargo and the nearly simultaneous requirement to switch to costly low-sulfur fuels triggered sharp increases in electricity prices. These met with growing public resistance, manifested in objections to further price rises, attacks upon fuel adjustment clauses, and suggestions for tinkering with electric rate forms so as to relieve one group or another from the burden of higher bills. The end result has been a steady deterioration of electric industry credit which may eventually restrict the industry's ability to attract capital.

Large future common stock financings

While the electric power industry in general has consistently held its average debt ratio below 55 percent, continued maintenance of this

Chart 5. U.S. electric power industry debt ratio (investor-owned sector)

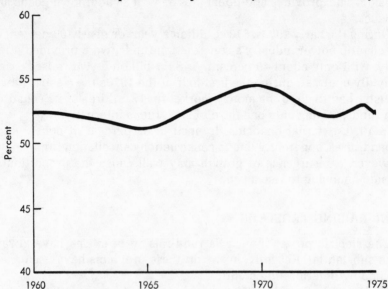

Year

Source: Federal Power Commission, *Statistics of Privately Owned Electric Utilities in the United States,* 1975 and prior editions.

ratio below 55 percent translates into the need to issue large amounts of new common stock.

In 1976, the electric power industry sold approximately $4 billion of new-issue common stock, up sharply from the $1 billion to $2 billion level characteristic of prior years. This was an all-time high, $500 million more than had ever before been sold in a single year. Over the next decade, however, new issues of electric utility common stock must average between $5 billion and $6 billion every year.

Consequences of issuing common stock below book value

Many electric utility common stock offerings are now being marketed at less than book value. This reduces the average book value of outstanding shares. Since electricity rates are generally based on book value, any such reduction in the book value of outstanding shares reduces the real value of those shares. Hence it results in a loss to earlier shareholders and is tantamount to a conscription of capital. This discourages new investors by strongly suggesting that they too may suffer similar losses in the future.

Resulting construction cutbacks

Reduced credit ratings may restrict the future market for electric utility debt securities, and continued sales of new-issue common stock below book value may similarly restrict the future market for electric utility stocks. Both have resulted from inadequate earnings. In turn, both have been accompanied by electric plant construction cutbacks. Inevitably, there has been a growing reluctance on the part of management to commit itself to the costly, long-lead-time plant expansion programs needed to meet the increased power needs anticipated for the mid-to-late 1980s. This is particularly the case today, when public opposition to such expansion is repeatedly expressed in the news media.[7]

During the past 12 to 18 months, there has been a virtual moratorium on nuclear power plant orders. In 1976, only three nuclear power reactors with an aggregate capacity of 3,700 megawatts were ordered in the entire United States. Since all three of these new orders were simply reinstatements of previous cancellations, in a sense no new nuclear capacity was ordered during the year. Early in 1977, 1,800 megawatts of nuclear capacity were canceled by Virginia Electric and Power Company.

During 1976, orders for new turbine generator units powered with coal amounted to only 4,900 megawatts. Almost no new oil- or gas-fired generation was ordered.

Yet both electricity sales and peak loads increased significantly in 1976, the latter increasing about 15,000 megawatts compared with 1975. Moreover, the generating capacity being ordered today is intended for service in the mid-1980s, when load increases are expected to exceed 30,000 megawatts annually.

Future supply shortages

Failure to order enough long-lead-time generating equipment today is a serious matter, because if power shortages develop in the mid 1980s, the traditional fallback method of avoiding shortfalls of electricity supply by building new oil-fired capacity on 18 to 30 months' notice will no longer be available. This suggests that we will confront an electricity supply problem in the mid-1980s which we simply will not have the tools to resolve.[8]

The financing problem in brief

In a nutshell, we see an industry whose immediate needs for new money are double what they were just a few years ago. We see an industry with declining credit which nevertheless must raise a third or more of all the new money raised by U.S. corporations over the next decade. We see an industry whose earnings are inadequate and of declining quality.

Earnings quality

The electric power industry's reported earnings are double what they would be if book depreciation were based upon replacement cost rather than historical cost. Moreover, unique to the electric industry is the fact that nearly 30 percent of its $6.9 billion of annual earnings is represented by bookkeeping credits for interest and return on funds used during construction. Both of these factors tend to reduce the quality of reported earnings.

Chart 6. U.S. electric power industry: Nominal versus real net income (investor-owned sector), 1976

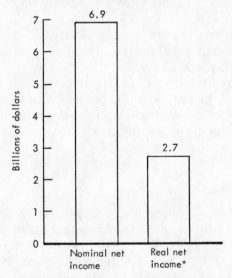

* Reflects depreciation on a replacement cost basis.

The 1976 figures for this chart, as well as for certain other charts in this chapter, were estimated by projecting data for earlier years on the basis of past trends.

Source: Edison Electric Institute, *Statistical Yearbook of the Electric Utility Industry for 1975.*

WHAT SHOULD BE DONE?

First, we must, as a nation, take full advantage of abundant opportunities for sensible energy conservation. Government authorities should take steps to stop waste. Local suppliers should show customers how to save energy. Space heating fuel suppliers should provide insulation packages. Research on the utilization of waste heat should continue at an accelerated pace.

Second, economic pricing of all energy forms should be adopted promptly. This includes peak-load penalties coupled with off-peak discounts. But it also includes raising overall energy prices to the point where additional supplies can be financed. The future energy supply problem is being needlessly overblown by our simple unwillingness to use the price mechanism to stimulate production and reduce demand.

Third, we must take steps to increase internal cash generation by substantially increasing depreciation provisions for book, tax, and regulatory purposes. The Securities and Exchange Commission is to be commended for requiring disclosure of the effect of higher replacement costs upon 1976 operating results, in particular the effect of increased depreciation charges under replacement cost accounting. A modest step toward full replacement cost accounting might be to follow a last in, first out (or Lifo) procedure for computing depreciation, depreciating the most recently installed (hence most costly) property items first. This would tend to reflect, to a degree, the replacement value of plant used up in day-to-day operations, while not requiring either appraisal write-ups or departures from historical cost accounting principles. It would be improper, however, to base depreciation charges upon replacement costs for financial reporting purposes unless such charges are also recognized for tax and rate-making purposes. A serious mismatch of revenues and expenses would otherwise result.

Fourth, we must avoid shortsighted steps which would reduce internal cash generation or slow its growth. For example, the practice of normalizing tax benefits from investment tax credits and accelerated depreciation provided almost a quarter of the electric industry's entire internal cash generation in 1976. This practice should be continued despite the growing criticism of so-called phantom taxes by those who do not understand their purpose and significance.

Fifth, the public must become aware of the need for adequate supplies of electric power in order to provide future jobs and economic health.[9] Without adequate electric power, we cannot expect to maintain our high rate of well-paid employment, while at the same time solving our inner-city problems and creating a better society for all.

We must not run short of electric power merely because of failure to set electricity prices high enough to attract the capital needed to ensure its production.

This must be explained in such a way that the public and the news media will stop criticizing regulators who allow needed rate increases. If we (the public) insist that electric rates be held down, the regulators will certainly do so, because they are responsible to the public. But if adequate electric power supplies are to be ensured for the future, our regulatory authorities must be free to make judicious determinations as to the proper prices to be charged for electric service. This does not imply some sort of special privilege, but it does suggest that it is difficult to achieve reasonable decisions in an environment where emotions and sensationalism drown out logic and reason.

Sixth, some or all of the electric industry's massive $40 billion investment in construction work in progress should be made a part of the rate base upon which a current return is allowed, thus gradually discontinuing the practice of saddling future ratepayers with the entire burden of paying off the "imputed earnings" on this uncompleted plant investment.

Seventh, we must (as covered elsewhere in this book) take effective steps to stimulate our lagging rate of savings. One such step, which would help resolve nearly half of the electric power industry's common equity fund-raising problems, is to provide for the simple tax-free reinvestment of dividends on stock.

Finally, as a last resort, we may have to turn to some form of allocation of capital funds, in order to ensure that we do not run short of electric power in the years to come. There have, of course, been capital allocations of one sort or another for many, many years. We have been allocating capital to the housing industry (both directly and indirectly) for over 40 years through the FHA and other federal agencies. It is hoped, of course, that this ultimate step will not have to be taken.

CONCLUSION

At first blush, the outlook for the U.S. electric power industry would seem rather dark. However, the industry is alive and functioning. It is providing reliable electric service in quantities never before provided to any society.

The market demand for electric energy is good. The need is great.

The industry's problems lie largely in the future—in the general area of the adequacy of electric power supplies during the decade of the 1980s and beyond.

The industry is not insolvent today, or even approaching insolvency. But there has been a ten-year decline in its earnings, credit standing, and fund-raising capability. This decline must be turned around if the industry is to obtain required capital funds to meet its 3rd-century challenge.

NOTES

1. Much of the projected financial data shown herein for the U.S. electric power industry was derived from the report and recommendations of the Technical Advisory Committee on Finance to the Federal Power Commission, *The Financial Outlook for the Electric Power Industry,* December 1974 (referred to herein as the TAC report). The $400 billion construction cost estimate for the period 1976 through 1985 is based upon the Case IA moderate-growth, low environmental cost projections used in preparing that report, increased by about $40 billion to reflect an 8 percent annual rate of construction cost inflation instead of the lower rates assumed therein.
2. All plant investment and asset valuation data are net after deducting depreciation reserves unless otherwise indicated.
3. The TAC report. The $30 billion and $60 billion figures are derived from table 4 and exhibit 3 of chap. 1, pp. 54 and 85. The $650 billion figure is based upon case IA, table 4, p. 54.
4. Ibid., exhibit 2 of chap. 1, p. 81. The "high" estimate was used in arriving at the $60 billion "high-side" estimate of environmental costs.
5. Ibid., pp. 27, 80.
6. See the report of the Ford Foundation's Energy Policy Project, *A Time to Choose,* 1974. The "Zero Growth" scenario, table F–6, p. 508, reflects a 3 percent annual electricity growth rate for 1975–85; the "Technical Fix" scenario, table F–3, p. 502, shows a 3.3 percent annual electricity growth rate for 1975–85.
7. It is occasionally suggested that electric firms are induced to overinvest in order to maximize profits. This is not true. If anything, the opposite is true. See Gordon R. Corey, "The Averch and Johnson Proposition: A Critical Analysis," *Bell Journal of Economics and Management Science,* vol. 2, no. 1, 1971, pp. 358–73.
8. See Federal Power Commission, *Factors Affecting the Electric Power Supply, 1980–85,* December 1, 1976.
9. See the report to the Federal Power Commission of the Technical Advisory Committee on the Impact of Inadequate Power Supply, *The Adequacy of Future Electric Power Supply: Problems and Policies,* March 1976.

Chapter 10

THE DOMESTIC STEEL INDUSTRY'S
PROJECTED CAPITAL REQUIREMENTS

Edgar B. Speer*

Our nation's future economic growth, the material well-being of our people, and the job opportunities available to them depend importantly on the rate of modernization and expansion of the tools of production. Some two thirds of steel shipments go directly or indirectly into capital goods markets. Thus an adequate and assured supply of steel is fundamental to improving and enlarging America's tools of production.

To understand the steel industry's capital requirements through 1985, it is first necessary to recognize that this nation's ability to produce steel remained virtually unchanged from 1960 through the mid-1970s. This lack of expansion in productive capability occurred during a period when the consumption of steel in this country was increasing by nearly two thirds. It reflected the very dismal prospects for steel profitability which existed throughout the period. Steel companies during those years simply were not able to justify large capital spending to create more goods and services and, in the process, more self-sustaining jobs. In 1974, steel companies operated virtually all-out. However, there wasn't enough steel production capability in this country to satisfy demand. Some 17 million tons of finished steel products were imported—at premiums averaging well over $100 per ton above domestic steel prices.

While some additions to productive capability have been made during the past two years, they have been relatively small in total. As a result, a tight supply-demand situation may recur later this year or in

---

* Chairman of the Board, United States Steel Corporation.

1978. This situation promises to become increasingly critical in the future as the growing demand for steel exceeds the growth in supply. The problem, then, is that this nation must either add sufficient productive capability within the domestic industry or become increasingly dependent on imported steel.

The worldwide steel shortage during 1974 provides a vivid illustration of what would be most likely to occur during future periods of tight supplies if we were to become more heavily dependent on foreign steel. During that year, foreign producers were able to charge sizable premiums for steel sold to American users—frequently 50 percent to 75 percent ($100 to $150 per ton) above domestic steel prices. All told, American steel users paid some $1.6 billion more for imported steel during 1974 than they would have paid if sufficient American steel had been available. *This more than offset many years of savings from lower-priced foreign steels. With inadequate domestic steelmaking capability, future shortages of steel may be more severe and long lasting than those of 1974.*

In addition, increasing our nation's dependence on imports for such a vital industrial product as steel is definitely not desirable from the standpoint either of national defense or of the balance of payments. For these reasons, it is clear that the wisest course of action is to build sufficient steel production capability in this country.

THE DOMESTIC MARKET FOR STEEL THROUGH 1985

To understand the steel industry's capital requirements, it is necessary to project future domestic steel consumption. Most steel companies base their facility and marketing plans on detailed analyses of the markets they serve. Although these analyses vary among steel companies for a variety of reasons, virtually all current steel company projections show an increase in steel consumption within the range of 2 to 2½ percent per year for the period 1977–85. The midpoint of 2¼ percent will be used in this chapter. (It is somewhat less than the average annual increase of about 2.8 percent experienced over the past two decades.) If anything, this projected rate of increase in consumption may prove to be on the low side, particularly if national economic policies are adopted to stimulate economic growth and seek full employment. (The estimated consumption of steel over the past two decades and its projected consumption by 1985 are presented in Chart 1.)

Although foreign steel—as mentioned earlier—cannot be considered a fully reliable source of supply, imports of steel have been a factor in steel availability since the late 1950s. Any measure of future demand and supply, therefore, must consider the possible level of for-

Chart 1. Estimated domestic steel consumption, 1957–1985

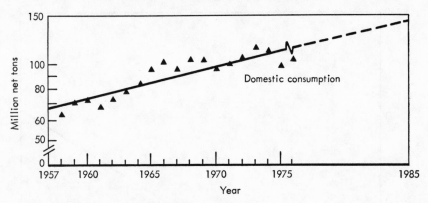

Source: American Iron and Steel Institute.

eign trade (imports and exports) in steel. Over the past five years (1972–76), imports averaged about 14 percent of domestic steel consumption. If this rate is sustained, imports would reach 20 million net tons by 1985.

It is necessary to keep in mind, however, that the foreign steel picture is changing. For example, more pronounced rates of inflation abroad seem to be pushing up production costs much faster abroad than in the United States. The high cost of adding new capacity abroad may prevent foreign steelmakers from building new mills to serve the U.S. market, as they have sometimes done in the past. More important, when domestic steel production costs are compared with those abroad, they show that our domestic producers are now fully cost competitive with foreign producers for steel produced for consumption in this country.

As to exports, they averaged about 4 million net tons during the years 1972–76. It is assumed that they will increase gradually in the period ahead, reaching perhaps 6 million net tons by 1985. This higher level reflects the more competitive position of the domestic steel industry in international trade. On balance, then, imports in 1985 are projected to exceed exports by 14 million net tons.

PRESENT STEELMAKING CAPABILITY

On an annual basis, raw steel production capability during the fourth quarter of 1976 (the latest data available) was 160 million net tons. The industry, however, cannot operate all-out continuously. Demand varies within a year, for seasonal and other reasons. Adverse

138

Chart 2. Public steel shipments: American steel industry, 1957–1976

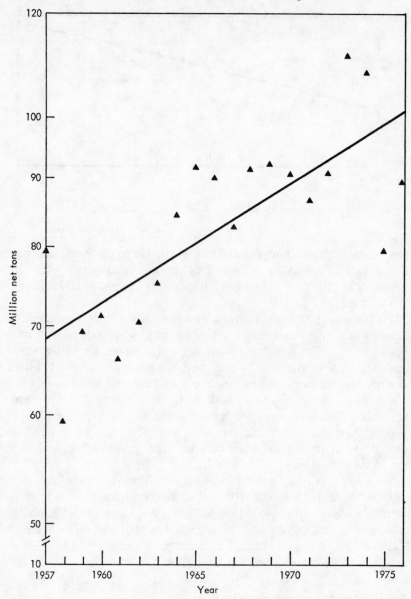

Source: American Iron and Steel Institute.

weather conditions, strikes, acts of God, and other factors can affect production from time to time. Therefore, steel companies generally estimate that a utilization rate ("peaking factor") of 92 percent on average must be used in order to determine a sustainable operating capability.

In addition, a yield factor is used by the steel industry to make allowances for processing losses in rolling and finishing operations. This factor is currently about 72 percent. Based on the technology of the new facilities expected to be installed over the period 1977–85, a slightly higher yield factor may be reasonably used for the year 1985 for facilities in place at that time.

Taking these peaking and yield factors into account, the industry's present sustainable finishing capability is about 106 million net tons per year. As shown in Chart 2, the long-term trend line of steel industry shipments for 1977 would be at this same level. Because the steel industry is still recovering from the recent recession, however, steel shipments by domestic producers are expected to be in the 95–100-million-ton range for the year 1977.

THE PROJECTED NEED FOR ADDITIONAL CAPACITY

With the growth in steel consumption projected at an average of 2¼ percent per year through 1985, finished steel consumption will average 142 million tons per year at that time, and imports may provide 14 percent of that amount. Obviously, then, approximately 30 million net tons of additional raw steel production capability will be required domestically by the year 1985 if the industry's raw steel "peak" capability is to be approximately 190 million net tons.

Tables 1 and 2 summarize what the domestic steel situation is expected to be by the year 1985.

Table 1. Projected consumption, foreign trade, and required shipping capability: Domestic steel industry, 1985

	Million tons
Finished steel consumption by 1985, based on average annual rate of growth of 2¼ percent per year	142
Net international balance of trade in steel products for 1985 (20 million tons of imports less 6 million tons of exports)	14
Annual shipping capability required to meet domestic demand for finished steel products in 1985	128

Source: American Iron and Steel Institute.

Table 2. Projected raw steel capability and sustainable shipping capability: Domestic steel industry, 1985

	Million tons		
	1976	1985	Increase, 1976–1985
Raw steel capability	160	190	30
Peaking factor	92%	92%	92%
Raw steel equivalent	147	175	28
Yield	72%	73%	78%
Sustainable shipping capability	106	128	22

Source: American Iron and Steel Institute.

THE PROJECTED CAPITAL REQUIREMENTS OF THE DOMESTIC STEEL INDUSTRY

Some capacity additions can be obtained within two to three years by "rounding out" existing facilities. But much of the additional capacity that this country will need will have to be obtained by building a full complement of steelmaking and supporting facilities. The period consumed by design, approval by various governmental bodies, construction, and break-in for these facilities could require as long as five to eight years in today's economic and political environment.

The steel industry is one of the nation's most capital-intensive in-

Chart 3. Investment per dollar of sales: Steel versus all manufacturers, 1976

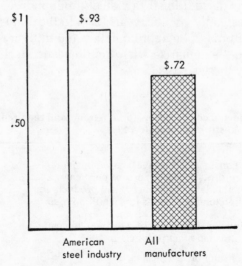

Source: American Iron and Steel Institute.

dustries. In 1976, the industry's investment per dollar of sales was $0.93 versus $0.72 for all manufacturing.

Although new plant and equipment in the steel industry may cost as much as several hundred thousand dollars per employee, depending on the nature of the plant or the equipment, even on a historical-cost basis the investment per worker in the steel industry is some $55,000. This is more than double the level of investment per worker as recently as 1965.

Chart 4.   Investment per worker: American steel industry, 1960–1976

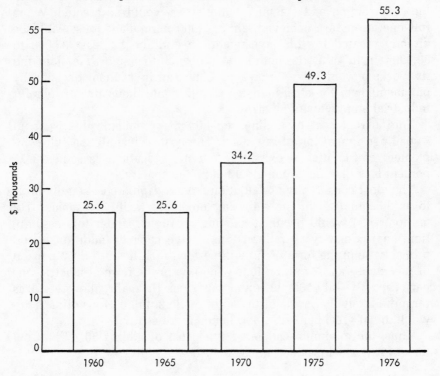

Source: American Iron and Steel Institute.

ADDITIONAL STEEL PRODUCTION CAPACITY

A survey conducted in early 1977 among member companies of the American Iron and Steel Institute (AISI) indicates that some 18 million additional tons of capacity could be obtained by "rounding out" operations at existing plant locations—that is, eliminating bottlenecks, upgrading technology, and otherwise improving production capability. While the exact cost of "round out" capacity would depend on many factors, recent additions to capacity by this method indicate that an average cost of some $375 per ton of raw steel could be representative.

Beyond "round out," new capacity can only be obtained by adding a full complement of facilities, including raw material support facilities—either at "greenfield sites" or at existing locations. Consideration must *now* be given to possible greenfield steelmaking capacity. We at U.S. Steel have been studying this subject in great detail for some time. We believe that a new integrated facility must be designed for at least 4 million tons. Some important employment prospects are involved. If a decision to proceed can be made, thousands of jobs in the construction and machinery industries would be created. When full operations are achieved, about 8,000 permanent jobs would be directly created by this investment. In addition, at least 25,000 to 30,000 jobs in industries both large and small to support the plant and its workers would also be created. Thus, an investment decision by one member of the steel industry would create thousands of jobs for industrial employers of all sizes.

The current cost of adding capacity at greenfield sites is about $1,050 per annual ton of raw steel. The cost of installing a full complement of facilities at existing production locations is some 10–15 percent less than installing greenfield site capacity.

The most conservative calculation from a capital-cost standpoint is to assume that all of the full complement of facility expansion (12 million tons) would occur at existing locations. Under this assumption, approximately 10 million tons of the capacity addition would probably be in the form of fully integrated facilities—at $900 per ton of raw steel—and 2 million tons would be in the form of electric furnace capacity—at $400 per ton of raw steel. (In reality, however, it is far more likely that some of the additional 12 million tons of capacity would be at greenfield sites and hence more costly.)

Thus, the minimum estimated total cost of adding 30 million net tons of raw steel production capacity is as follows:

18 million tons of additional capacity by "rounding out" existing facilities—at an average of approximately $375 per ton of raw steel	$ 6.75 billion
12 million tons of additional capacity by installing a full complement of integrated and electric furnace facilities—at an average of approximately $800 per ton of raw steel	$ 9.6 billion
Total	$16.35 billion

And on this basis, the average annual expenditure by steel companies would be $1.8 billion for the period 1977 through 1985. We believe that if we are to continue to have a healthy domestic steel industry, expenditures of this magnitude must be made.

REPLACEMENT AND MODERNIZATION OF PRESENT STEEL PRODUCTION CAPACITY

Calculation of the amount of capital needed to replace and modernize present steel production capacity is quite complex. This is primarily attributable to the independent yet interrelated factors that enter into the determination of a production facility's economic life. For example, a facility may be worn out physically. It may no longer be capable of producing a commercially acceptable product. It may be technologically obsolete. It may no longer produce a profitable product. It may need to be replaced or improved to conform with legislated requirements. Or it may need replacement for a combination of these reasons.

A reasonably accurate estimate of such future capital requirements can be derived, however, by examining the capital expenditures reported by AISI member companies during the 1966–75 period, when no appreciable increase in raw steel production capability occurred. This total can then be adjusted to exclude environmental control and non-steel-related expenditures, and the remainder can then be scaled up to a "total industry" basis and adjusted for inflation. On this basis, an average of approximately $2.5 billion per year, as shown in Table 3, will be required to replace and modernize present steel production capacity.

Some observers outside the steel industry might question the use of a recent ten-year period as a basis for projecting future capital requirements for replacement and modernization, on the ground that changing technology during that period resulted in the replacement of many open hearths by basic oxygen furnaces. However, the capital requirements of basic oxygen furnaces are less than 10 percent of the total capital requirements for producing finished steel products. Also, technology is constantly changing in steel, and such changes will require major capital expenditures even if total capacity is not expanding.

ENVIRONMENTAL CONTROL AND OSHA EQUIPMENT FOR EXISTING PLANT FACILITIES

In 1975, Arthur D. Little, Inc., published a study about the impact of existing and proposed air emission and water effluent regulations on the domestic steel industry.[1] This study, which had been commissioned by AISI, estimated that from 1975–83 the domestic steel indus-

Table 3. Future capital expenditure requirements for replacement and modernization of present steel production capacity ($ billions)

Year	Capital expenditures reported by AISI member companies			GNP price deflator for private nonresidential investment	Capital expenditures adjusted to 1976 dollars		
	Total	Environmental control	Steel and nonsteel		Steel and nonsteel	Nonsteel	Steel
1966	$ 1.953	$0.056	$ 1.897	76.8	$ 3.413	$0.160	$ 3.253
1967	2.146	0.094	2.052	79.3	3.577	0.186	3.391
1968	2.307	0.102	2.205	82.6	3.689	0.580	3.109
1969	2.047	0.138	1.909	86.6	3.047	0.375	2.672
1970	1.736	0.183	1.553	91.3	2.351	0.386	1.965
1971	1.425	0.162	1.263	96.4	1.810	0.308	1.502
1972	1.174	0.202	.972	100.0	1.343	0.287	1.056
1973	1.400	0.100	1.300	104.0	1.728	0.322	1.406
1974	2.104	0.199	1.905	116.1	2.267	0.366	1.901
1975	3.215	0.453	2.762	132.1	2.851	0.453	2.398
1976	n.a.	n.a.	n.a.	138.2	—	—	—
Total	$22.726	$2.178	$20.548		$26.076	$3.423	$22.653

	Steel and nonsteel	Nonsteel	Steel
Annual average of capital expenditures made by AISI member companies (1976 dollars)	2.608	0.342	2.266
Annual average scaled up to a total industry basis (assuming expenditures of AISI members to be 90.9 percent of total industry expenditures)	90.9%	90.9%	90.9%
Average annual amount required for steel and nonsteel replacement and modernization (1976 dollars)	2.869	0.376	2.493

n.a. = not available.

Source: American Iron and Steel Institute.

try would spend approximately $8.25 billion for the installation of pollution abatement equipment on existing facilities.

Using the Arthur D. Little study as a starting point, and adjusting for pollution control spending during 1975–76 as well as for inflation and OSHA and other environmental costs not covered by the Arthur D. Little study, we estimate the domestic steel industry's average annual requirement for pollution abatement during the 1977–85 period at $1.2 billion.

Under present interpretations of our laws, this level of capital expenditures for air and water treatment facilities represents nearly 20 percent of the domestic steel industry's expected capital requirements between now and 1985. It should be noted that these pollution abatement commitments are not discretionary. In most cases the laws are in place and the dates for compliance have been established. In addition, the commitments are ongoing. One-time compliance does not mean that the expenditures for compliance are over. In many instances the technology is new, and in some instances it is not yet in existence. It is quite likely that the obsolescence factor will be very high for pollution and safety equipment and that replacement of such equipment will continue to drain away capital funds from more productive facilities.

The steel industry also faces the fact that the operating costs for these facilities will be very substantial on a continuing basis. For these reasons, we believe that expenditures for air and water treatment facilities and newly legislated health and safety devices should be tax-deductible as incurred. This will permit the cash generated to be reinvested in additional job-creating production facilities.

NON-STEEL-RELATED CAPITAL EXPENDITURES

Many steel companies are engaged in activities other than steel manufacturing, activities which have made important contributions to internal cash flow. These companies anticipate spending approximately $500 million per year for facilities to produce goods and services other than steel. As shown in Table 3, this estimate is consistent with actual experience on capital spending for these purposes, updated to 1976 dollars and allowing for modest growth in expenditures for nonsteel activities.

WORKING CAPITAL NEEDS AND DEBT REPAYMENTS

Increased shipments of steel will inevitably require additional working capital in the forms of inventory and accounts receivable.

These are estimated to require $0.2 billion per year, and approximately the same amount will be required annually to retire long-term debt as it becomes due.

The projected average annual capital requirements for the steel industry are summarized in Chart 5. They total $6.4 billion annually, stated in dollars of 1976 purchasing power. Any inflation occurring after 1976 would further increase steel's needs for capital.

Chart 5. Projected average annual capital requirements: American steel industry, 1977–1985

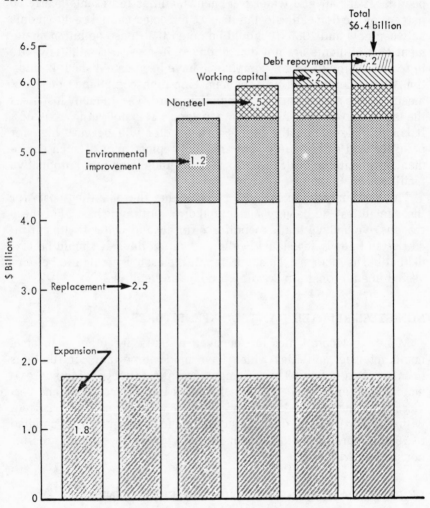

Source: American Iron and Steel Institute.

FINANCING FUTURE CAPITAL REQUIREMENTS

If the steel industry is to meet these capital requirements, domestic steel companies, beginning in 1977, will need to generate substantially more capital from internal sources (reinvested earnings and depreciation). They will also need to raise much more capital from external sources (long-term borrowing and the issuance of additional capital stock).

As shown on Chart 6, internal cash flow during the years 1965–76 averaged only $1.9 billion per year. Profits were adversely affected during this period by many factors, including imports and formal and informal price controls. Depreciation was limited to the recovery of

Chart 6. Actual internal cash flow versus projected cash requirements: American steel industry, 1965–1985

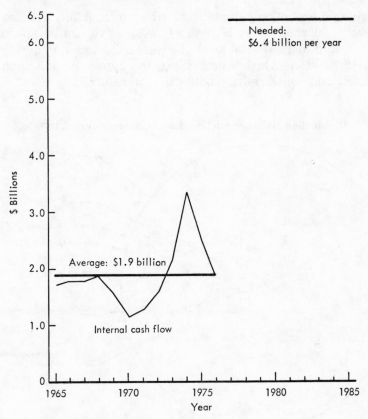

Source: American Iron and Steel Institute.

original cost, yet engineering studies by U.S. Steel and others indicate that it requires as much as three times as many dollars today to replace worn-out facilities as has been allowed as a cost of depreciation.

Long-term debt increased during the past decade by an average of $300 million per year—primarily to help offset the inadequate level of depreciation. Only an insignificant amount of additional capital was raised by domestic steel companies during this period.

Total cash flow during the past decade has thus averaged only about $2.2 billion a year—about one third of the expected annual capital requirements during the years ahead.

Obtaining greater internal and external capital necessarily hinges directly on earning higher profit rates. During the most recent years, the American steel industry's profits averaged only 4 percent of sales, with about half paid to stockholders as dividends and the other half reinvested in the business. The distribution of the sales dollar during 1976 is shown in Chart 7.

Higher profits not only directly contribute to cash flow but also improve the financial attractiveness of prospective capital spending, which in turn increases the level of depreciation and the investment tax credit. Likewise, higher profits help to improve the environment for raising additional capital—both debt and equity.

Chart 7. Distribution of the sales dollar: American steel industry, 1976

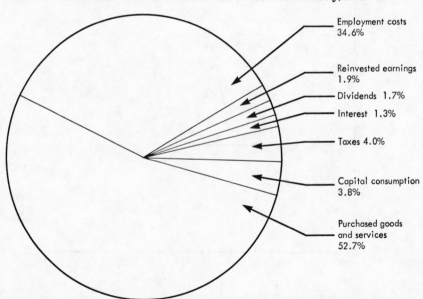

Employment costs 34.6%

Reinvested earnings 1.9%

Dividends 1.7%

Interest 1.3%

Taxes 4.0%

Capital consumption 3.8%

Purchased goods and services 52.7%

Source: American Iron and Steel Institute.

In addition to higher profits, a solution to the problem of capital and job formation for steel and other industries will also require changes in federal income tax laws to lessen or eliminate the many present disincentives to investment. Examples of the necessary changes include faster depreciation, first-year write-off of pollution abatement facilities, a permanent investment tax credit of at least 12 percent, and elimination of the double taxation of dividends. Although a full discussion of each of these changes is beyond the scope of this chapter, they nevertheless are an integral part of the solution to the problem of capital formation in the steel industry and, indeed, in American industry as a whole.

If steel companies are unable to obtain sufficient capital for the purposes discussed above, a number of undesirable economic effects will occur: a growing scarcity of domestically produced steel, higher levels of steel imports, fewer jobs within steel companies, and a slower rate of economic growth. These consequences can be avoided—but only if our nation's public policies encourage profitability and capital investment. *The challenge is substantial, but so too are the prospective rewards.*

NOTE

1. Arthur D. Little, Inc., "Steel and the Environment: A Cost-Impact Analysis," May 1975.

Chapter 11

GROWING NEEDS FOR INVESTMENT CAPITAL FOR U.S. ENERGY

*Rawleigh Warner, Jr.**

SUMMARY OF THE PROBLEM

The United States is short of secure energy. We need to invest more in U.S. energy development. If we don't, the shortage will grow worse.

As recently as 1967 the United States was essentially energy self-sufficient. In 1976 it imported more than 20 percent of its total energy consumption and about 42 percent of its oil. Its dependence on imported energy is growing, and its dependence on OPEC sources in the Middle East is growing very rapidly.

At one time the United States was the largest producer of oil in the world. Today it is the largest importer of oil in the world. In 1956, when Premier Khrushchev announced to the United States, "We'll bury you," the United States produced more than four times as much oil as the Soviet Union. Today the Soviet Union produces more oil than the United States. United States oil reserves and oil production are declining. United States gas reserves and gas production are declining. United States development of alternative sources of energy has been slow.

Our security and our standard of living are increasingly dependent upon imported oil. This need not be so, in view of our potential domestic energy base. It is wrong for us to needlessly rely on imported oil, not only because this puts our security and our standard of living in jeopardy, but because it is unfair to friendly nations which have no alternative but to rely on imported energy.

---

* Chairman of the Board, Mobil Corporation.

There are many reasons why the United States has moved from a position of energy strength to energy danger in the postwar period, *but the basic reason is that we have not invested enough to develop adequate additional U.S. energy supplies.* Investment has been inadequate because of lack of adequate economic incentives and because of governmental inhibitions. We need to spend considerably more in the next ten years than we spent in the last ten years, or we will become increasingly reliant on foreign sources of energy. We cannot "conserve" our way out of this problem. Conservation is important, but increased supplies are essential if we are to have the economic growth and jobs that the vast majority of Americans want.

SUMMARY OF THE SOLUTION

Improvements in the economic environment are necessary if we want the huge investment that will be needed to arrest the decline in the U.S. energy position.

The Federal Energy Administration (FEA), in its *National Energy Outlook, 1976,* has forecast that in the next ten years the U.S. petroleum industry will need to invest at least $244 billion (1975 dollars) in the development of U.S. petroleum supplies in order to hold imports at approximately their current level. This is almost twice the amount of money (1975 dollars) that was spent in the last ten years. If anything, the FEA estimate is low.

The supplies to be developed are conservatively forecast by the FEA because its assumed demand for petroleum arises from realistic estimates of GNP growth, challenging estimates of improved energy efficiency, and optimistic estimates of the development of nonpetroleum energy supplies. Higher GNP growth or slower progress on energy efficiency or alternative energy supplies will increase the need for more petroleum supplies.

The dollars required to develop the needed supplies of petroleum are also conservatively forecast. The FEA forecast implies that more U.S. supplies can be developed per dollar spent in the coming decade than were developed per dollar spent in the past decade.

Although the dollar investment required to keep imports from growing is debatable, the policy implications of even the conservative FEA estimate are clear. The only way we will get the increased investment to provide the indicated increase in U.S. petroleum supplies is to:

1. Improve the profitability of U.S. petroleum investment.
2. Increase the availability of government land for exploration.

3. Decrease the delays and inhibitions (environmental and other) that impede exploration and development.
4. Revise existing tax rules to facilitate aftertax cash flows and improve the balance sheets of the petroleum industry.

The sine qua non for a turnaround in our current unsatisfactory energy posture is to deregulate newly discovered petroleum (both oil and gas) as soon as possible and to let the U.S. consumer pay as much for secure U.S. energy as he will otherwise pay for insecure imported energy. Controlled prices for U.S. energy will continue to produce inadequate conservation, inadequate development of alternative supplies, and inadequate U.S. petroleum investment.

DISCUSSION

U.S. energy capital requirements depend in the first instance upon U.S. economic growth policy

The no-growth proponents of the Club of Rome notwithstanding, the United States must have an economic growth policy. The American people want an economic growth policy that will comprehend an increasing gross national product (GNP) to supply adequate jobs and an adequate standard of living for our people. The supply of adequate jobs for a growing working age population is critical. All administrations in Washington have taken and will take this position.

We think it unlikely that the American public will be satisfied with a GNP growth for the next ten years of less than 4 percent. The energy policy implications of a 4 percent GNP growth are inescapable.

U.S. energy demand will grow if the U.S. economy grows

Economic activity requires the use of energy. One of the major factors in the growth of the United States to the greatest industrial power in history has been the abundance of secure and inexpensive energy. Relative life-styles and economic output throughout the world are closely related to energy use. In the United States over the period since the early 1950s, a 1 percent increase in real GNP has involved close to a 1 percent increase in energy use.

There is reason to hope that the ratio of energy use to GNP will decline in the future because of greater awareness of the need to conserve and because energy has become more expensive. There is no realistic basis, however, to expect that the ratio of energy growth to

Chart 1. Ratio of energy use to GNP in the United States (thousand BTUs per dollar of GNP in 1958 dollars)

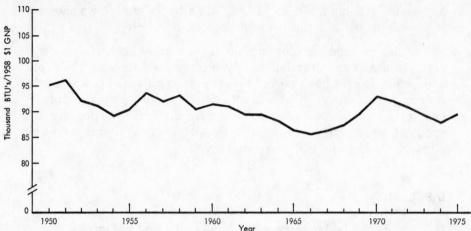

Source: Bureau of Economic Analysis; Bureau of Mines.

GNP growth will approach zero. I have assumed that for the next ten years a 1 percent increase in GNP will result in a three fourths of 1 percent increase in energy use. In other words, 4 percent annual growth in GNP will result in 3 percent annual growth in energy use. *This will not be easy to achieve, and in my opinion it will only be achieved if the U.S. government promptly ceases and desists from hiding the true energy costs from the U.S. consumer.*

Prices for newly discovered oil and gas need to be deregulated as soon as possible so that the prices the consumer pays will help him to make sensible conservation decisions. Commentators who oversell the potential of conservation are friends neither of the earth nor of the people. The consequence of being mesmerized by that siren song will lead directly to diminishing U.S. supply, growing imports, and declining jobs.

Nonpetroleum energy supplies (especially coal and nuclear) need to grow at a rapid rate

To make sure that we do not come up short, we should have a redundancy of effort to increase all of our U.S. energy supplies, especially nonpetroleum supplies. Research should go forward on solar, fusion, tidal, and wind energy. Further work should be done on the cost/benefits of oil/shale development.

The simple fact is, however, that if nonpetroleum energy supplies are going to make a significant contribution in the next decade, it is coal and nuclear that will do it.

Coal. In 1945 oil and gas supplied about 44 percent of total U.S. energy requirements, compared with 51 percent for coal. By 1975 oil and gas were supplying about 75 percent of total demand, and coal only about 19 percent. The absolute level of coal consumption in the United States decreased from 610 million tons in 1945 to about 560 million tons in 1975—this for the energy source with which the United States is most richly endowed.

In the postwar period, cheap and abundant oil and natural gas drove coal out of many of its traditional markets. Natural gas price controls instituted in 1954 played a major role in this displacement. Pollution control regulations also contributed to the displacement of coal. Natural gas was a clean-burning fuel, easier to handle than coal, and much less expensive because of government price control policy. These regulated prices encouraged the country to draw heavily on gas reserves for uses which could just as well have been handled by coal.

At the expected prices of unregulated new petroleum supplies, coal will attract substantial new investment; we believe that unsubsidized private investment will be forthcoming and that domestic coal supplies can grow at approximately 5 percent over the next decade. This is a formidable task because tremendous capital investment in mining, transportation, and personnel will be required, but it can be done in a proper economic environment. In addition to the price uncertainty, there are two major clouds on the horizon. The first relates to environmental restraints on the use and development of coal, and the second relates to the proposal that companies in the petroleum industry should be precluded from coal investment and should be obliged to divest themselves of the coal investments they have already made.

Environmental restraints. Coal supply growth objectives will rely heavily upon the development of western low-sulfur coal and upon moderating the environmental uncertainties and restraints on burning high-sulfur eastern coal. The ability to mine western coal through open-pit methods is hampered by the lack of a rational policy on strip mining. We need a balanced policy on environment and development if coal supplies are to play their appropriate role in the future energy supplies of the United States.

Divestiture restraints. Logic dictates that petroleum companies be permitted to do their part in the development of our coal reserves. Petroleum companies are accustomed to making large capital outlays and to managing large, high-risk projects. Petroleum companies have the size, the financial capacity, and the technical and managerial skill needed for rapid coal development. They have already invested heavily in coal exploration, development, and research. The gasification and liquefaction of coal will provide one means of meeting our growing energy requirements. Petroleum companies have special credentials for handling the research, development, and financing of these costly, high-technology developments.

Considering the great importance to the country of developing large supplies of energy other than petroleum, it would be a tragedy if Congress were to enact legislation requiring horizontal divestiture of the oil industry. This would shut off the participation of the oil industry in developing the alternative sources of energy needed now and in the future. Research by oil companies in these areas would cease (and incomplete research is virtually worthless); cash flows would be channeled elsewhere; and the management expertise of the oil industry would be lost to this critical need of the country. Horizontal divestiture is anticompetitive. It would create an artificial division of energy markets. It would raise barriers to entry into various energy industries. It would mandate the misallocation of resources, diminish supplies, and raise costs. It would make it very unlikely that coal supplies would grow at the rate that is possible and that the FEA assumed.

In summary, I believe that our coal energy sources can be developed at a rapid rate (that is, 5 percent per annum) in the next decade, provided that:

1. Coal is not required to compete with subsidized petroleum.
2. Reasonable trade-offs between development and environmental considerations are promptly made.
3. All potential investors, including petroleum companies, are permitted to participate.
4. All who wish to conduct research are encouraged and are assured that they can benefit from the fruits of that research.

Nuclear. I believe that nuclear power can grow at approximately 15 percent over the next decade, but the considerations that can constrain nuclear growth to less than this rate are similar to those applicable to coal. The forecast growth rate is challenging but achievable in the context of an appropriate energy policy.

Oil supplies to grow at 2 percent per annum— huge capital required

The foregoing discussion shows that a realistic GNP growth, coupled with substantial improvement in energy efficiency and a vigorous growth of coal supplies and nuclear power, will still require a growth in oil supplies of approximately 2 percent per annum over the next decade. Total petroleum (oil and gas) supplies will need to grow at 1.5 percent per annum, but since the potential growth for gas supplies is believed to be limited, oil supplies will need to grow at 2 percent per annum. In its 1976 study, the FEA assumed that this entire growth could be supplied from U. S. sources (implying a growth in U.S. production of more than 3.5 percent per annum), provided that $244 billion (1975 constant dollars) were invested in the U.S. oil and gas industry. For purposes of the later discussion of the policy decisions needed to produce such an investment and such a growth in supplies, I will assume that the FEA forecast of the supplies that will be generated by a $244 billion investment is valid, but frankly I believe

Chart 2.   Petroleum industry: Capital and exploration expenditures in the United States ($ billions)

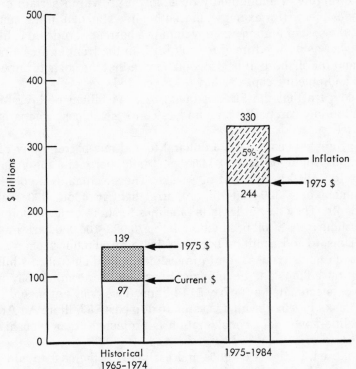

Sources:
   1965–74—current dollars, Chase Manhattan Bank, *Capital Investments of the World Petroleum Industry*; 1975 dollars, by application of price deflators for private fixed nonresidential investment.
   1975–84—1975 dollars; Federal Energy Administration, *National Energy Outlook, 1976.*

that the FEA forecast of the amount of petroleum supply that can be developed for that amount is optimistic.

During the ten years 1965–74 the capital and exploration expenditures of the petroleum industry amounted to $97 billion in the United States (in 1975 dollars this represents $139 billion). The quantity of oil produced in the United States in 1976 was about the same as the quantity produced in 1966, and crude oil reserves were at about the same level in both years. Gas production was higher, but gas reserves declined by about 25 percent. In recent years, gas production has also been declining. It is important to note also that 25 percent of the 1975 oil reserves figure and more than 10 percent of the 1975 gas reserves figure are represented by what may be a unique find on the North Slope of Alaska. These results mean that during the last decade the investment of $139 billion (1975 dollars) resulted in less than no growth in the U.S. petroleum supply—all of the growth was supplied by imports.

While there will undoubtedly be a slower growth in certain petroleum investments (for example, marketing investments) in the coming decade, the cost of finding and developing a barrel of crude oil is likely to be higher as we are forced to look for it in the frontier areas in the Arctic and far offshore. It is also well known that the costs for new refineries and pipeline capacity have skyrocketed.

My concern that the FEA estimate of $244 billion of investment may be too low can perhaps be understood if some cost comparisons are recited.

The estimated cost (in 1976 dollars) to add one barrel a day of oil production would be from $4,000 per daily barrel in the Atlantic offshore to $7,800 in the Gulf of Alaska. These estimates involve the development of a 300–400-million-barrel field in about 400 feet of water depth. They do not include pipelines to shore or lease bonuses. They assume rates of oil production in the 75,000–100,000 barrel-a-day range. Thus, to add 1 million barrels a day of production from a number of such fields would require investments totaling from $4 billion to about $8 billion. The development cost for the Prudhoe Bay field in Alaska is estimated at nearly $14 billion. This does not include the Trans Alaska Pipeline, which is estimated to cost $8 billion. An Arctic gas pipeline now under consideration is projected at an even higher cost.

By contrast, in the late 1960s and early 1970s the cost to add one barrel a day of oil production in the Gulf of Mexico was in the range of about $2,000 to $2,500. Onshore, in the lower 48 states, it was in the range of $1,000 to $1,500. Compared with the average cost of about $10 million a mile for the Alaska pipeline, large-capacity pipelines were built in the lower 48 states for $200,000 to $300,000 a mile.

In the oil industry it is extremely difficult to predict the amount of supply a given level of expenditures will produce. It is always risky to quote supply and cost estimates based upon possible or probable reserves. In spite of the technological progress the industry has made, the only way to find out for certain whether hydrocarbons exist is to drill. For example, in 1973 three companies in a joint venture paid the government a lease bonus of $623 million for the right to look for oil on what seemed to them to be promising acreage in the Gulf of Mexico off Florida. Then they spent $15 million to drill some wells. No oil was found, and the operation was abandoned. An investment of nearly $650 million in an attractive-looking area produced zero supplies of petroleum.

Large investments will be needed not only to find and develop oil and gas reserves, but also to build new refineries and upgrade existing refineries. Even with moderate consumption growth, some additional refinery capacity will be needed. A completely new, modern, competitive refinery would cost well over $500 million today. One of the last large, modern refineries built in the United States was completed in 1973 by Mobil at Joliet, Illinois, at a cost of $300 million. It would cost more than twice as much to duplicate this plant to day.

Much greater investment will be required to modify existing refineries than to add capacity. We are using up our traditional-source supplies of light low-sulfur crude oil faster than we can replace them. Crude will be coming from different places (for example, the North Slope of Alaska), and more of it will be heavy crude with high sulfur content. Very heavy investment in new facilities will be required to make just the same amount of gasoline out of this crude and to remove the sulfur. Removing lead from gasoline will also require the installation of expensive equipment.

Marshaling $244 billion (1975 dollars) in the next decade— a big challenge

My feeling is that it will take more than $244 billion (constant 1975 dollars) investment in U.S. petroleum to keep oil imports from growing, but even if the optimistic FEA forecast of requirements proves to be correct, it will take a major change in the environment to produce that level of investment.

In the last decade the oil industry invested $139 billion in 1975 constant dollars and achieved no growth in reserves or the level of production. Clearly there was less investment than we now know would have been desirable. It is important for us to determine why there was underinvestment so that we can correct the situation.

1. During the last decade the oil industry's return on equity investment was just about the average for manufacturing industry in general, notwithstanding charges of "obscene" profits.
2. During that decade the oil industry's tax bill was drastically increased, primarily as a result of the elimination of percentage depletion.
3. The prices for crude oil and petroleum products were placed under price control and continued under price control even when all other industries were freed of such control. Natural gas remained under price control, and only slow progress was made in adjusting its controlled prices in the direction of more realistic levels.
4. Refinery construction, port development, and pipeline construction were delayed by environmental groups. Construction costs increased as a consequence of the delays.
5. Offshore leasing was slowed down by legislation and government moratoriums.
6. Offshore operations were made riskier for large companies by the prohibition against joint bidding.

In light of all these developments it is surprising that the industry invested as much as it did. Happily, despite these disincentives, the industry has stepped up its rate of capital expenditure, especially in exploration and production. As a result of relatively low returns on investment and increased rates of expenditure, the internally generated cash flows of the industry have covered a smaller and smaller portion of capital expenditures in recent years. Debt/equity ratios have risen when they should not have done so, since the industry was investing more of its money in the higher risk areas of the business.

The industry increased its investment in recent years, in my opinon, because it saw the U.S. supply/demand gap widening in a menacing manner. Consequently it concluded that sooner rather than later, the United States would adopt an energy policy that would free indigenous petroleum prices from controls and restore a more rational procedure to consider development/environment trade-offs. *These optimistic conclusions must be validated and strengthened if investment is to grow. If we expect the industry to spend $244 billion (1975 constant dollars) in the next decade, much less the higher amount that will probably be required, changes in the regulatory environment are going to have to be made.*

First and foremost, newly discovered U.S. supplies of oil and gas need to be free of price controls. There are simply not going to be $244 billion private dollars available for investment in the current regulatory environment. Furthermore, if prices are controlled at a level too

Chart 3.   Petroleum industry debt/equity ratio

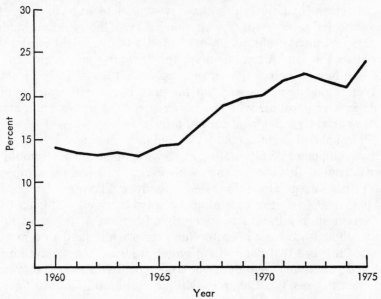

Source: Chase Manhattan Bank, *Financial Analysis of a Group of Petroleum Companies.*

low to give the supplier a fair rate of return, the public is not going to make efficient use of energy. Waste will continue and national requirements will grow.

Under our economic system, competition assures that prices producing more than a fair and adequate rate of return cannot and will not persist over any reasonable period of time.

If prices for new U.S. supplies are decontrolled, the price for U.S. oil will tend to approach, but not exceed the current prices for imported oil. I believe that such a price level is needed to assure adequate investment and conservation. In fact, because of rising costs I am not at all certain that adequate returns can be earned and adequate supplies developed in the United States if U.S. prices merely equal the current prices for imported oil. (This assumes, of course, that the U.S. government will always maintain the power to reimpose controls on U.S. prices should OPEC prices skyrocket in the future.)

Furthermore, an automatic adjustment system virtually guarantees that there will not be an unreasonably high rate of return for the industry if prices for new U.S. oil and gas are decontrolled. Much of the potential for significant new petroleum supplies in the United States will come from land owned by the federal government. The rights to explore these lands are auctioned. To the extent that unreasonably high rates of return for new exploration investment seem to be indicated at the expected price levels, the auction bids will increase and bidders will pass on much, if not all, of any "windfall" that might be thought to exist to the landowner, namely, the federal government. In essence, we have a before-the-fact excess-profits tax already in place. The fact is that bonuses will not increase because the profitability of offshore exploration will not be excessive at prices comparable to those currently being paid for imported oil.

Earlier, I stated that the country would be well advised to have too much development of alternative energy supplies, since it would be better to cope with a surplus than with a scarcity. I feel the same way about prices. A regulated price that is too low (and our experience has been that regulated prices are almost always too low) will keep us in our current supply bind. An uncontrolled price that might in hindsight be thought to have been too high for a while (and I do not believe that this is a real risk) will at worst produce "too much" investment and "too much" supply. I am confident that if those conditions ever come to pass, our Congress will have little difficulty in figuring out a solution. In short, we should adopt an energy policy that is in the national interest and stop worrying about the unlikely possibility that the petroleum industry will become too profitable.

If reasonable prices are not rapidly achieved, nothing else will produce the required investment in the private sector. Higher prices, however, will only create the willingness to invest; they will not assure the ability to invest. In addition to fair prices, we need:

1. Certain and rapid access to government lands that have energy potential (and this applies not only to Alaskan and offshore oil and gas but also to coal and other mineral resources).

2. Revision of the tax laws to eliminate the tax penalty against equity versus debt capital. Under current law, interest is deductible but dividends are not. This has all but compelled industry to finance as much of its expansion as possible through the issuance of new debt rather than new equity. This distortion hurts all industries, especially during economic downturns. In the future it could be a special problem for high-risk investors who seek to marshal capital to finance exploration and the development of petroleum supplies in hostile environments requiring new technology.

3. We need liberalized depreciation rules and investment tax credits in order to eliminate the current discrimination against long-term investment in an inflation-prone society. A system in which an investment in 1975 dollars gives tax relief in 1985 dollars taxes more than

income. It taxes capital—capital that should be available for investment in U.S. energy sources.

Conclusion

The United States is short of secure energy, and the situation is getting worse. This need not be the case if we face the facts: (1) we must have reasonable economic and employment growth; (2) we must achieve improved energy efficiency; eliminate the impediments to the rapid development of coal and nuclear power; decontrol the prices of new supplies of U.S. oil and gas; convert government delay to support for the development of U.S. energy supplies, particularly those which are owned by the U.S. government itself; and eliminate the bias against long-term investment and equity investment in our taxing system. If these policies are adopted, there is a good chance that we can marshal the capital that the FEA has forecast will be required to keep foreign imports from being higher in 1985 than they were in 1975. And, in my opinion, if these policies are adopted, there is a good chance that we can marshal the greater amounts of capital that are more likely to be required in order to do the job.

International postscript

While we plan and, hopefully, act to implement new policies to develop U.S. energy supplies, we should keep in mind two factors in connection with foreign supplies.

First, under the best of circumstances we will be importing tremendous quantities of foreign oil throughout and at the end of the next decade. Second, to the extent that the U.S. energy supply/demand goals implicit in the FEA analysis are not achieved, the shortfall will be translated into greater reliance on foreign imports.

Foreign imports in today's world do not represent secure supply, but if they are developed by U.S. companies they are more secure for the U.S. than if they are developed by non-U.S. companies. I don't mean to imply by this statement that U.S. companies will discriminate in favor of the United States and against friendly nations. I do mean to state, however, that as was the case during the 1973 embargo, U.S. companies will assure that the United States will not suffer from discrimination. As we formulate our commercial laws, our foreign policy, and our tax legislation, we should keep in mind that American security and the American balance of payments and the American consumer are going to be better off if foreign oil is imported from U.S. companies than if it is imported from foreign companies. Obviously, this is going to take large investments by U.S. companies in foreign areas.

Furthermore, all foreign sources of energy will be more secure if the sources of foreign energy are widely diversified. Recent enactments by Congress, proposed legislation, and new regulations and rulings by the Internal Revenue Service have made U.S. companies less competitive in foreign exploration and producing ventures. At the same time that we improve the environment for investing in U.S. energy development, we should also call a halt to the deterioration in the competitive posture of U.S. companies that have the capability and the willingness to invest in foreign sources of energy to supplement U.S. supplies and to provide the needed requirements of friendly nations.

Chapter 12

CAPITAL NEEDS OF THE
TELECOMMUNICATIONS INDUSTRY

*Theodore F. Brophy**

INTRODUCTION

It is more than coincidence that the pattern of expansion and industrialization which characterized America's progress in its second century was closely matched by the growth and development of the U.S. telecommunications industry during its first century of existence.[1]

The telephone has played an increasingly important role in all aspects of American life for the basic reason that it has given nearly everyone in the United States the means for communicating immediately and inexpensively with almost anyone else. The ready availability and dependability of telephone service have enabled it to exert tremendous influence on the economy as our nation evolved over the past 100 years from a rural, agrarian country into an urbanized, industrial society.

While the telephone was contributing in a major way to the nation's growth and progress, all segments of the population, in turn, were making the telecommunications industry highly successful through their rapidly increasing use of its services. This has been especially true in the business sector, where entire industries have grown up and thrived on a foundation of reliable, versatile communications facilities. Today, the telephone is an integral part of everyday life throughout America.

The contribution of the telephone and its derivative technologies to the growth and enrichment of our economy and our society cannot

---

* Chairman and Chief Executive Officer, General Telephone & Electronics Corporation.

be measured adequately in numbers. However, numbers can give some indication of the extent to which the telephone has become a necessity of everyday life.

In 1950, when U.S. telephones totaled 43 million, Americans made an average of 176 million phone calls every day. By the end of 1976, the number of U.S. telephones had increased to 155 million, and an average of 637 million calls were made daily. In a quarter of a century, more than 110 million telephones had been added to the communications resources of the nation. In addition, operating revenues climbed from $3.7 billion to approximately $40 billion, plant investment jumped from $11.5 billion to nearly $120 billion, and employment grew from 616,000 to nearly 940,000.

The industry's historical goal of "universal service"—the provision of high-quality telephone service to the maximum number of people at the lowest practicable cost—has become a reality. As the United States enters its third century, virtually the entire population is now served by the finest telecommunications system in the world.

The composition of the U.S. telecommunications industry

The U.S. telephone industry is comprised of the Bell System companies and the Independent telephone companies. The Bell System, which serves nearly 82 percent of the nation's 155 million telephones, consists of the American Telephone and Telegraph Company (AT&T), 21 principal operating telephone subsidiaries, and two minority-owned companies. AT&T also owns the Western Electric Company, the Bell System's manufacturing and supply unit, and jointly with Western Electric, it owns Bell Telephone Laboratories, the research and development organization. The Long Lines Department of AT&T provides interstate and international long-distance services in cooperation with the operating companies.

The remaining 18 percent of the nation's telephones, primarily in smaller cities, towns, and rural areas, are served by almost 1,600 Independent telephone companies. The largest of these is General Telephone & Electronics Corporation, which, at year-end 1976, served nearly 13 million telephones through 20 operating subsidiaries in portions of 33 states.

In addition to providing local service in more than 11,000 communities, the Independent companies join with the AT&T Long Lines Department and the Bell System operating companies in handling interstate and intrastate long-distance calls and share the resulting toll revenues with AT&T.

The United States leads in technology

The attainment of customer satisfaction depends not only upon a dedication to high-quality service; it also depends on a concentrated effort to achieve high levels of efficiency in all areas of operation and to introduce innovative methods of serving the public. Ever since the invention of the telephone itself by Alexander Graham Bell in 1876, the U.S. telecommunications industry has been heavily committed to providing more efficient and versatile services. As a result, the industry is the world leader in communications technology.

The U.S. telecommunications industry pioneered in developing and utilizing automatic dial systems which resulted in far more efficient local telephone service and ultimately led to faster and more economical long-distance service. The introduction of coaxial cable systems and microwave radio networks made possible the high-capacity long-distance network which extends throughout the nation today. "Carrier" systems capable of handling numerous conversations simultaneously on a single circuit represented another notable achievement. More recent innovations include computer-controlled switching systems which have greatly broadened the variety of available services, and satellite systems which have further expanded the capacity of the long-distance network. A newer development which has resulted from extensive research both in the United States and abroad is the use of fiber optic techniques to bring even greater capacity to the telecommunications network. Prototype systems utilizing hair-thin glass fibers to carry voice, video, and data signals are now being field-tested by several U.S. telecommunications companies.

Comparison of the United States with other nations

Reflecting the high efficiency and the economies of scale available in this country, the cost of telephone service in the United States compares favorably with that of the other industrialized nations of the world. Although in recent years charges for local service in the United States have been rising, they remain considerably below such charges in most European countries and they have increased at a far lower rate than has the cost of American consumer services as a whole. The same is true of new-service installation charges and of charges for extension telephones and specialized services. Waiting time for the installation of new telephone service in the United States is generally only a few days, whereas in many other countries the delay can run into months or even years.

The reasonable cost, ready availability, and high quality of service have encouraged Americans to take full advantage of the telephone. This country, with 40 percent of the world's telephones, leads all other industrialized nations in the number of telephones and in telephone "density." More than 90 percent of the nation's households have telephone service—a higher proportion than that of any other country.

THE PROJECTED DEMAND FOR TELECOMMUNICATIONS SERVICES

The tremendous upsurge in the use of telecommunications during the past quarter century has placed heavy demands upon the industry's resources.

In 1950, 30 million telephones were in residences and 13 million in business establishments. By 1976, there were 114 million residential telephones and 41 million business telephones. According to a recent forecast, there will be more than 133 million telephones in homes and 43 million in businesses by 1980 and about 156 million in homes and 48 million in businesses by 1985.

THE CAPITAL NEEDS OF THE TELECOMMUNICATIONS INDUSTRY

The dynamic growth trend projected above presents the telecommunications industry with many challenges as the industry enters its second century. The overriding challenge is the necessity for raising, on an economical basis, the large amounts of new capital required to finance the continued expansion and improvement of service in the years ahead.

Historical and future capital requirements

Demands for service translate into capital requirements. This relationship can be illustrated by both the historical and the projected plant and equipment expenditures of the telecommunications industry. As shown on Chart 1, the industry's construction expenditures totaled approximately $89 billion in the 1966–75 period and are expected to reach $240 billion in the 1976–85 period, an increase of 170 percent. Department of Commerce figures show that total expenditures for plant and equipment have been rising more rapidly for all utilities, including the telecommunications industry, than for the economy as a whole.

Chart 1. Telecommunications industry construction expenditures, 1966–1985 ($ billions)

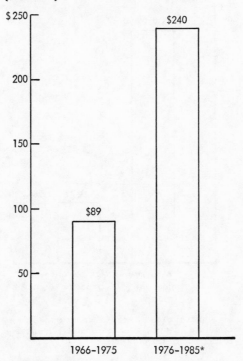

* Estimated.
Sources: American Telephone and Telegraph Company; United States Independent Telephone Association.

Industry leaders are concerned about the availability and the price of funds required to support these essential expenditures. This concern will intensify as the competition for funds and the cost of capital increase in the future.

A highly capital-intensive industry

Because of the large investment required to meet service demands, the telecommunications industry is highly capital-intensive. A comparison of the assets required to generate $1 of revenue in the telecommunications industry with the assets per $1 of revenue for all manufacturing companies illustrates this characteristic feature of the telecommunications industry. Chart 2 shows that the telecommunica-

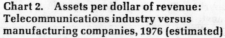

Chart 2. Assets per dollar of revenue: Telecommunications industry versus manufacturing companies, 1976 (estimated)

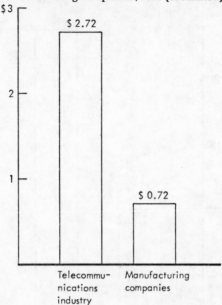

Sources: American Telephone and Telegraph Company; *Fortune;* General Telephone
& Electronics Corporation.

tions industry requires approximately 4 times as many dollars in assets to generate a dollar in sales as do manufacturing companies. As
a consequence, this industry, as compared with manufacturing companies, has relied and will probably continue to rely much more heavily on the external capital markets. In fact, utilities, including the telecommunications industry, account for a major segment of the private
external capital financing in the United States.

Other factors affecting capital needs

The capital requirements of the telecommunications industry are
affected not only by the growth in demand for service and the capital-
intensive nature of the industry but also by other important factors,
such as the shorter useful life cycles of plant and equipment, the inadequate depreciation allowed for rate-making purposes, the impact
of competition, and the need for investment that will enable productivity to keep pace with wage increases.

Shorter useful life cycles. In past decades, customer demands for totally new services were met by orderly advances in technology, and depreciation rates were based largely on the historically long physical service life of plant and equipment. But changes are now occurring at a far faster rate, a trend which seems certain to continue. Exploding technology, the ever-increasing customer demand for sophisticated new services, and the need to improve productivity have greatly increased overall capital requirements. Telephone companies will be unable, economically, to retain equipment developed with past technology, not only for operational reasons, but also because of demand and competition. It is, for example, more costly to operate and expand some existing telephone switching systems than to install entirely new systems.

These conditions are causing economically justifiable desires on the part of telephone companies to accelerate the replacement of existing equipment with electronic telecommunications systems. In fact, studies have justified the replacement of toll switching systems that have been in service less than ten years. Historically, the expected "normal" service life of such systems has been 30 years. Such replacements on a large-scale basis, spurred by expanding service demands, competition, and new technology, could result in severely curtailed capital recovery unless regulators change depreciation practices to permit the recovery of capital expenditures over a shorter and more accurate service life. When the economic life of plant and equipment is depleted faster than the investment in such plant and equipment is recovered through depreciation allowances, the difference must be made up through additional external financing, increased revenues, or reduced operating costs. These alternatives are either undesirable or difficult to achieve.

The need for reasonable depreciation practices.   In view of these trends, action must be taken to establish reasonable depreciation practices for rate-making purposes, and supporting rate structures should be adjusted to allow adequate recovery of plant and equipment investment dollars.

In the telecommunications industry, depreciation is by far the largest single component of internally generated funds. Reasonable depreciation rates that reflect shorter life cycles will assure the ability of the telecommunications industry to meet growing competition and increasing customer demand, while taking advantage of evolving technology and associated cost benefits at an early stage. In terms of both service and cost, the ultimate and principal beneficiaries of adequate depreciation practices will be the customers.

The impact of competition.   The Federal Communications Commission's recent introduction of competition into the intercity transmission market will also require increased capital spending to satisfy the nation's telecommunications needs. The introduction of multiple carriers on the same route, for example, New York to Chicago, divides the traffic among them. This serves to reduce the economies of scale otherwise available. Moreover, the division of telephone traffic postpones the day when any one carrier will have the traffic density necessary to support the next generation of lower cost, high-volume technological improvements.

Productivity and wage increases. Another factor affecting capital needs is the recently demonstrated inability of increases in productivity to keep pace with wage increases. Bureau of Labor Statistics data indicate that the productivity of the U.S. telephone industry has more than tripled in the past two decades, rising at a rate substantially higher than that of the private economy as a whole. Output per employee hour for the telephone industry grew at a compound annual rate of 6.1 percent between 1955 and 1975, whereas the growth rate for the total private economy was 2.7 percent.

However, despite these impressive increases in productivity, wage increases have far exceeded the rate of productivity improvement in recent years, largely because of the general inflationary trend throughout the country. Between 1969 and 1976, wages in the telephone industry rose at a compound annual rate of 10.8 percent, with the increases in selected years being well above the average. These increases compare with the telecommunications industry's productivity increase of a 6.0 percent compound annual rate over the same period.

The rapid increase in wage rates has been one of the factors which has led the telecommunications industry to be adventurous in seeking technological improvements and aggressive in seeking rate increases, while continuing its high level of investment in plant and equipment.

Investment per employee

Despite its relatively high level of productivity and its capital-intensive nature, the telecommunications industry is one of the largest employers in the United States, employing nearly 940,000 people in 1976, or over one half of all employees in the utility industry as a whole. The telecommunications industry achieved improvements in productivity well above the national average, for the most part, by significant and growing investment relative to the number of employees.

Chart 3 shows that gross plant investment per employee in the telecommunications industry was $127,000 in 1976, compared with only $42,000 in 1960. This increase of over 200 percent is based solely on *historical* costs. On a *replacement* cost basis, the 1976 investment per

Chart 3. Telecommunications industry gross plant investment per employee, 1960–1976 ($ thousands)

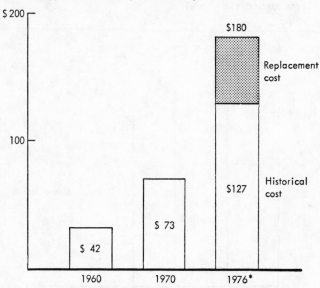

* Estimated.

Sources: American Telephone and Telegraph Company; Moody's Investors Service, Inc.; United States Independent Telephone Association.

employee would be far greater—$180,000 compared with the 1976 historical figure of $127,000. Because of projected demands for service, technological improvements, and inflation, it is expected that the investment per employee in the telecommunications industry will continue to increase.

PROBLEMS IN MEETING CAPITAL NEEDS

External capital requirements

Due to the large amounts of plant and equipment needed to satisfy customer demands and the highly capital-intensive nature of the telecommunications industry, total capital requirements far outstrip internally generated funds. Chart 4 shows that in 1976 a total of $14.1 billion of capital was required. Total internal sources of funds, comprising retained earnings, depreciation and other internal sources, provided only $9.9 billion, leaving $4.2 billion to be obtained from the external capital markets.

174

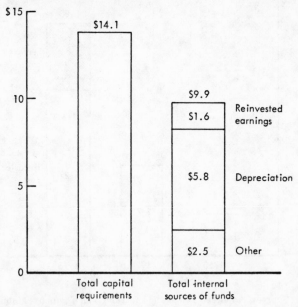

Chart 4. Telecommunications industry: Comparison of
capital requirements and internal sources of funds, 1976
(estimated) ($ billions)

Sources: American Telephone and Telegraph Company;
General Telephone & Electronics Corporation.

Competition for capital

The telecommunications industry must compete in the capital markets with other industries and with governmental bodies for the limited supply of investor funds. Because of the ever-increasing demand
for funds at all levels of society, competition in these markets has
intensified dramatically over the past ten years. This competition,
coupled with worldwide inflation, has increased the cost of capital
significantly. For example, the interest rate on "Aaa" telecommunications bonds increased from an average of 4.50 percent in 1965 to a
high of 9.50 percent in 1974, and was at the 8.15 percent level at the
end of 1976—well above historical norms.

The effect of inflation on the cost of plant and equipment

Inflation not only increases the cost of capital; it also substantially
raises the price of needed plant and equipment. Chart 5 shows that

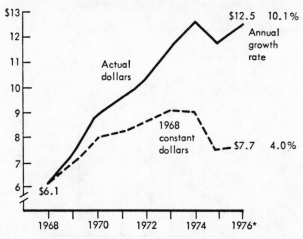

Chart 5. Telecommunications industry: Effect of inflation on construction expenditures, 1968–1976 ($ billions)

* Estimated.

Sources: American Telephone and Telegraph Company; General Telephone & Electronics Corporation; United States Independent Telephone Association; U.S. Department of Commerce.

actual construction expenditures grew at a rate of 10.1 percent between 1968 and 1976, whereas in terms of 1968 constant dollars the percentage growth was only 4.0 percent per year. The additional capital requirements resulting from inflation place an added burden on the telecommunications industry and tend to further intensify competition in the capital markets.

The effect of inflation on net income

Another consequence of inflation is the significant overstatement of reported net income in the telecommunications industry. As illustrated on Chart 6, reported net income for the industry in 1976 was $4.4 billion, whereas net income adjusted for the replacement cost depreciation of plant and equipment was 41 percent less, or $2.6 billion. Net income may be overstated either because it represents fewer real dollars or because depreciation is inadequate to recover the replacement cost of plant and equipment. In either case, the result is a situation in which the corporation is overtaxed, its internally generated sources of funds are depleted, and in some instances, its capital is consumed.

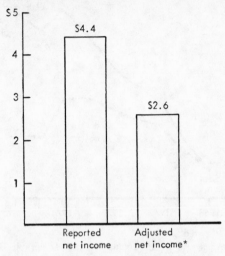

Chart 6. Telecommunications industry:
Reported net income versus adjusted net
income 1976 (estimated) ($ billions)

* Adjusted for replacement cost depreciation.

Sources: American Telephone and Telegraph Company; General Telephone & Electronics Corporation.

The effect of inflation on interest rates

Historically, interest rates on long-term utility bonds have fluctuated with changes in inflation. In Chart 7, the upper line shows the current interest rates for "A"-rated utility bonds. The bottom line reflects the same figures adjusted for inflation. The chart shows that in terms of real dollars, long-term interest rates have amounted historically to approximately 3.0 percent. The inflation premium has obviously widened sharply since 1966, reflecting the investors' concern regarding inflation.

Higher interest costs increase operating expenses and thereby reduce internal generation of funds. This, in turn, increases the amount of funds required by the industry, thus placing a further burden on the capital markets. In addition, the increased costs make it more difficult to meet service demands and, ultimately, will result in higher costs to telephone customers.

Strained debt/equity ratios

Due to the large capital requirements, the effects of inflation, and federal tax discrimination against dividend costs as compared to in-

Chart 7. The "inflation premium" in utility bond rates

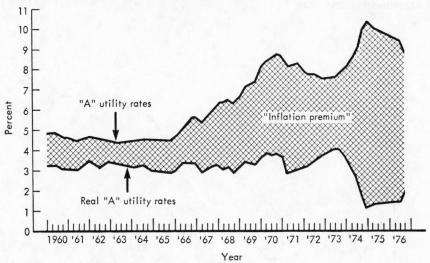

Sources: Moody's Investors Service, Inc.; U.S. Department of Commerce.

terest on bonds, the telecommunications industry has come to rely more and more heavily upon the use of debt capital. Chart 8 illustrates this increase in the burdensome level of corporate debt, which rose from 35 percent of total capitalization in 1965 to over 50 percent in 1975. Many corporations in the telecommunications industry are, in fact, approaching or have reached the limit of reasonable debt levels and will not be able to increase their reliance on debt capital in the future.

Declining interest coverage

Interest coverage is widely considered to be the single most important criterion utilized in the evaluation of the investment quality and creditworthiness of debt securities. The increased reliance on debt, coupled with rising interest costs, has resulted in a severe long-term decline in the interest coverage afforded investors. Chart 9 shows that in 1960 the average pretax interest coverage of the telecommunications industry was approximately 9.2 times, whereas by 1976 this coverage had fallen to only 3.7 times. Declining interest coverage reduces the quality and attractiveness of such securities and at the same time increases the risk to the investor. As a direct result, telecommunications companies have found it more difficult and more expensive to raise needed capital.

Chart 8. Telecommunications industry: Debt as a percentage of total capitalization, 1960–1976

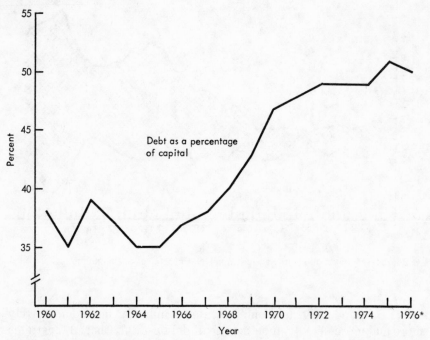

* Estimated.

Sources: American Telephone and Telegraph Company; General Telephone & Electronics Corporation; United States Independent Telephone Association.

Although interest coverage showed modest improvement in 1976 compared with 1975, it is still dramatically below historical norms. If the industry were to return to a decline in interest coverage, individual companies in the telecommunications industry could reach the point where they would be restricted by indenture limitations from issuing additional long-term debt.

The effect of regulation on return on equity

A major factor in the ability of the telecommunications industry to meet its capital needs is the effect of regulation. As a "natural monopoly," the telecommunications industry is regulated by federal and state authorities. Regulation serves as "the law's substitute for competition," which arises naturally in other industries.

A nonregulated business is free to adjust its prices immediately in response to increasing costs, whereas a regulated business must first

Chart 9. Telecommunications industry: Pretax interest coverage, 1960–1976

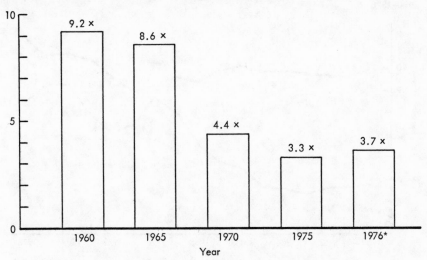

* Estimated.

Sources: American Telephone and Telegraph Company; General Telephone & Electronics Corporation; Moody's Investors Service, Inc.; United States Independent Telephone Association.

obtain approval from a regulatory agency. The inevitable delay resulting from the regulatory process is especially damaging during periods of high inflation. Because of this delay and continuing inflation, very few telephone companies have been able to achieve the allowed rate of return on common equity, in spite of repeated rate increases.

The key to maintaining the financial integrity that will attract capital at reasonable costs is the achievement of adequate earnings. Under pressure from consumers to maintain current price levels, regulatory commissions have been reluctant to heed the advice of financial experts and allow utilities the opportunity to earn the return needed to assure a continued flow of investor capital. Much evidence has been presented to regulators indicating that a common equity return of approximately 15 percent is currently necessary to attract capital at reasonable costs.

Chart 10 shows that during the 1960–65 period, a relatively equitable relationship existed between the returns provided the common equity investor and the returns afforded the investor in less risky debt securities. Since then, however, the returns to common equity investors have simply not proved to be adequate compensation for the increased risk of equity security ownership. Although some improvement has occurred since 1970, this improvement must continue if the

180

Chart 10.   Telecommunications industry: Shrinking return on equity premium,
1960–1976

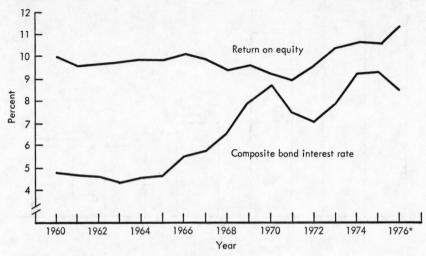

* Estimated.
Sources: American Telephone and Telegraph Company; Moody's Investors Service,
Inc.; United States Independent Telephone Association.

telecommunications industry is to attract needed capital to satisfy
the legitimate demands for customer service at reasonable rates.

THE ROLE OF THE TELECOMMUNICATIONS INDUSTRY
IN THE CENTURY AHEAD

If the U.S. economy is to expand and to compete effectively in the
world markets in the century ahead, and if this nation is to continue
to develop and grow socially and culturally, then the economy and the
nation must have the infrastructure which only a dynamic and vigorous telecommunications industry can provide.

The foundation of a healthy telecommunications industry will continue to be its ability to attract, at reasonable cost, the capital it requires to meet its obligations and assume its responsibilities.

It is clear that to achieve this objective pervasive changes in the
nation's tax policies will be required. In the decade ahead the telecommunications industry's capital needs will be some 2½ times as
great as they were in the past ten years. Obtaining capital on that order
of magnitude will require both the elimination of past discrimination
against investors and new tax incentives equal to those of other leading industrial nations.

NOTE

1. Although the Federal Communications Commission's introduction of competition into the telecommunications industry has perhaps expanded the industry definition to include companies other than the regulated telephone companies, for the purposes of this chapter we will use the more limited definition.

Chapter 13

CAPITAL PROBLEMS IN THE FOREST PRODUCTS INDUSTRY

*George H. Weyerhaeuser**

INTRODUCING THE FOREST PRODUCTS INDUSTRY

Processing trees into products is one of the oldest industries. Even though the manufacture of forest products would thus seem to be a mature industry, it is very likely to outlive many of the more recent industries, since the resource it processes is renewable and the industry's primary energy source is the sun, the one essentially inexhaustible energy source. Despite its age, the forest products industry is subject to constant technological innovation, as both its processes and the uses of wood products change.

The very feature that provides the industry with its endurance also characterizes its uniqueness as a capital investment. No other industry makes large investments comparable to reforestation expenditures, investments which will provide very little payback from current outlays for as long as 50 years, when the mature timber is harvested.

Investment in timber growth

Over the last two decades, with better markets (especially internationally) and heavy investments in forest management, the industry has begun to grow trees at more than twice the average rate of growth achieved naturally. This has been achieved by better planting, the use of improved nursery stock, fertilization, thinning, brush control, and other practices. The last includes genetic selection, still in its infancy, which will further increase the rate of growth.

---

* President and Chief Executive Officer, Weyerhaeuser Company.

Employment: Product impact is crucial

The forest products industry currently employs directly 1.3 million persons in growing timber on industry land; in producing solid wood products, such as lumber and plywood; and in manufacturing wood fiber products, including paper, packaging, shipping containers, and construction boards. Lumber, plywood, and particleboard are still the principal materials used in the construction of single-family homes, even though during the last several decades steel and cement have become increasingly important in the construction of large multifamily residential dwellings and large commercial and industrial buildings. Pulp, the source of paper, paperboard, and other wood fiber products, is used throughout the economy in the production processes of other industries, in the publications media, and in the packaging of most consumer products and many industrial products.

The forest products industry is a critical supplier of shelter and the whole spectrum of paper products used by consumers. These range from newspapers, books, and magazines, through tissues and the boxes used to ship most nonpaper products, to photographic film. When one considers, in addition to the direct jobs provided by the forest products industry, the indirect supplier and service jobs that support the industry, the total job impact of the forest products industry encompasses a work force of more than 3 million, or more than 3 percent of the current U.S. labor force.

CAPITAL INVESTMENT IN THE PAPER AND PAPERBOARD MILLS

The paper and paperboard industry appears on the surface to be moderately above the average capital intensity for a manufacturing industry (see Chart 1). Total capital investment per worker for the industry has risen in recent years to $42,000 (see Chart 2). If the plant and equipment investments carried on the books were restated to recognize past inflation, then the industry investment per worker would be $64,000. If existing plants are replaced with up-to-date mills that satisfactorily meet known pollution standards, then the industry would have $73,000 invested in plant and equipment for each member of the current work force, and since the replacement of many of the older mills would undoubtedly decrease the work force somewhat, the investment required per worker would be raised even further.

If we include the inflation in land and timber management costs, the investment per worker increases to about $81,000. However, since the timber resource has been held and managed for so many years, it

**Chart 1.   Paper and paperboard industry:
Average investment per dollar of sales**

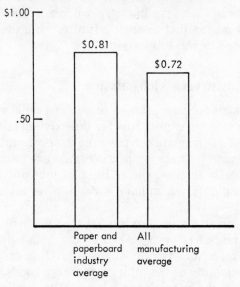

Source: FTC quarterly financial reports.

Chart 2.   Paper and paperboard industry: Investment per worker, 1960–1976

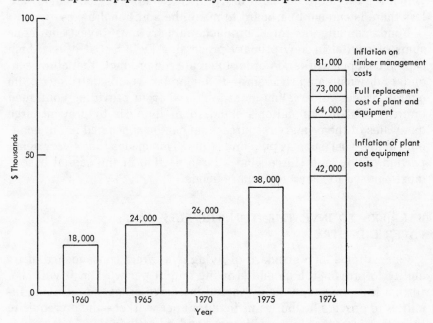

Sources: FTC quarterly financial reports; American Paper Institute.

would be impossible to replace it by purchases in today's market without paying much more than the restated historical cost. Clearly the full capital costs of the paper industry are much higher than we have indicated. This means that financing future job growth represents a challenge of monumental proportions.

The capital intensity versus jobs illusion

The capital costs for *new* primary processing mills are considerably higher than the average capital cost for the *existing* mills—rising to as much as $1,000,000 per worker for a new newsprint or paper mill. Products from such primary processing mills are required before we can expand capacity to allow the addition of jobs downstream in converted-products plants, which have a much lower investment cost per worker.

In recent years, the enormous capital cost per worker for some of these primary mills has been looked at disparagingly by those who want to create more jobs per dollar invested. It is easy to forget that without the availability of the primary resource goods, it is impossible to create jobs in the more labor-intensive converting plants, since materials-limited converting plants would not be able to operate. In short, one can't establish more box shops, or expand other industries which require more boxes to move their goods to the consumer, unless there is enough linerboard to make the additional boxes.

Fundamentally, the forest products industry must invest enormous sums of capital in new primary processing facilities, at a very high capital cost per worker, in order to create the products that allow secondary downstream processing—if the industry is to contribute to the overall process of creating more jobs. A key to providing continued improvement in our nation's standard of living is to provide large quantities of the primary resources that can be consumed in our economy at low cost, such as pulp and paper. This means that a very small portion of the labor force—but a large portion of the capital base—must be used to generate primary goods.

BARRIERS TO INVESTMENT IN THE PULP AND PAPER INDUSTRY

Our nation's high standard of living is a direct consequence of its ability to provide a high and growing output per worker. It will take further investments in highly capital-intensive primary processing facilities to provide further gains in output per worker—the prerequisite to further increases in our citizens' standard of living.

In recent years a number of new problems have developed in sustaining investment in new primary processing facilities. These include pollution abatement costs, difficulties regarding site availability, and the energy shortage. As our past standard of living rose, so too did pollution levels. Pollution became so objectionable by the 1960s that major capital investments have been directed to pollution cleanup ever since. During the last five years nearly 30 percent of the pulp and paper industry's plant and equipment investment has been diverted to the cleanup of existing mills. As a consequence, capacity expansion has slowed.

Because of this trend, capital requirements for the next decade will be larger if we wish to source the goods needed from this and other primary industries to allow the economy to grow closer to full employment, without major and inflationary materials shortages. The industry is also investing more in energy conversion, especially to use the low-grade forest wastes, normally left behind in harvesting, as a source of fuel for energy. Perhaps another 7 percent of the required plant and equipment investment will be for energy conversion, incremental to the expenditures made on energy in the past. There is also an urgent need to invest more in new energy sources. At the same time, more energy will be needed to minimize the pollution produced by some types of mills.

THE ESCALATION IN INVESTMENT REQUIREMENTS

Chart 3 shows that the industry's investment need for plant and equipment will increase from $17 billion over the last decade to a staggering $74 billion in the next decade. As shown on the chart, a significant part of this represents inflation expected during the next decade. But the increase is nevertheless dramatic, with very large pollution cleanup capital requirements if the industry is to reach current 1983 standards. New OSHA standards and new levels of energy independence will further increase the problem of finding enough capital to provide the primary capacity needed to support a fuller employment domestic economy.

CAN THE CAPITAL BE OBTAINED?

Sourcing the funds to meet those capital requirements now appears almost impossible. Given a continuation of the historical profit margins in the industry, even in the unlikely event that debt borrowing remains at the very high levels sustained over the past few years, the industry will source only about half of the required funds for invest-

Chart 3.   Spending for plant and equipment: Paper and paperboard industry requirements

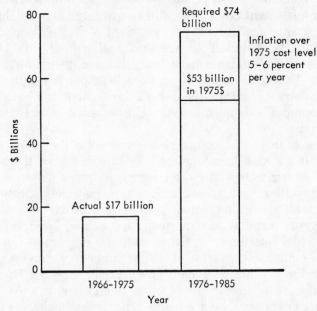

Sources: Study for API—URS and API staff update.

Chart 4.   How the paper and allied products industry sales dollar is distributed

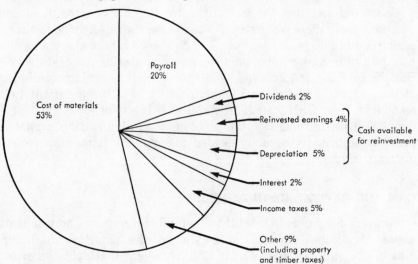

Sources: FTC quarterly financial reports; IRS Statistics; and annual survey of manufacturers.

ment. Reinvested earnings have represented only 4 percent of the sales dollar (see Chart 4), and debt ratios have been running high at 30–35 percent of total capital (Chart 5). This has already put a strain on the industry's credit standing. Any significant increase in debt ratios would probably cause lenders to worry about the industry's creditworthiness. This could result in a downgrading of the bond ratings for many companies, greatly increasing interest costs. But more important, it would serve to limit the amounts of borrowed capital available to those companies—especially during tight money periods.

Chart 5.   Paper and paperboard industry debt ratio

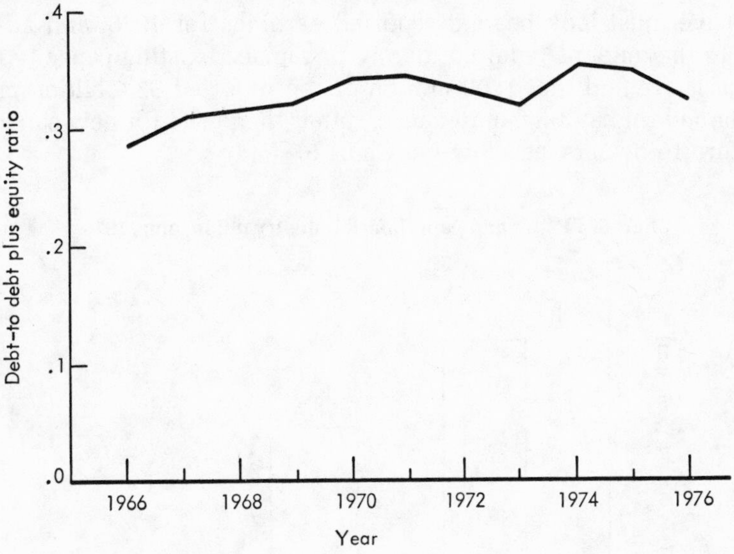

Source: Moody's Industrials.

Corporate cash flow consists primarily of reported net income before depreciation and depletion charges. These charges are based on the fact that no institution can long survive if all of its annual earnings are made available for shareholder dividends. In effect, depreciation and depletion charges are designed to recover, over the life of the investment, the original invested capital. These funds are reinvested in the business. And historically, depreciation and depletion charges were large enough to represent adequately the cash required to replace facilities as they were used up. However, with high inflation rates over recent years, actual replacement costs are now much larger than depreciation reserves. This means that supplemental funding must be appropriated from earnings otherwise available for dividends to share-holders. Historically, earnings reinvested, rather than paid to share-owners, have been used to finance *growth*. But in the current inflation-ary situation, a growing portion of reinvested earnings must instead be used simply to maintain existing capacity—rather than to expand. This puts a further drag on new capital formation for expansion—with an obvious concomitant drag on new jobs. Net income for 1976 did reflect an increase from 1975 levels, although it was lower than the 1974 peak. That peak resulted from a year of very tight markets with severe price inflation in all commodity products. However, *on the sur-face* 1976 margins still appear to be slightly higher than those of the late 1960s.

But we must look beyond reported earnings for 1976, and adjust them to the amount required merely to replace existing capacity. On this basis we find that $700 million of the reported $2.4 billion must be retained for capital maintenance, rather than used for new capacity or return to owners, as shown in Chart 6.

Chart 6. Paper and paperboard industry net income, 1976

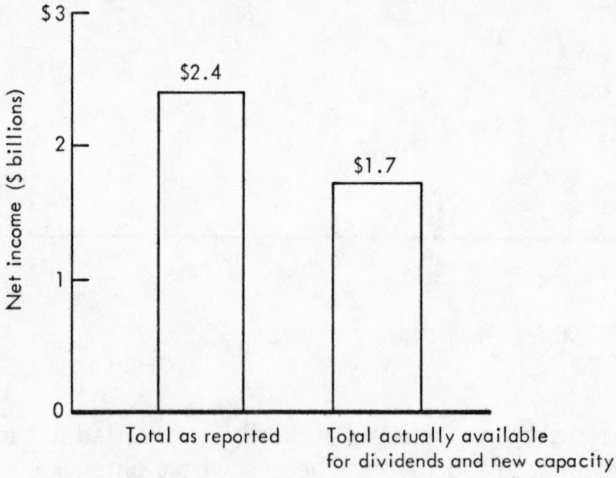

Sources: FTC quarterly financial reports annualized nine-month rate; API data on depreciation.

SEARCHING FOR A FREE ENTERPRISE SOLUTION

In effect, the tight markets of 1974 did produce a slight increase in profit margins. But this increase was insufficient even to correct for recent inflation—let alone to provide the increased source of capital necessary to pay for pollution cleanup equipment, to offset technical obsolescence, and to provide the expansion necessary for healthier employment levels in the economy.

What can be done to restore a more reasonable growth path for capacity in primary goods such as paper? Tough decisions—but proper ones—by business, government, and consumers can still help close the gap.

Product use or demand will decline somewhat as a result of current conservation efforts. Over the next few years industry managers can get a little more capacity out of incremental expansion of existing plants, which costs less than would new plants. But it must be recognized that the postponement of new mill investments will result in an even greater need for totally new plants with higher capital costs per unit of capacity by the mid-1980s.

The industry simply can't go on trying to expand old plants for very long. In fact, it can no longer expand plants as easily as in the 60s without overloading some portion of the system. This produces unsatisfactory pollutant by-products. With a little luck, replacement capital costs might be held down a bit for a few years. It might also be possible to defer timberland purchase and regeneration costs for a few years in order to get as much expansion in the near term as possible. However, this would lead to a future penalty in capital costs and capital needs. The use of debt and equity sources to the maximum extent possible will also contribute to industry expansion.

GOVERNMENT'S RESPONSIBILITY

While all of these measures can contribute to increased expansion, taken collectively they are insufficient. Equally important, or even more important, are environmental measures, site availability problems, and taxation measures. For example, deferral of the 1983 water quality standards, except in those cases where significant water quality improvement would result, would forestall a major source of capital diversion. The capital involved would be enough to enable a nearly 4 percent increase in expansion to be under way by 1985. Since water quality will not be measurably improved (with a few regional exceptions) by the uniform implementation of the 1983 technology standards in all mills, such implementation seems a very poor trade-off between the use of capital for new capacity and the improvement of environmental quality. Similarly, some site availability problems, usually related to environmental and zoning regulations, preclude expansion alternatives. Standards should be directed toward measurable improvements in the *total* environment. This seems preferable to absolute and inflexible "uniform" formulas—each designed to influence a single aspect of the environment without relation to other equally important aspects.

Federal tax policy can make a major contribution in this area. Tax credits obviously increase the cash available for expansion. If adequate tax credits were given for specific pollution abatement spending, it would allow bringing old plants up to standards—which is a technical necessity to avoid their premature obsolescence. This appears to make economic sense, and it would avoid diverting capital away from capacity expansion.

Because of the long-term nature of timber-growing investments, it is crucial that federal, state, and local tax systems not become so burdensome as to discourage these investments—the basis of future timber harvests. Such fiscal measures are as important as amendments to the 1983 standards that will allow recognition of water quality priorities rather than simply enforcing a uniform technology.

Another important element in creating jobs and improving the environment is the need for additional cash flow with which to modernize facilities and equipment. Existing capital cost allowances under the tax law are inadequate and fail to recognize the investment demands caused by inflation. Revised allowances, based on replacement costs of assets appear to offer a logical and urgently needed solution to this problem.

Options that will reduce the potential shortage of primary goods are still available. But it must be emphasized that a sound tax and regulatory program is needed to support more capacity expansion in the primary processing industries. Otherwise, all attempts to push economic growth toward full employment will result in major shortages of basic materials and another escalation in inflation rates. The problem, in a nutshell, is public understanding. In the absence of public understanding, the necessary options simply cannot be exercised.

CAPITAL INVESTMENT IN HOUSING AND WOOD PRODUCTS MILLS

Any changes in the capital requirements that impact the paper industry or overall manufacturing will have a significant impact on the solid wood products industry and its capital markets. Although long-term housing *demand* is directly dependent upon population growth and labor force trends, the *supply* of housing has always been very strongly impacted by the availability of credit. Consequently, excessive demands in capital markets relative to the supply of funds have resulted and will continue to result in a supply of mortgage money and housing construction far below long-term demand—as in the 1974 housing slowdown. At that time housing starts fell rapidly to only 50 percent of previous peaks. Housing starts have exceeded long-term demand only in those years when the available supply of credit has greatly exceeded government and business needs for capital. Housing has often been "crowded out" by heavy government borrowing and heavy business investment needs.

Unlike the paper industry, the wood products industry can respond fairly rapidly to demands for increased capacity. The capital required for a new solid wood products mill is almost always less than $20 million to $30 million—or one tenth of the amount required for a new fiber products mill. Also, the lead time between planning and mill production in the wood products industry is one to two years, in contrast to the more than three years required to get paper and paperboard mills in operation. The periodic shortages and price cycles in lumber and plywood have not stemmed from any fundamental problem of the lumber or plywood industries in meeting long-term demand trends, but have been a direct response to the enormous fluctuations in housing construction that have resulted from past governmental fiscal and monetary extremes.

Consequently, any solution that minimizes the gap between the demand for investment capital and the sourcing of investment funds in the paper industry and other primary processing industries will also help to stabilize the operating efficiency and the capital needs of the wood products industry. Based on current economic life expectancy and the normal expansion needed to support a long-term demand for just under 2 million housing starts, the capital needs of the wood products industry will approach $13 billion over the next ten years.

However, if the markets are not stable—if they zigzag as wildly as they have in recent years—the very inefficient use of production capacity in the solid wood products industry could greatly increase the estimated capital needs.

But the more significant question is: Can the capital markets produce the $800 billion–$1,000 billion in new mortgage money required to meet the long-term housing demand of 1.8 million–2 million conventional housing starts for the next ten years? The people born in the "baby boom" of the late 1940s and the 1950s are now moving into the family formation stage. This will result in a sustained strong demand for housing for the next ten years—a stronger demand than we have ever experienced for such an extended period.

SUMMING UP

Our economy is much more interconnected than most of us wish to realize. But if we can address the enormous capital needs in primary processing and energy during the next ten years, we should also be able to stabilize the capital markets' support for our housing needs. In my view, this can be achieved if tax penalties on saving and investing are removed. It cannot be accomplished if, in the name of "reform," tax penalties are made more severe.

The forest products industry traditionally makes investments for the long-term. Hundreds of dollars per acre are invested over the timber growth cycle, and millions of acres are harvested each year. We don't expect a return from our investments for many years. But it is important to the American way of life that we continue to invest in the renewable resources that will be critical to our future standard of living. Over the next ten years every aspect of government policy that affects capital needs will have an impact on the willingness of the American people to save and invest.

Failure to look at the full problem of how to source the funds for needed investments can only result in periods of shortages, inflation, recession, and severe housing cycles, with an overall shortfall in the production of homes to meet the needs of the current generation. This, in turn, would trigger still more government intervention and controls over free markets.

The American people simply cannot afford to sit back complacently. The future will not be just an extension of the past. Business leaders have a civic duty to make clear the nation's needs for capital and job formation. But above all else, we urge the body politic to recognize that capital and job formation is not industry's problem—it is society's problem.

Chapter 14

THE CHEMICAL INDUSTRY'S CAPITAL NEEDS

*Irving S. Shapiro**

The chemical industry has been a vigorous and increasingly important element of the U.S. economy in recent decades. At the turn of the century it represented 1 percent of the country's gross national product; today it represents 6 percent. Because of the basic position of the industry, its importance extends well beyond its immediate boundaries. It is a large, complex industry that supplies materials and products to virtually every sector of the modern U.S. economy.

The industry's products fall into three general categories: (1) basic chemicals, such as acids, alkalies, salts, and organic chemicals; (2) chemical products to be used in further manufacture, such as synthetic fibers, plastic materials, and pigments; (3) finished products for consumer use, such as drugs, cosmetics, and soaps; and items that other industries use as materials or supplies, such as paints, fertilizers, and explosives. Major customer industries include textile mill products and rubber and plastic products; the apparel, automotive, packaging, and health care industries are among the larger end-users.

The chemical industry's importance to the domestic economy is summarized in Table 1.

The industry's importance extends far beyond its direct activities. As indicated above, it is estimated that about one third of the jobs in manufacturing industries are closely related to the chemical industry.

* Chairman, E. I. du Pont de Nemours & Co., Inc.

Table 1. Chemicals and allied products, 1976

	Amount	Percent of total manufacturing
Value of direct shipments	$102 billion	8.6%
Employees		
Direct	1 million	5.4%
Including dependent industries (estimated)	6 million	30–35%
Total assets	$ 85 billion	10%
Total assets per employee	$ 82 thousand	$45 thousand (actual)
Net profit margin	7.8%	5.5% (actual)

Sources: Federal Trade Commission quarterly financial report; U.S. Department of Labor, Bureau of Labor Statistics.

HISTORICAL TRENDS

The industry's vigor is reflected in its performance compared to total industry (see Table 2).

Table 2

	Chemicals and allied products	Total industry
1955–73:		
Annual growth rate	8%	4.3%
Annual change in selling prices	0.6%	2.1%
Annual increase in productivity	6.1%	2.5%
Current output:		
Per employee	$100M	$62M
Per dollar of investment	$1.23	$1.42

Sources: Federal Reserve Board index of quarterly output; U.S. Department of Labor, Bureau of Labor Statistics.

The chemical industry's high growth rate has resulted in major part from its innovative products. Since World War II, the industry's level of self-funded research and development effort (expressed as a percentage of sales) has been about twice that of manufacturing as a whole. This effort produced man-made products that displaced traditional materials by offering unique physical properties and processing advantages at attractive prices. Familiar examples are synthetic fibers replacing cotton and wool; plastics replacing paper and glass in packaging and replacing metals and wood in fabricated products; detergents replacing soaps based on natural oils and fats; and chemical fertilizers replacing organics. The new products also allowed people to do things that were previously impossible, in fields such as health care and food production. The industry's contribution to living standards is apparent when one considers the practical impossibility of serving the needs of today's population solely with products that exist in nature.

The high growth rate of the industry has required the continuous construction of new plants and the expansion of existing plants. In addition, major research and development efforts have been devoted to improved process technology and the reduction of operating costs at existing plants. As a result, established products have been constantly modified and improved in quality, price, and processibility. For example, the price of a product as basic as polyethylene dropped from 39 cents/pound to 14 cents/pound over the 1955–73 period. Over half of today's polyethylene output is in product types that are less than ten years old, and the newer grades have contributed to quality and processing benefits for customers.

Innovations in process technology and economies of scale led to reduced costs through improved productivity, yields, energy efficiency, and the effectiveness of capital. As an example, between 1955 and 1973 the cost of manufacturing nylon salt was reduced by more than half. In constant dollars, the cost was reduced by a factor of four.

Table 3

	Exports less imports ($ billions)	
	Chemicals and allied products	Total U.S. industry
1955–75	$39	$64
1965–75	29	20
1976	5	(6)

Source: U.S. Department of Commerce, *Survey of Current Business*.

Another important dimension has been the industry's contribution to the nation's balance of trade (see Table 3). The chemical industry, which represents less than 10 percent of total U.S. industry, contributed 60 percent of our positive balance of trade from 1955–75 and has contributed relatively greater proportions in recent years.

Despite these positive factors, there have been disturbing trends in the industry. For example, its financial position has deteriorated (see Table 4).

Profitability since 1955 has been relatively even at about an average 8 percent net return on total assets, but internal cash generation has not been adequate.

Table 4

	1955	1976 (estimated)
Total equity	$12 billion	$51 billion
Total debt	$ 3 billion	$22 billion
Debt as a percentage of equity	25%	43%
Earnings coverage of interest expense	30 times	8 times

Source: Federal Trade Commission quarterly financial report.

There have also been some negative trends in our international position. Our industry's share of the worldwide market for chemicals has declined; our share of total technical effort is less today; and our plants tend to be older.

The recent sharp increase in energy costs has had a major impact on the chemical industry. The implications of this increase for the future are not entirely clear, and will require several years to sort out, but energy costs pose a major challenge.

Finally, there is the chemical industry's deep involvement in environmental considerations, which will require an increasing share of future resources.

THE CURRENT STATUS AND FUTURE OUTLOOK OF THE INDUSTRY

After the unprecedented dislocations in the energy area in 1973, followed by the 1974 recession, the industry currently has a financial breathing spell as it operates at levels well below capacity. But recent and current trends in the areas of research and development and capital investment give cause for concern about the future.

Innovative technology has been the driving force behind the superior growth rate and the deflationary price performance of the chemical industry. The source of this innovation has been a high level of investment in research and development, but the recent trend has been downward. Research and development by the chemical industry declined from 3.7 percent of sales in 1966 to 2.9 percent in 1976, and as capital constraints have emerged, the thrust of the research effort has favored the improvement of existing product lines as opposed to the development of totally new products. The motivation to assume the risks of new product development is being weakened by concerns over the availability of adequate investment capital in a very capital-intensive industry. It is pointless to accept the expense of new product research if adequate production facilities cannot be funded.

Recently, other developments have had major impact on the outlook for the industry:

1. *Energy and other raw materials have become much more expensive.* The chemical industry, and to a lesser extent industry in general, has owed much of its rapid progress to cheap energy and natural resources. This has changed, and the higher costs are reflected in price increases for chemical products. Looking forward, although the general inflation rate is expected to increase about 6 percent per year through 1986, the prices of oil, natural gas and energy are expected to increase at least 9 percent per year. The chemical industry is especially affected, in that a majority of its energy and feedstock is based on oil and natural gas. Historically, cheap feedstocks—made possible by government regulation and abundant supply—have given the industry some competitive advantage vis-à-vis foreign competition, but deregulation is expected to eliminate this advantage in the next few years.

2. *Environmental considerations and related government regulations are escalating.* The chemical industry has responded to the need for a cleaner environment by investing $2.4 billion—10 percent of total capital expenditures—in pollution abatement facilities during the last four years. Significant costs will be incurred to operate these facilities, to put products through stringent toxicity-testing procedures, and to meet occupational safety and health regulations. In some cases, major additional investments will be necessary to replace some chemical product lines with safer products that will perform the same functions. Over the next decade the chemical industry faces costs in the range of $20 billion–$30 billion to meet projected pollution abatement regulations—hopefully, it will be possible to attain some reasonable balance between environmental and economic considerations, so that limited resources will not be wasted in attempts to attain arbitrary or unreasonable objectives. In any event, the projected capital requirements are staggering.

3. *Growth is slowing.* Slower growth in the general economy, the higher cost of energy, environmental considerations, and the maturing of certain segments of the industry (such as man-made fibers and synthetic rubber) are expected to hold annual growth to 5 percent in the next decade, compared to the historic rate of 8 percent.

The upshot is that the chemical industry is entering a new era. Simultaneously, emerging human needs will require contributions from a strong and competent chemical industry—in such areas as food production, the effective use of natural resources, health care, the balance of trade, and employment. The question arises whether the industry will have the capital to meet these growing needs.

CAPITAL FORMATION

The ability of the industry to generate sufficient capital is subject to conflicting pressures. As indicated earlier, the industry's financial position steadily weakened in the 1950s and 1960s during a period of rapid growth and limited inflation. The current outlook is for somewhat slower growth and stronger inflationary pressures, with the added dimension of major capital outlays to meet environmental objectives. Table 5 compares our estimates of capital needs in the years 1976–85 with the actual results in the prior decade. For this purpose a range has been defined between two limits—a 6 percent inflation rate with a sustained 7 percent net profit margin, and a 10 percent inflation rate with a 5 percent net profit margin.

Table 5. Capital requirements of the chemical industry ($ billions)

	1966–1975	1976–1985 6 percent inflation	10 percent inflation
Average annual real growth	7%	5%	5%
Net profit margin	7%	7%	5%
Capital generation	$50	$125	$125
Capital needs			
Construction:			
Productive facilities	$52	$100	$120
Environmental	4	25	30
Total	$56	$125	$150
Working capital	9	30	50
Total	$65	$155	$200
Capital shortfall	($15)	($30)	($75)

Sources: Federal Reserve Board Index of Quarterly Output; Federal Trade Commission Quarterly Financial Report; and Du Pont Company estimates.

These projections illustrate the continuing pressures on adequate capital formation. At December 31, 1976, we estimate that the industry had an equity base of $51 billion and a debt-to-equity ratio of 43 percent. If inflation holds to around 6 percent and profit margins are sustained at 7 percent, there is a possibility that adequate capital would be available during the 1976–85 period. But the price of this financial balance is a 40 percent decrease in annual growth rate, curtailed product development and innovation, and a sharp reduction in new employment opportunities both in the chemical industry and in its customer industries. The chemical industry's contribution to the U.S. balance of payments, which is especially critical in light of our dependence on foreign sources of energy, will decline. Other countries with superior capital formation rates will fill the vacuum in production and in new product development.

Beyond this, if inflation is aggravated by the present emphasis on current consumption versus future investment, and accelerates to 10 percent or more, the industry will be unable to finance even a 5 percent growth rate and further curtailments will be required. The threat of such inflation, posed by recent fiscal policies, has a strong inhibiting effect on the industry.

CONCLUSIONS AND RECOMMENDATIONS

The chemical industry has struggled to maintain its financial viability over the past decade, but increasing capital needs and strong inflationary pressures limit our confidence in the future. The outlook for capital investment, employment, and research and development is increasingly negative. We sense a strong need to:

1. Increase the rate of capital formation in the United States even at the expense of current living standards. The future standard of living can be no greater than the nation's productive industrial base. At current and prospective levels of inflation, profits are overstated and income taxes assess not only real income but underlying capital. Under these circumstances, special effort is required to offset the cumulative process of capital erosion. Adequate depreciation for tax purposes, including the recognition of replacement costs, an emphasis on investment tax credits, and the elimination of double taxation (as reflected in taxes on dividends), would contribute significantly to this objective.

2. Develop a government policy that encourages basic research and development to offset the current trend toward limited, short-term objectives.

3. Ensure that governmental regulations and controls are based on realistic assessments of costs and benefits—for example, action to improve the environment must take into account the capital cost and energy requirements, as well as potential effects on domestic employment and the ability of U.S. manufacturers to compete in world markets.

Considering the scope of the problems and the stakes, it is clear that an effective and continuous industry/government dialogue is essential in sorting out the problems and effecting their solution.

Chapter 15

THE ALUMINUM INDUSTRY'S
GROWING CAPITAL REQUIREMENTS

W. H. Krome George*

Aluminum is the most abundant metallic element in the earth's crust. Measured in either quantity or value, the use of aluminum exceeds that of any other metal except iron. This highly versatile light metal is used to some extent in nearly all segments of the world economy, and its continued availability is critical to many broad aspects of our national life.

The aluminum industry has displayed remarkable growth over the past decades, as users converted to aluminum from other metals and materials. Continued growth is forecast in the major markets which use aluminum's basic properties in the energy-constrained society of the future.

Research and development are being specifically aimed at markets which use aluminum's energy conservation qualities to advantage. Some of the current applications are:

- *Housing.* Aluminum is in growing demand for roofing, siding, window frames, and insulation to aid in the reduction of heating and cooling requirements.
- *Durables.* Growing tonnages of aluminum are required to reduce energy consumption by improving the efficiency and service life of consumer durable goods and machinery and equipment.
- *Electrical.* Virtually all of the nation's overhead power requirements are carried by aluminum conductor systems, and increasing amounts are going into the underground systems. These applica-

---

* Chairman and Chief Executive Officer, Aluminum Company of America.

tions are expected to grow as the nation turns to electrical energy for the conservation of dwindling petroleum resources.

- *Transportation*. Designers, manufacturers, and operators of automobiles, commercial vehicles, and mass transit systems are specifying more aluminum parts to reduce weight, thereby improving fuel consumption and payloads. The 1977 car models averaged 100 pounds of aluminum, and consumption is expected to more than double by 1980.
- *Packaging*. Although not often viewed as an energy conservation product, the all-aluminum beverage can makes an important contribution to energy conservation, since the cans are recyclable. Currently, the industry recycles more than one out of every four cans manufactured. Recycling saves 95 percent of the energy required to produce new metal from ore and conserves raw materials as well.
- *Energy*. Aluminum is being used to broaden our nation's ability to increase the power supply in the processing and containing of liquefied natural gas and in the generation of power from the sun and the wind.

In addition, through an industry-wide program the per pound energy requirements have been reduced by 6.5 percent in the past four years. The goal is a reduction of 10 percent by 1980.

SUPPLY AND DEMAND

The U.S. supply of aluminum consists of domestic primary production, primary imports, metal recovered from domestic and imported scrap, and imports of mill products.

During the period from 1958 through 1975, domestic primary production increased annually at the rate of 5.5 percent and the number of primary producers doubled. Secondary recovery rose 7.3 percent per year.

The remarkable long-term growth of the aluminum industry is due to competition (both within the industry and with substitutable materials), innovative marketing, strong research and development, high productivity, and relative low price. Chart 1 illustrates that prices of aluminum products, although rising sharply after 1973, did not keep pace with the U.S. general price indexes. Few industries in the United States have had a better performance record over the past two decades.

While the U.S. industry has displayed remarkable growth, productive capacity has grown even faster in the rest of the world. As shown

Chart 1. Index of aluminum prices versus general price indexes (1958 = 100)

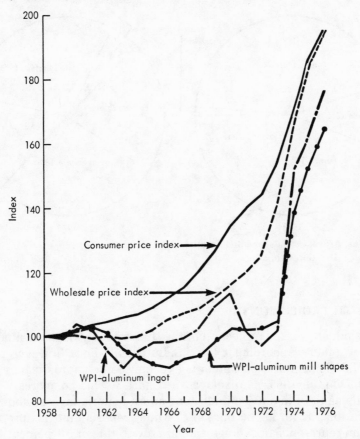

Source: U.S. Bureau of Labor Statistics.

in Chart 2, new-capacity locations have been shifting from the United States and Canada to Europe and the less-developed countries. The Soviet sphere has remained relatively constant over the entire period.

This shift has been due both to the social pressure to locate in less-developed countries and to the tendency to situate new aluminum capacity near relatively cheap and reliable power, whether due to natural abundance or to government-subsidized programs.

The United States has traditionally been the leading world consumer of aluminum, although its share of world demand has decreased from 42 percent in 1958 to 30 percent in 1975.[1]

Chart 2. Primary aluminum capacity, 1958 and 1975, by selected areas

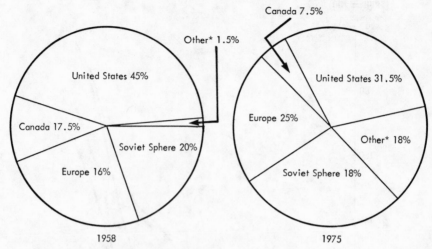

1958   1975

* Asia, Africa, Oceania, and South America.
Source: U.S. Bureau of Mines.

GROWTH PROJECTIONS

An industry-based projection of the future supply-demand situation
is not available. According to the U.S. Bureau of Mines, however, probable U.S. demand for aluminum is expected to be approximately 11.8
million tons in 1985, as displayed in Chart 3. This compares with a
1975 demand of about 5 million tons and a historic high of about 6.5
million tons in 1973. The Bureau of Mines reports that this probable
demand represents an average annual growth rate of 5.1 percent from
the 1973 high. From 1958 through 1976, demand grew at better than
7.2 percent annually.

Future growth in demand in the rest of the world is expected to be
above the U.S. average, or at an annual rate of just under 6 percent.[2]

The ability of the aluminum industry to meet this projected demand
—to build the new capacity necessary for an avoidance of shortages
and for the provision of additional jobs—is directly related to the industry's ability to secure a return on investment that will permit major
investments for both modernization and the addition of capacity. Such
efforts to improve the return on invested capital are being thwarted
by a number of forces. Some of these forces are unique to the aluminum industry, and some are common to all capital-intensive industrial enterprises operating in today's inflationary and turbulent world
economy.

Chart 3.   U.S. primary aluminum demand

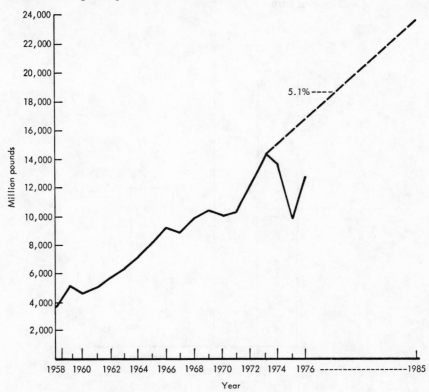

Sources: Aluminum Association; U.S. Bureau of Mines.

It takes three to four years to bring new capacity onstream. Because only a small amount of capacity is currently scheduled, even the most conservative forecasts of aluminum demand indicate that through 1980 imports must increase dramatically. The void filled by imports will result in an adverse effect on the U.S. balance of payments and in potential new domestic employment. On the other hand, should the needed imports not be available, a shortage of this most vital metal could result.

PROFIT PERFORMANCE

Although major investments must be made in order to assure adequate supply, the historical record of the aluminum industry's rate of return on equity capital presages difficulties in financing. As shown in Chart 4, the industry's rate of return for the period 1970 through 1976

Chart 4. Rate of return on equity capital, average 1970–1976

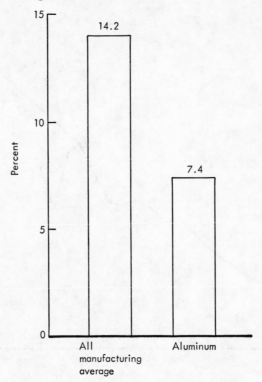

Sources: S&P average earnings on common equity and annual reports.

(represented by the performance of the three largest aluminum producers, since composite financial data for the aluminum industry are not available) was approximately half that of all manufacturing. Whether measured as return on equity capital or on total invested capital, which includes debt, the results give virtually the same picture.

Investment (herein defined as total assets) per dollar of sales is a commonly used measure of capital intensity. In 1976, aluminum's investment per dollar of sales was dramatically higher than that of the average of all manufacturing as shown in Chart 5.

The low return percentages are more critical when viewed in terms of replacement costs as opposed to the conventional historical-cost basis. Alcoa prepared replacement cost data for its *1976 Annual Report* to comply with the new requirements of the Securities and Exchange Commission. The 1976 depreciation calculation on a replacement cost basis was 75 percent higher than the amount reported. The

Chart 5.   Investment per dollar of sales, 1976

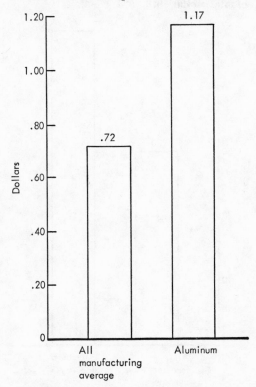

Sources: Federal Trade Commission and annual reports.

price of replacing existing unmined minerals, structures, and equipment would be more than double the historical cost. It should be noted
that these calculations may not be strictly applicable to other aluminum producers, but they are noted to show the wide differences.

These replacement cost figures underscore the contention that the
rates of return are not high enough when measured against future capital requirements and that there is a critical need for tax reform, cost
reduction, and increased revenues.

Despite the low levels of return on capital, the aluminum industry
has in the past managed to install sufficient facilities to maintain productivity and to expand capacity to meet demand. This was accomplished to a large extent through the use of borrowed funds. Chart 6
shows the extent to which the aluminum industry, as compared with
all manufacturing, has relied on such borrowings from 1970 through
1976. Borrowings are defined here as long-term debt; total capital, as
the sum of shareholders' equity and long-term debt.

Chart 6.   Average borrowings as a percentage of total capital, 1970–1976

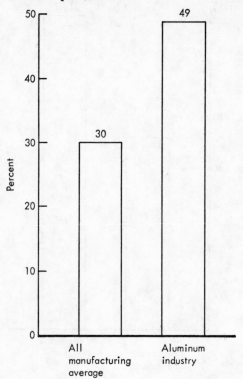

Sources: Federal Trade Commission and annual reports.

CAPITAL REQUIREMENTS

In a report issued in 1976, the 25-member-nation Organization for Economic Cooperation and Development stated that aluminum's "biggest problem, in terms of insufficient resources, is not so much energy or raw materials, but rather capital accumulation."[3]

Historically, costs to construct new primary aluminum capacity have placed aluminum among the most capital-intensive of basic industries. Alcoa currently estimates the cost to install a ton of primary aluminum capacity—including mining, refining, and smelting, but excluding power-generating facilities—to be well over $2,000, compared to about $1,400 three years ago. This appears to be a conservative estimate, since other producers and researchers have publicly cited much higher numbers.

Based on Alcoa's estimate, a typical new primary plant with an annual capacity of 200,000 tons (which would add only about 4 percent additional production in the United States) would require a minimum investment of $400 million. This amount does not include substantial investment in power generation facilities and in facilities required to process aluminum into mill products.

In the past few years, capital expenditures of aluminum producers have been sharply increased by additional government-mandated expenditures. These expenditures have been made necessary by the programs set up to improve environment, health, and safety. Although no one questions their intended benefits, such programs are expensive and cut heavily into the amount of capital available for job-creating outlays. Furthermore, these programs do nothing to improve productivity or to increase production. Alcoa alone has spent almost $170 million over the past five years on environmental programs.

Alcoa's total capital expenditures, depreciation and depletion, and retained earnings for the years 1972 through 1976 are shown in Chart 7. It is evident that capital expenditures during the past five years far

Chart 7.   Alcoa's capital expenditures, depreciation, and retained earnings, 1972–1976

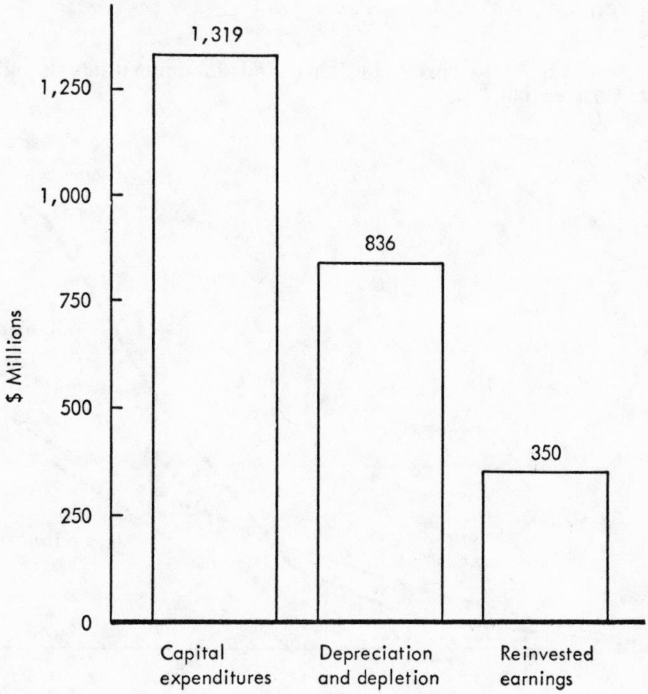

Source: Alcoa.

exceeded depreciation expenses. In fact, the sum of both allowable depreciation and retained earnings during this period was less than 90 percent of capital expenditures, thereby necessitating external financing. Furthermore, a substantial portion of Alcoa's total capital outlays during the past five years was expended for environmental and sustaining (largely replacement) programs. Those outlays diverted the limited capital resources that might otherwise have been available for new-capacity additions and cost reduction projects.

OPERATING COSTS

Along with the increased costs of building new plant and equipment, the aluminum industry has experienced rapidly escalating operating costs. Cost elements for the industry are not published, but the representative Alcoa experience is shown in Chart 8, which graphs the changes in the company's costs in three major categories: energy; purchased materials; and salaries, wages, and benefits. These costs amount to almost 75 percent of Alcoa's total revenues. Each of these cost elements has escalated faster than the prices of the company's fabricated products, which are the source of over 70 percent of its total revenues.

Chart 8. Index of Alcoa's prices for fabricated aluminum products and major cost elements (1970 = 100)

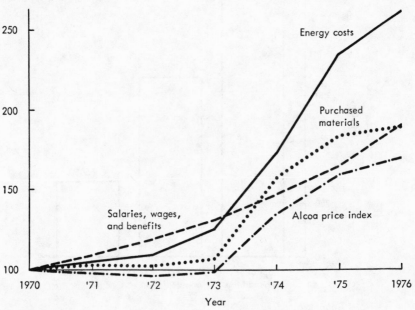

Source: Alcoa.

Operating costs and paperwork costs have also been influenced by consumer safety legislation and worker health and safety legislation. Such mandated increases in the employment of resources often go beyond the point where the costs of these factors are equal to their benefits.

As pointed out by a Brookings Institution paper,[4] the aluminum industry experienced its largest increase in operating costs as a result of actions by two cartels, the Organization of Petroleum Exporting Countries and the International Bauxite Association. The Brookings author noted that price increases from 1971 to 1975 did not keep pace with operating costs, although he noted that they may have caught up in 1976. Chart 8 illustrates that at least for Alcoa, there was no catch-up in 1976.

ENERGY

Although U.S. industry in general has experienced major problems due to the world energy crisis, there are energy problems unique to the aluminum industry which place extraordinary demands on its capital requirements.

In the Pacific Northwest, fully one third of the industry's domestic smelting capacity faces the possibility of losing much of its present supply of electricity. The Bonneville Power Administration has notified the aluminum producers that it will be unable to supply power to the region's smelters as present contracts expire over the next decade. Although the industry is working to solve this problem, without fair and favorable power rates as well as an assured supply of energy in the Northwest, the producers in that region will not be able to compete. Existing facilities will have to be closed as they grow older and less productive. In any case, energy cost increases of major proportion are expected.

Another regional problem has been created by the impact of rising natural gas costs in the Southwest. There is currently idle smelting capacity because the cost of natural gas precludes the production of metal at current prices. Producers may be forced to turn to other forms of energy, adding another major cost.

Yet another threat is the possibility of rate restructuring of electric power, which has historically been priced in relationship to the delivered cost to customers. A change in the rate system could result in the inability of industries that rely on electric energy to compete with foreign producers. Interestingly, the aluminum industry, being a steady, large-scale energy user, has been considered a necessary adjunct to the development of many major electric power facilities throughout the world.

Because aluminum producers are particularly vulnerable to the loss of electric power, the assurance of uninterruptible power is important. To firm up available constant and economical power, aluminum companies have been making substantial investments in alternative sources of supply, such as coal reserves, and in joint power-generating projects. These investments divert current capital funds from the expansion of new primary aluminum smelting facilities.

Such energy-related problems could result in the construction of virtually all future aluminum capacity outside the United States.

RECOMMENDATIONS

Despite higher earnings and the somewhat improved financial position of the U.S. aluminum industry in 1976, the industry is confronted by significant deeply rooted problems which must be resolved to assure aluminum's maximum contribution to society. The industry must improve its economic base to a level that will attract the extensive capital necessary for the replacement of obsolete facilities and the construction of new capacity to meet future demands. Only in an economic environment favorable to private investment and competitive marketing can the aluminum industry or, in fact, any industry thrive.

A number of things can be done to aid capital formation and job creation and to provide the stable supplemental environment conducive to a healthy economy.

1. *A return to wage and price controls should be avoided.* Recent experience continues to demonstrate that such controls discourage industrial expansion and modernization. Controls have also created shortages of critical materials and serious distortions in the production process, and over the long term they contribute to inflation.

2. *Greater control should be exercised over federal spending.* Federal budget deficits result in "crowding out" the private productive sector of the U.S. economy and thereby reduce the savings available to support investment for jobs by the private sector. In addition, the resulting heavy tax load on U.S. aluminum producers impairs their competitive posture in world markets.

3. *Compliance schedules on environmental standards should be extended.* Unnecessarily stringent standards as to quality requirements and the time allowed to meet them should be eased. Provision should be made for the immediate write-off of expenditures made for pollution control purposes, since such outlays do not result in additional production or revenues.

4. *The present system of capital recovery should be restructured and extended.* Depreciation rates allowed for federal income tax pur-

poses are clearly not keeping up with inflated replacement costs. This is especially burdensome to highly capital-intensive industries, such as the aluminum industry, since the price inflation of heavy capital goods has accelerated to a much greater degree than the overall price level. The tax laws of most other industrialized nations ensure much faster capital recovery than do those of the United States. This is clearly reflected in the poor comparative productivity growth rates of the United States over the past 15 years.

5. *The investment tax credit should be increased and made a permanent part of the tax structure.* The Tax Reduction Act of 1976 extended the investment tax credit to 10 percent through 1980. A further increase to 12 percent for business can be supported on the grounds cited above, and this change should be made a permanent part of the tax structure.

6. *The double taxation of corporate dividends should be eliminated.* The corporation pays taxes on its pretax profits, and the owners of the corporation's stock are taxed on the dividends they receive on the corporation's aftertax profits. At present, shareholders only receive a $100 dividend exclusion. In view of the pressing need for U.S. business to generate additional capital through equity financing and retained earnings, the elimination of the double taxation inequity is required.

7. *The corporate income tax rate should be reduced from its current 48 percent level.* A steady and progressive reduction in the rate over a period of time would energize investment and have a significant impact on job creation. The depression-instituted increase of the federal corporate income tax rate from 38 percent to 48 percent should finally be recognized as the serious economic error it has proved to be.

8. *Additionally, a number of changes in the existing tax structure are being proposed that should not be effected.* Among these are:

■ The tax credit allowable to U.S. companies for foreign taxes paid on income from foreign sources should not be repealed or reduced.
■ The percentage depletion on foreign mineral income should not be eliminated.
■ The payment of U.S. income tax by U.S. shareholders on foreign subsidy income before such income is repatriated as dividends should not be required.

Such changes in the existing tax laws would impede U.S. job formation; they would damage the competitive position of U.S. companies in world markets, reduce exports, and destroy export-related jobs. In the case of the aluminum industry, these changes would also result in making less cash available for investment in facilities and related jobs—both of which are vital to meet the nation's demand for aluminum in the future. In short, the proposed changes would vitiate this nation's ability to meet its twin third-century challenges of capital and job formation.

NOTES

1. *Metal Statistics, 1957–1966* and *Metal Statistics, 1965–1975* (Metallgesellschaft Aktiengesellschaft, 1967 and 1976).
2. John W. Stamper and Horace F. Kurtz, "Aluminum," in *Mineral Facts and Problems,* 1975 ed. (Bureau of Mines, 1976).
3. Organization for Economic Cooperation and Development, *Industrial Adaptation in the Primary Aluminum Industry,* 1976.
4. Barry Bosworth, "Capacity Creation in Basic-Materials Industries," *Brookings Papers on Economic Activity 2* (Brookings Institution, 1976).

Chapter 16

THE AIRLINES' SOARING NEED FOR INVESTMENT CAPITAL

*Edward E. Carlson**

AIRLINE CAPITAL REQUIREMENTS

The airline industry of the United States is facing potential capital needs over the next 15 years which dwarf its existing investment base and raise critical questions concerning the future of the industry. Capital investment estimates for 1976–85 range from $21 billion to $47 billion, in current dollars, while forecasts for the entire 1976–90 period call for expenditures exceeding $65 billion. Simply stated, the industry will be moving from total capital expenditures of $9 billion in the 1960s to $15 billion in the 1970s and $60 billion in the 1980s.

These estimated expenditure requirements are the product of a number of assumptions relative to traffic growth, load factors, inflation, and other elements. Much of the needed funds will come from internal sources. Depreciation, retained earnings, and the sale of obsolete aircraft could account for as much as 70 percent of the total. The rest must come from outside sources—as much as $18 billion for the 1980s. These vast needs occur in an environment of great uncertainty for the airlines, caused by a history of inadequate return on past investment, an inflationary economy, a political environment hostile to business, and possible changes in regulatory process. The airline industry must obtain the capital to meet these needs if the United States is to maintain the finest air transport system in the world. The problem is twofold—first, to replace aging aircraft with new, more productive, and fuel-efficient planes, and second, to provide for added capacity to meet the ever-growing transportation needs of our nation's economy.

* Chairman of the Board, UAL, Inc.

Chart 1.   Comparative capital investment by decade: U.S. scheduled airlines

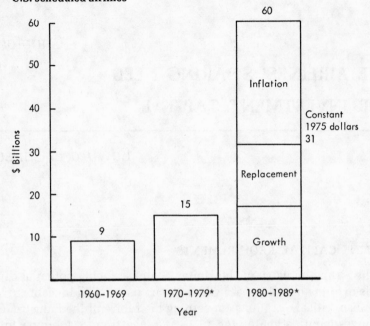

* Estimated.

Source: Air Transport Association of America, *The Sixty Billion Dollar Question*, 1976.

mestic manufacturers may find it necessary to enter into joint programs with plane builders overseas. This would reduce employment
in our domestic aerospace industry and have an appreciable impact on
the nation's balance of trade. Aerospace products are one of the largest exports of the United States, amounting to $6.2 billions in 1976.[1]

PAST SOURCES OF FUNDS

Private financing has provided the funds which have enabled the
airline industry to grow from infant to giant. Lenders to the industry,
principally banks and insurance companies, along with equity investors, have made our present airline system possible. In the early days,
when equipment lives were shorter, short-term bank borrowings
played a major role. As service lives lengthened and dollar outlays
grew, banks were largely excluded from long term financing. Hence,
institutional lenders, principally insurance companies, made substantial long-term loans. The sale of equity and convertible securities in
the public market was used to balance debt-equity ratios.

Through the 1950s and on into the 1960s these sources of funds
were adequate for the fast-growing needs of the carriers. Strong traffic
growth and the great efficiencies brought by the jet airplane resulted
in a period of profits and the anticipation of still greater profits. Equity
showed strong market appreciation, reflecting the expectation of continued growth and productivity gains. However, at the end of the
1960s, with the decline in airline earnings which followed lower year-
to-year traffic gains and inflating costs, the picture changed abruptly.
The declining market prices of airline stocks made sale of equity unattractive, and subordinated convertible offerings declined. However,
aircraft leasing helped fill the gap as carriers sought to preserve their
investment tax credits by leases where tax advantages to the lessor
were passed back to the carrier in the form of lower lease rentals.

With the decline in industry earnings, the major insurance companies, which had supplied the major part of carrier long-term debt, with
over $2.5 billion in loans and leases outstanding at year-end 1976, have
shown great reluctance to expand their airline investment.[2] If the airlines are to raise the capital needed for the 1980s, the insurance companies must again come into the marketplace, along with the other
long-term lenders. For shorter-term financing, bank loans must also
play a part. However, for all this to come to pass, airline industry
financial leverage, expressed as a ratio of total debt (including capitalized aircraft leases) to net worth, must be improved from the 1.75 to
1 leverage ratio which existed at the end of 1976 to more prudent levels. Only 5 of the existing 11 carriers (trunks plus Pan American) have

ratios below 1.75 to 1, and only four have ratios of under 1.5 to 1.[3] Unless these debt ratios can be reduced, the financing task appears awesome. An obvious need for a majority of the carriers is an infusion of new equity capital. Since book value per share is higher than the market price for most carriers, the direct sale of equity is unlikely without major improvement in the level and stability of airline earnings.

FORECASTING FUTURE CAPITAL NEEDS

Any estimate of future airline capital investment requires forecasts of traffic growth, the expected service lives of aircraft now in use, possible changes in flight service patterns, environmental requirements and their costs, and, of great importance, and the effect of inflation on the capital cost of new aircraft.

The cost of meeting federally mandated noise standards for aircraft fleets would impose an added financial burden. It is estimated that the replacement of capacity which does not meet present noise requirements under Federal Air Regulations Part 36 would take over 200 aircraft and cost nearly $6.3 billion in 1984 dollars.[4] Although it is possible that the phaseout of aircraft to be replaced may be delayed or the rules modified to blunt their full cost impact, this potential cost does overhang the industry. It would appear that the noise standards for three-engine aircraft are unrealistic in view of the almost imperceptible noise reduction gained by a high-cost and fuel-inefficient retrofit program.

PHASES OF CAPITAL NEED

A number of recent studies have addressed the size of the airline fleet and capital investment need by 1985 and beyond to 1990. Those studies are summarized in Table 1. Over the next 15 years the airlines will experience several phases of equipment acquisition and capital requirement. There are two distinct phases of capital need—one from 1976–80 and a longer outlook to 1990, the former representing the near-term need, and the latter a realistic period for longer-term financing programs. Although a substantial part of the total need may be met on an interim basis by short-term financing, a realistic program should anticipate the entire decade of the 1980s. This is a decade in which new-type aircraft are expected to be introduced into airline fleets in quantity. From the present to 1980, replacement and expansion needs will be relatively modest, as load factors will rise and the seating density and utilization of aircraft will increase. This will largely accom-

Table 1. Summary of selected studies of airline capital requirements

Study	Airlines	Traffic growth (percent)	Aircraft service life (years)	Capital requirements ($ billions)	
				1976–1985	1976–1989
Donaldson, Lufkin, & Jenrette	Trunks and Pan Am	6	20	21	—
United Airlines	Trunks and Pan Am	5	20	21	60–65
DOT–NTCC	U.S. airlines	7		30	85
Boeing	Trunks and Pan Am	6	16	47	—
CAB	Trunks and local	5.6	Present depreciable basis + 3	32.5	—
ATA	U.S. airlines	5	18	26	65

Sources: Air Transport Association of America, The Sixty Billion Dollar Question, 1976; U.S. Department of Transportation, Trends and Choices, 1977.

modate anticipated growth. Some older aircraft will also be replaced with newer aircraft having greater capacity. However, until the decade of the 1980s, new cash requirements will be moderate and, given reasonable earnings, airline liquidity should improve and balance sheets strengthen.

By the 1980s, however, the full effect of a major aircraft reequipment cycle will be felt and it will be impossible to accommodate growth by greater seating density, expanded utilization, or higher load factors. By that time, those resources will have been used up. The full impact of the reequipment cycle, augmented by the need to accommodate traffic growth, will bring on a massive increase in capital requirements and a sharp decline in liquidity, making large external financing programs a necessity.

THE INTRODUCTION OF NEW TECHNOLOGY

Equally important to future capital needs is the anticipated introduction of new aircraft types, the 7X7s and the DC–Xs, which are expected to go into service in the 1980s—given sufficient go-ahead orders by the air carriers to justify the very large development costs which will be required to bring these new planes into being. Estimates of such development costs range from $1 billion to $1.5 billion—sums which could give pause to prudent aerospace managements unless substantial firm orders are on the books.

All of the forecasts shown in Table 1 are based on an unconstrained environment, on the assumption that adequate airport and airspace facilities will be available to permit the economic operation of future fleets. And perhaps even more important, none of the estimates reflect possible restrictions in fuel supply. Most of the published estimates of capital need include the ten trunk carriers plus Pan American. Others include local service, all-cargo, and unscheduled carriers. The inclusion of these latter groups has less influence on anticipated total spending requirements than do the assumptions on anticipated service lives and inflation. However, even small variances in assumed traffic growth rates do have a significant effect on investment requirements.

The flight equipment replacement and growth requirements through 1982 assume the purchase of aircraft now in production through 1982. Beginning about that time, deliveries of new-type, advanced technology aircraft could commence. These new planes would meet the need for an aircraft with from 180 to 200 seats, and conceptual designs include both medium- and long-range types. However, at this time it is not clear that productivity gained through new technology will be sufficient to offset the higher investment required for these more advanced designs. Even as aircraft now in production are becoming more expensive year by year, inflation is expected to result in still higher costs per seat for the advanced technology aircraft of the 1980s. It is this equation of higher capital cost versus greater productivity which must be solved if the new technology is to have a payoff. If productivity gains cannot justify the higher purchase prices, the industry must choose to meet its needs with existing-type aircraft and be content with such productivity gains as derivative designs can develop—an obvious step toward less economic and environmental efficiency.

WHY NEW TECHNOLOGY?

Why is it necessary to make these large capital investments in new aircraft, particularly by an industry which will be hard pressed to obtain the new funds required to finance a program of the magnitude indicated? First, a substantial number of aircraft now in service are already economically obsolete because of high per seat operating costs, a condition created in part by fuel prices which have tripled since 1972 and are headed even higher. Either the air carriers or the consumer must bear a growing economic penalty until these aircraft can be replaced. Second, as traffic grows, even at the moderate rates anticipated by most forecasters, smaller planes in the 100-plus passenger class in present fleets will become too small to serve their markets without adding unneeded schedule frequencies. The substitution of larger aircraft in the 180–200 passenger class for these older, less efficient 100-passenger aircraft, would produce substantial operating economies.

The increase in fuel cost is important, but the need for fuel conservation is an added imperative. Greater seating density and operating techniques which maximize fuel efficiency are already playing a large role in conserving our vital fuel resources. To gain maximum savings, however, new fuel-conserving technology must be developed and placed in service in the national interest.

Even now the air carriers are moving to anticipate fleet replacement and growth needs. Orders are being placed for existing aircraft types at a rate not anticipated a year ago. Seating density is increasing as first-class compartments shrink and total seats per plane increase. Wide-body 747s and DC–10s are being converted to seat nine and ten across rather than the present eight and nine across. Aircraft are flying more hours per day—up from the utilization cutbacks created by the fuel allocations of a few years ago. Carriers are already operating at higher load factors and anticipate further increases in the utilization of existing capacity.

224

PRICE INFLATION AND SERVICE LIVES

In determining the size and timing of the investment required, two critical assumptions are a forecast of aircraft price and a forecast of the expected service lives of aircraft now operating in airline fleets.

In forecasting aircraft price, investment per seat is the best measure of aircraft costs over the 1977–90 period. Per seat cost tends to be relatively independent of aircraft size—given standard assumptions on seating density. By using per seat price we avoid the need to forecast future requirements by fleet type. Moreover, the required industry investment tends to be the same whether airlines move to larger aircraft and less frequent flights or smaller aircraft and increased frequency. During 1975, a new aircraft cost about $90,000 per seat. To that $90,000 we have applied an escalation factor of 6 percent per year. This assumes that aircraft prices will rise in response to the inflationary pressures in our economy to a per seat cost of over $200,000 by 1990. An investment requirement for spare parts and ground equipment and facilities, similarly inflated over time, is also included.

The next key assumption in determining airline capital needs is a forecast of expected aircraft service lives. Maintenance costs and fuel consumption rates tend to increase as aircraft grow older. Other predictable factors are structural life and potential competitive displacement by new aircraft with greater passenger appeal. Environmental considerations will be a serious constraint on the operation of certain aircraft in the 1980s. Analysis of technical data from past and present fleets, combined with judgment of future less tangible considerations indicates a 20-year life as the basis for aircraft replacement and resulting capital expenditure needs. This is not to say that present-day airliners will not be airworthy after they reach their 20th year of service—they will—but that the economic and environmental factors will dictate their retirement.

On the basis of a 20-year aircraft service life, the trunk airlines of the United States face an aircraft replacement program of $16 billion in 1976 dollars. Adjustment for continuing inflation increases this replacement cost to $30 billion. This amount of capital will be needed merely to replace present-day aircraft on a seat-for-seat basis.

MEETING TRAFFIC GROWTH

Even this $30 billion total contains no allowance for capacity to meet anticipated growth in demand. At a conservative 5 percent annual growth rate, scheduled traffic will double from 1976 to 1990, to a total of 313 billion revenue passenger-miles. At a forecast load fac-

tor of 60 percent over 520 billion seat miles will be required if the
trunk airlines are to meet this conservative estimate of our country's
requirements. To provide for that expanded need an added $35 billion
in inflated dollars must be invested, bringing the total trunk industry
investment requirement for replacement and growth between now
and 1990 to $65 billion.

Great as this sum appears, it does not cover the entire industry—
the local service carriers, the supplementals, and the all-cargo carriers
will all add to the total, although some of these needs may be supplied
by used or converted aircraft. On the other hand, certain trunk carriers
have relatively modern fleets and face a more moderate need for aircraft replacement.

To put this $65 billion total in perspective, it should be compared
with total current trunk airline fixed assets of $15.5 billion plus leased
aircraft in service valued at about $2.2 billion. *Thus the funds required
over the next 15 years amount to over 3½ times the present investment
in fixed assets.*[5] Internal generation of funds, although substantial, will
fall well short of meeting these needs unless historical returns are sur-
passed in the future. Major reliance must be placed on obtaining new
funds from external sources, that is, investors in the marketplace.

OBSTACLES IN THE COMPETITION FOR CAPITAL

The ability of the airline industry to compete for capital in a highly
competitive market obviously depends on the financial position and
the profit performance of the carriers. Here the industry record is not
encouraging. With a few notable exceptions among individual carriers, airline industry earnings have fallen far short of the levels needed
to provide a reasonable return on invested capital and thus give much-
needed strengthening to industry balance sheets.

Airline profitability has been low—the lowest of any major industry, whether measured in terms of return on investment or of margin
on operating revenue. As shown in Chart 2, from 1967 through 1976,
a period which covers two of the industry's most profitable years, the
pretax profits of the 11 trunklines were only 1.5 cents per dollar of
revenue.

The highest return on investment was 11.7 percent. The average
was only 6.1 percent, and it has trended downward, as shown in Chart
3. At the same time, the carriers produced an average revenue growth
of 11 percent over the period. This is respectable growth, but growth
without adequate profit. Present regulatory rate-making practices,
which adjust an actual rate of return on invested capital of 4.4 percent
to a fictitious return of 11.8 percent, and thus deprive the industry of

Chart 2. Profit margin: Airlines versus U.S. manufacturing and railroads, 1965–1976

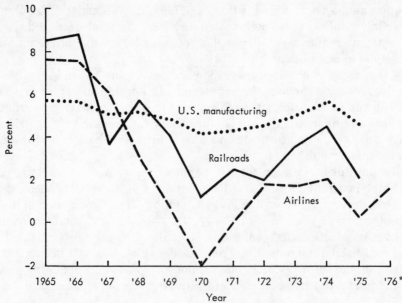

* Estimated.

Source: Air Transport Association of America, *Airline Financial Performance, 1976–1977*, 1977.

fare increases adequate to sustain reasonable earnings, contribute to the industry's dilemma.[6]

DEBT IN THE AIRLINE CAPITAL STRUCTURE

Predictably, this history of inadequate profits has made its mark on airline balance sheets. Many airlines are top-heavy with debt and lease obligations. The latest available data, for the 12 months ended December 31, 1976, show an industry capital structure of 61 percent debt, including subordinated debt and the capitalized value of aircraft leases.

Fortunately, some carriers face the 1980s with relative liquidity. However, others face heavy debt repayments and severe restrictions on new borrowing. Lack of adequate earnings has left the domestic trunk industry with two obstacles to financing fleet replacement with debt. One is the effect of debt ratings by Moody's and Standard and Poor's. While much airline debt is unrated by virtue of private placement, examination of the 23 trunkline issues currently rated by Moody's discloses the following: 5 issues rated Baa; 12 rated Ba; 5

Chart 3. Return on investment: Domestic trunks and Pan American*

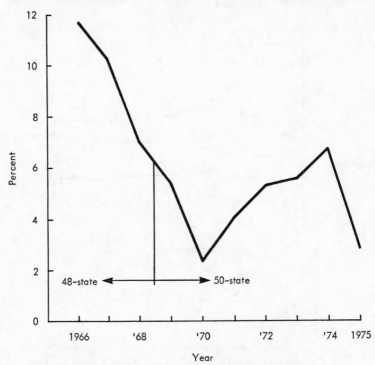

* CAB "unadjusted" return on investment for system operations.
Source: Bureau of Accounts and Statistics, *Airline Industry Economic Report.*

rated B; 1 rated Caa. Of the U.S. certified carriers, only Flying Tiger enjoys an A rating—on two equipment trust issues—whose rating is based on a secured obligation.

A second obstacle to debt financing is a New York State insurance regulation which requires that a corporation earn 1½ times fixed charges in one of the two most recent years and on the average for the past five years. Of the 32 scheduled and 8 supplemental U.S. certified carriers, only 8 qualify under the New York regulation, and none of the 5 largest carriers are included in those 8.

WHY NOT GOVERNMENT ASSISTANCE?

If the carriers are unable to finance the new fleets through the sources available to them in the past, what about some form of government support of guarantee? Isn't there ample precedent with Amtrak or Title XI of the Merchant Marine Act or the guarantees available to

228

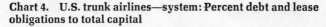

Chart 4.   U.S. trunk airlines—system: Percent debt and lease
obligations to total capital

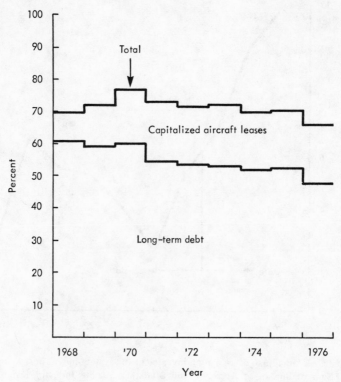

Source: McDonnell Douglas Finance Corporation, *Airline Industry Data.*

subsidized local carriers to mount a government-backed program to
solve the problem?

As a last resort it could come to this, since our nation must have an
airline system, but the price could be high in terms of bureaucratic control over the vital aircraft acquisition process—political decisions on
matters that are essentially technical and economic. In the end, carriers
could wind up being told what type of aircraft to buy, how many, and
from whom—in short, the airlines would be wards of the state. One has
only to look abroad for examples of what happens when political
factors dictate decisions which can best be made by those who have
the responsibility for safe and economic operation of aircraft fleets.
In our judgment government involvement in such decisions would be
only a preamble to eventual takeover and nationalization. The last
thing this country needs is an Amtrak in the sky!

REGULATORY REFORM

In 1977 the debate on regulatory reform of air transportation may be resolved by congressional action. It is well that it be resolved, for so long as uncertainty concerning the nature of future economic regulation hangs over the industry, the prospects of obtaining external funds will be clouded. Lenders have long relied upon the route franchise system established by Congress nearly 40 years ago as a basis for their impressive role in financing the meteoric growth of air transportation. The prospects for a sufficient period of adequate and stable carrier earnings depend heavily on the final shape of regulation which emerges from these years of debate. If Congress legislates greater freedom of pricing along with the ability to rationalize route structures, carrier results could respond favorably. Much depends on the rate at which added "competition," which is essentially "cream-skimming" on heavy-duty routes, is permitted to enter the marketplace. Much also depends on the ability of the existing carriers to adjust to the new rules.

CONCLUSION

In spite of the recent earnings record of the air carriers and the uncertainties which beset the industry in mid-1977, there is sufficient time between now and the end of the decade to strengthen the ability of the airlines to accomplish the external financing required for the 1980s. The key is a sustained period of reasonable earnings. Enlightened action by Congress and the regulators can and should be directed toward rebuilding lender confidence and stimulating investors to supply needed private capital in the very large amounts needed. Airline managements must take a major share of the responsibility and direct their energies toward a maximum effort to control costs, maintain responsible pricing, and improve productivity if they are to build the record of stable and adequate profits that they need in order to compete in the capital markets. Wage and fuel cost pressures continue, as do airport charges. Up to now, productivity gains have simply not been able to keep pace with higher wage costs, higher taxes, higher fuel costs, and so on. The 6.1 percent industry rate of return of the past decade must be improved to nearly twice that level for the 1976–90 period.

Unless the airline industry can achieve this result, it will experience a severe capital shortage and become a shrinking resource unable to serve the needs of our nation in its third century. This would serve to curtail job opportunities in the airline industry as well as the many industries furnishing it goods and services. An obvious first step to prevent this from happening is to institute the tax reforms required to stimulate greater capital formation.

NOTES

1. U.S. Department of Commerce, Bureau of the Census, *Highlights of U.S. Export and Import Trade,* December 1976.
2. Statement by William A. McCurdy, vice president, The Equitable Life Assurance Society of the United States, to the U.S. Senate Aviation Subcommittee Hearings, March 25, 1977.
3. Testimony of Frederick W. Bradley, Jr., vice president, Citibank, N.A., to the Senate Aviation Subcommittee, March 25, 1977.
4. Ibid.
5. McDonnell Douglas Finance Corporation, *Airline Industry Data,* September 30, 1976.
6. Civil Aeronautics Board, Order No. 77–1–93.

PART III _____

Working toward
a solution

Chapter 17

PUBLIC POLICY FOR A FREE ECONOMY

*Darryl R. Francis**

Although this discussion will be limited to economic freedom, the ideas expressed herin have a bearing on all freedoms—economic, social, and political. In my view the three are interdependent, and no one of them can exist without the others.

Let me begin by stating the basic premises upon which the discussion will rest. I view economic freedom as the freedom to determine and to seek to satisfy one's own wants as one sees them. I view economic freedom as a desirable end in itself, and I subscribe to the widely held doctrine that the promotion of economic freedom is consistent with the attainment of the maximum possible standard of living for society. According to this doctrine, *state regulation should be viewed with suspicion as a potential enemy of society's material well-being.* On the other hand, maximum freedom for individuals to act in their own self-interest should be viewed as a source of the variety and diversification of ideas, experiments, and innovations which lead to the discovery of new products and more efficient means of production. If one accepts these premises, then a free economy should be viewed not only as precious in itself, but also as the most promising means by which the standard of living of all members of society can be raised.

THE ROLE OF GOVERNMENT—IN THEORY

If we accept the foregoing propositions, as I am sure most of us do, what, then, is the role of public policy in assuring a free economy? I

---

* President, Federal Reserve Bank of St. Louis, 1966–76.

233

see the role as follows. The maintenance of maximum economic freedom demands the organization of our economic life largely through individual participation in a game with definite rules. The need for rules arises because absolute economic freedom is impossible. One man's freedom can conflict with another's security and property rights. Hence, each person must give up some freedom in order to resolve individual conflicts. The major problem is determining what freedoms the individual should give up in order to resolve conflict with others.

Just as a good game requires that players accept both of the rules and of an umpire to interpret and enforce the rules, so a free society requires that its members agree on the general rules that will govern relations among themselves, and on some device for enforcing compliance with those rules. Unfortunately, we cannot rely on custom or consensus alone to interpret and enforce the rules; we need an umpire. These, then, are the basic roles of government in a free economy—to provide a means whereby we can establish some set of general rules, and to enforce compliance with those rules on the part of those few who would otherwise not play the game.

The present-day advocate of a laissez-faire policy realizes that there is a constructive role for government in the economy; he is not an anarchist. He recognizes that a system which promotes maximum economic freedom may not be a godsend and that its existence depends, in part, upon affirmative government action. However, he also recognizes that each new governmentally enacted rule of the game involves a loss of some freedom. Herein lies the problem: Where do we draw the line? At what point does affirmative government action begin to have a net negative impact on economic freedom?

I can offer you no hard-and-fast principles on how far it is appropriate to use government to maximize economic freedom. However, I would suggest to you that in any particular case of proposed intervention, we should make up a balance sheet, listing separately the advantages and the disadvantages of the proposed policy. Most important we must always enter on the liability side of any proposed government intervention its effect in threatening freedom, and give this effect considerable weight. For it is an indisputable—yet frequently overlooked—reality that every new rule has its costs in terms of a loss of some freedom.

THE ROLE OF GOVERNMENT—IN PRACTICE

We have witnessed in many foreign countries the culmination of movements from constitutional government to dictatorship or from freedom back to authority. One need but look behind the Iron Curtain, or the Bamboo Curtain, to see the results of the former. And there is perhaps no clearer example of the latter—at least in the economic sphere—than that of our English cousins. Most of us are revolted by these movements and regard them as something to be avoided at all costs. Yet, faced with the same problems as these other nations, we too have often adopted measures which call for more government authority and less individual freedom. *As a nation we have often been too eager to justify and rationalize policies that propel us in a direction which we overwhelmingly disapprove.* As an indicator of how far and how fast we have moved in that direction, consider for a moment just a few facts and figures which are indicative of the tremendous growth of the government's influence on our economy.

1. It took 186 years for the federal budget to reach the $100 billion mark, a line we crossed in 1960, but in only 9 more years we reached the $200 billion mark, and in only 4 more years after that we broke the $300 billion barrier. And unfortunately, the $400 billion milestone was passed in the first year of our nation's third century.

2. In 1930, prior to the New Deal, government spending at all levels accounted for just 12 percent of our gross national product. Today government spending accounts for over 32 percent of our gross national product, and if present trends continue, government spending could account for as much as 60 percent of GNP by the year 2000.

3. As the role of government has increased, the bureaucracy has also grown, so that today one out of every six employed persons in this country works directly for the federal, state, and local governments. And despite all the political rhetoric to the contrary, the growth in the number of government employees—federal, state, and local—shows no evidence of slowing down.

Why is it, in light of the record, that the burden of proof still seems to rest on those of us who oppose new government programs which curtail our freedoms? Why is it that society seems so bent on curtailing the very freedoms that have netted us the highest standard of living and the highest degree of economic freedom in the entire world?

I submit that the reason for this drift is that there are natural biases in its favor. One of these biases has to do with what I will call "the regulatory reflex," a reflex which seems to have grown to almost epidemic proportions in our country. The other has to do with the same political realities which led that eminent Harvard economist Joseph Schumpeter to argue 30 years ago that there was "an irreconcilable conflict between democracy and free enterprise."

THE REGULATORY REFLEX

The regulatory reflex operates in the following manner. Upon observation of what some individuals deem an undesirable result produced by the free enterprise system, government officials or the media suggest that the government should "do something." This has usually meant the creation of a strong new government agency or an increase in the functions of an existing agency. The agency is empowered to make decisions regarding the allocation of resources according to its own interpretations of "what is best," rather than leaving such allocation to determination by the market process. The latter would give consumers the right to decide how the nation's scarce capital resources should be allocated.

Implicit in the reflex process is the assumption—invalid in my view —that "the free market system produces undesirable results" and that "government planning" achieves more desirable results. Unfortunately, the results sought by a group of regulators are frequently not those which the members of society would choose for themselves. The process often enables some group of zealots to decide that others should not have what they want, but should accept what the regulators consider "best" for them. This type of thinking, combined with the power to implement it, poses a tremendous and very basic threat to freedom. Yet such thinking is becoming increasingly common. Witness, for example, the proposals for compulsory national health insurance, seat belt interlock mechanisms, and the issuance of food stamps instead of money to the poor and the not so poor.

The regulatory reflex also arises from the fact that many people still subscribe to the medieval notion that all business is a zero-sum game. That is, many people believe that one person's profit is another person's loss. This notion underlies the frequently heard demands that the government should intervene in the market to limit what some consider to be—without defining the term—the "obscene" profits of entrepreneurs and to "protect" the "powerless consumer." These demands are based on a notion that is absolutely false. Their acceptance requires that we also accept the proposition that one or more parties to all transactions are either "irrational" or "victims of a fraud."

Free individuals will enter a transaction only if they can benefit by doing so. Business transactions are never a zero-sum game as long as the participants are free to choose for themselves and as long as they have alternative choices. It is true, of course, that there are shoddy practices in every profession and that market economies produce goods that are often poorly made or are undesirable to some individuals. However, the beauty of the free market system is that if the consumer does not want to purchase such products, *he or she has alternatives, and businesses will either shift to accommodate consumer desires or they will fail.*

The fact is that the alternative to free markets, planning by government bureaucracies, also results in the production of shoddy and expensive products (the U.S. postal service and Soviet agriculture are good examples). The crucial difference, however, is that the plans pursued by government bureaucracies are not subject to the forces of market competition, and therefore there is no way to test their relative efficiency or acceptability.

Advocates of "government planning" often cite "economic efficiency" as a basic goal. But they overlook the fact that the "dollar votes" of consumers make the market system far more responsive and sensitive to human needs than any government rules could possibly be. Each day the market receives millions of "buy signals" and "no-sale signals" showing consumers' needs and desires. This system is actually far more complex and sensitive than the most sophisticated computer yet designed or dreamed of.

I believe that much of the blind faith in the efficacy of government intervention stems from the impatience and shortsightedness of many individuals, reinforced, of course, by the lobbying of those who stand to gain directly from a particular regulatory proposal. Most policies are formulated with an eye to the short run. In a familiar pattern we see situations arise in which the short-run outcome of free market forces is considered by many to be less than socially optimal. The key question is, What is the alternative? For example, we have experienced several years of inflation. Impatience leads many to clamor for the quickest solution to the problem. In this case many people believe that wage and price controls fit the bill, and a rigid system of wage and price controls will, in fact, keep reported prices from rising in the short run. Unfortunately, as recent history shows, such controls will also create shortages and distortions in the economy that result in severe bottlenecks in the production process. Reported prices are temporarily fixed, but the consumer is robbed of the right to purchase those items which are in short supply. However, everyone concentrates on the immediate impact of the controls on the movement of reported price indexes and says, "You see how simple that was?"

So it is with most cases of state intervention. The seemingly beneficial effects are direct, immediate, and visible. On the other hand, the undesirable effects are often gradual and indirect, and are frequently considered only when they actually occur, if even then. However, the ignored long-run costs of state intervention eventually surface. And when they do, there is a call for more short-run intervention to correct the problems which arose as a result of the *earlier* government policies. Over a long period of time there is a cumulative and disastrous erosion of freedom and economic efficiency. Unfortunately, most of these situations seem just too complex to be readily grasped by the average citizen—or even by the average expert in the media who conveys a daily diet of instant "solutions" to the citizenry.

Unfortunately, regulation begets further regulation and regulations outlive their original rationale. Though most government regulation was enacted under the guise of protecting people from abuse, much of today's regulatory machinery only provides jobs for the regulators, increases the cost of doing business, and shelters those who are being regulated from the normal consequences of free enterprise competition. In some instances—the Interstate Commerce Commission for example—the original threat of abuse no longer exists. The railroad "monopoly" of 80 years ago has passed into history. In other instances, the machinery was a mistake from the start. In any case, the individual, whatever the presumed abuse from which he or she is being spared, pays for regulation through both a loss of freedom and a loss of material well-being.

Nevertheless, we have acknowledged that from time to time the "umpire" has to step in and enforce the rules of the game. This means that under some circumstances *some* regulatory rules are necessary. The rules devised for one historical era may, indeed, be responsive to the perceived problem. What occurs all too often, however, is that the rules persist through other eras even though the nature of the problem has changed—as in trucking, communications, air travel, and so on. The social invention of one era will very likely be the social stasis of another.

Recent events suggest that the concept that over time, social inventions become static, bureaucratic, and unresponsive, is being widely understood. For example, President Carter, among others, has suggested deregulation of the trucking and airline industries "as much as possible." The *Wall Street Journal* has commented that "present deregulation efforts might serve to remind us how often yesterday's progressive thinking becomes today's albatross."[1]

Although many regulatory programs seem to accomplish their goal (desirable or not) in the short run, they are seldom successful in the long run. The central problem with all of these measures is that they all involve an abridgment of some freedoms. They seek through government to force some individuals to act against their own immediate interests in order to promote a supposedly "public interest." They substitute the values of outsiders for the values of participants. Some people are telling others what is "good" for them, or else the government is taking from some to benefit others. These measures therefore run counter to the efforts of millions of individuals to promote their own interests and to live their lives by their own values. This is the major reason why such measures have so often had the opposite of their intended effects.

THE POSSIBLE CONFLICT BETWEEN DEMOCRACY
AND FREE ENTERPRISE

Despite the fact that the regulatory reflex contaminates so much of our society, I do not believe that it would be as pervasive as it has been were it not provided with a political framework conducive to its proliferation. Consider the situation that would exist in a community in which the mass of the people favor economic freedom of choice in their daily lives and oppose government direction.

What normally happens, however, is that many groups are formed which perceive an opportunity for material gain through a particular form of government intervention. Under the guise of such slogans as "consumerism," "equitable wages," or "fair trade" laws, these groups seek protection from the sources of competition. In such situations a political party hoping to achieve and maintain power will have little choice but to use its power to buy the support of these special interest groups by catering to their legislative demands. It will do so, not necessarily because it thinks that the majority of society is interventionist, but rather because *it cannot achieve and retain the support of a majority without promising special advantages. This means, in practice, that even a statesman who is wholly devoted to the maintenance of freedom and who realizes that every new regulation is an abridgment of freedom, will be under constant pressure to satisfy the interventionist demands of organized minority groups.*

Some special interest groups undoubtedly favor intervention, not for personal gain, but for what they consider to be the "good of society." These groups labor under the illusion that they can draft a law to prevent every outcome that they, and frequently only they, deem undesirable. In such cases, the operation of the regulatory reflex merely feeds an insatiable appetite for power on the part of those who wish to impose their values on the rest of society. When regulation fails to accomplish its goals, as it almost inevitably does, these people do not call for the repeal of the laws. Instead, they push to amend them into infinite complexity until the purpose of the original law is lost. As a result, the hand of regulation ends up touching every aspect of human action. This process is not only wasteful, but it serves to destroy incentive and to discourage ingenuity—as recent history has so amply shown.

CONCLUSION

It is ironic that groups which constantly look for problems in our nation insist on inhibiting the ability of the economy to respond to those problems. For example, present technology does not permit us to have both surgically clean air and plentiful electricity at less cost. However, there is no reason to believe that future technology could not provide those benefits. The essential ingredient is freedom to react to incentives and an understanding that individual liberty is not only precious but efficient. Just as thought control is the great enemy of the freedom of inquiry in academia, economic controls are the great enemy of economic freedom and the entrepreneurial spirit which is needed to solve our economic and social problems.

As the nation begins its third century, rediscovering the indivisibility and efficiency of political and economic freedom will take time. In the past 50 years we have become a society accustomed to overreliance on government interventions. The political and intellectual bias against the free market has become strongly entrenched. One can look to the newspapers, the magazines, or the TV newscasts to witness this first-hand, and there are always some who will find a platform to continue to feed this bias out of a complete misunderstanding of both the political and the market function.

More often than not, those of us who firmly believe in the preciousness and efficiency of a system which maximizes economic freedom find ourselves on the defensive. Given the biases that seem to continuously propel our society away from such a system, being merely defensive is not nearly enough. We must take the offensive and encourage others to restudy the philosophy of free enterprise. We need to drive home the point that every new rule of the game involves the loss of some freedom and that one cannot erode freedom in one sector of society without adversely affecting all other sectors. In other words, we must insist that public policy be based on a recognition of the desirability, the efficiency, and the interdependence of political, social, and economic freedom.

These truths have served our citizens quite well through 200 years. But, if our third century is to be a fruitful one, it is clear that free markets must again be nurtured and revitalized. In short, the lesson of history must be relearned—or we and our children will be condemned to relive it.

NOTE

1. "Jimmy Carter, Deregulator?" *Wall Street Journal*, April 11, 1977, p. 16.

Chapter 18

DIVIDEND REINVESTMENT: KEY TO AN UNTAPPED RESERVOIR OF NEW CAPITAL

*John D. deButts**

What is most surprising about dividend reinvestment is that it was so long in coming to the corporate world. Long a fixture of the mutual fund industry, where dividend reinvestment proved a convenient and inexpensive way for participants to buy additional shares, it was the late 1960s before American corporations first sensed the potential of automatic dividend reinvestment. Even then, that potential was seen for the most part in terms of offering a gesture of goodwill toward shareowners who found it costly and troublesome to make small stock purchases in the capital markets.

More recently, however, a combination of factors—a more bearish stock market, capital shortages, and an increasing appetite for scarce equity capital on the part of corporations—has led an increasing number of American businesses to adopt this vehicle for attracting new capital and encouraging long-term investment in American business. In short, what first appeared to be only a convenience for small shareholders is now seen by some companies as the key to an untapped reservoir of new capital.

In the years ahead, dividend reinvestment will surely play a larger role in the formation of capital than it has in the past, generating even larger amounts of new equity to help create jobs and spur economic growth, while offering investors of every economic level a greater share of American enterprise.

---

* Chairman of the Board, American Telephone and Telegraph Company.

An estimated 800 businesses now offer their shareholders the opportunity to have dividends reinvested for the purchase of additional shares. Chart 1, which depicts the growth of corporate dividend plans over the last ten years, illustrates this upsurge in corporate interest. Some of the plans permit only the reinvestment of dividends; others offer shareowners the option of buying additional shares with cash as well as reinvested dividends. Still others permit the purchase of shares without service fees or brokerage commissions.

Chart 1.   U.S. corporations sponsoring dividend reinvestment plans

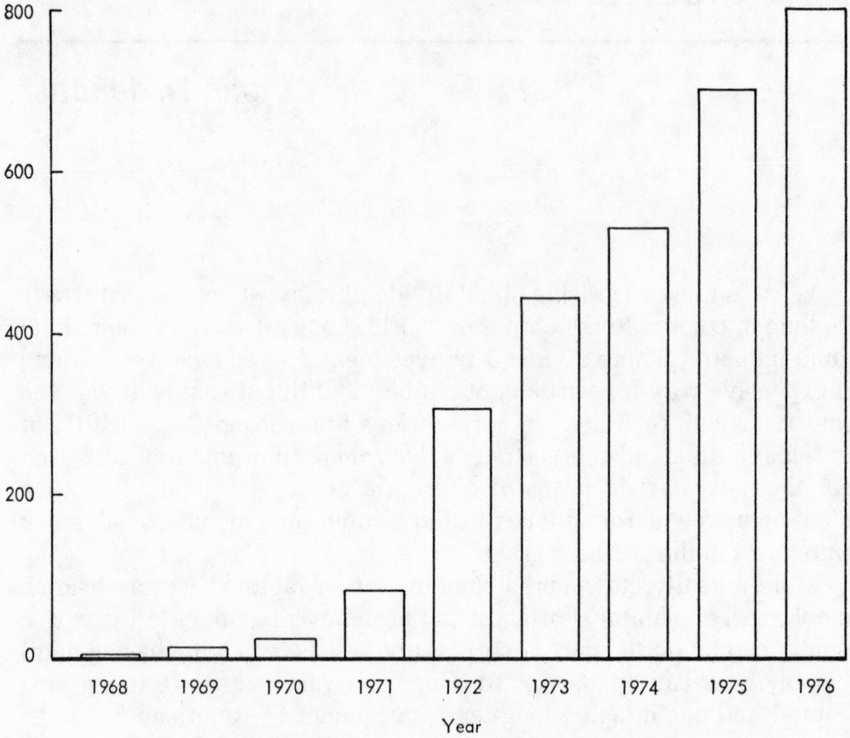

Year

Source: American Telephone and Telegraph Company.

Among U.S. corporations offering dividend reinvestment are some of the nation's biggest and most prestigious. Of the 30 corporations whose stock activity is tracked by the Dow Jones industrial average, all but 4 offer their stockholders some form of dividend reinvestment plan. Overall, it is estimated that in 1976 some 1.5 million investors then enrolled in reinvestment plans made stock purchases amounting to more than $1 billion.

THE FIRST REINVESTMENT PLAN

The potential of a large market of shareowners who would be interested in having their dividends reinvested was first perceived by Citibank, which in 1968 approached a number of widely owned, capital-intensive businesses with the proposal that it establish and administer for the companies an investment program modeled on the mutual fund reinvestment concept. The first business to accept the proposal was Allegheny Power System, a holding company for electrical utility firms, which inaugurated the first corporate dividend reinvestment plan in September of that year.[1]

American Telephone and Telegraph Company was not far behind, announcing a similar plan in April 1969 for its then more than 3 million owners of common shares. Under the bank-administered plan, AT&T shareowners were invited to reinvest their quarterly dividends to buy additional shares of AT&T common stock on the open market at prevailing prices. For that service, they were charged a flat 75-cent service fee and a proportionate share of whatever brokerage commissions the bank had to pay on bulk purchases of the stock in the marketplace. Some 130,500 shareowners signed up for the service.[2]

Enrollment in AT&T's Dividend Reinvestment and Stock Purchase Plan rose slowly until 1972, when the company negotiated a lower service fee with the bank. Later that year, the plan was again modified to enable shareowners to add cash payments of up to $1,500 a quarter to their reinvested dividends. By the year-end over 220,000 shareowners had signed up for the plan.

TYPES OF REINVESTMENT PLANS

At the start, dividend reinvestment plans offered only existing shares of stock bought on the open market by brokers for the banks and others that served as agents for sponsors of the plans. Beginning late in 1972, a second type of reinvestment plan was inaugurated by the Long Island Lighting Company. Under this type of plan, in which newly issued shares of stock were offered, the stock was sold directly to the shareowner by the corporation.

The Long Island Company plan prompted other companies to follow suit. AT&T moved in that direction in 1973, taking over administration of its plan from the bank that had been acting as trustee. At the same time, the company introduced a number of new features for its plan: shareowners could henceforth buy new shares and make cash payments of up to $3,000 a quarter. In addition, they could invest income from other Bell System securities as cash payments.

244

For AT&T shareowners, the revised plan meant the end of service fees and brokers' commissions for stock purchased through the plan; from then on, every dollar invested would buy stock. For the company, which because of difficult financial markets, had been relying principally on debt issues of one kind or another to meet its capital requirements, the plan was a move that strengthened the equity side of the capital structure.

Further improvements in the plan followed in 1975, with the introduction of a 5 percent discount on shares purchased with reinvested dividends, and in 1976, with new features that permitted shareowners to buy shares each month with cash and to reinvest less than all of their dividends. These steps made AT&T's plan even more convenient and attractive to many shareowners. And for the first time, AT&T had provided a substantial incentive for institutional investors to enroll.

Chart 2. Enrollment in AT&T's Dividend Reinvestment and Stock Purchase Plan (shareowner accounts)

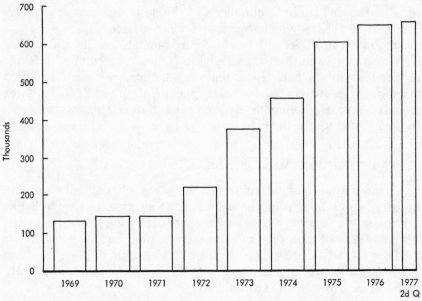

Source: American Telephone and Telegraph Company.

With these changes, enrollment and investment rose to new levels. By the end of 1976, enrollment, as shown in Chart 2, had increased to 650,000—almost one out of every four shareowners. Equity investment through the plan, as shown in Chart 3, rose to $432 million in 1976, and $265 million was invested in the first six months of 1977.

Chart 3.   Equity investment in AT&T's Dividend Reinvestment and Stock Purchase Plan

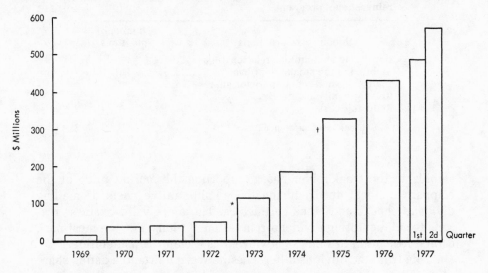

* Issuance of new AT&T common shares initiated July 1973.
† Five percent discount on reinvested dividends inaugurated April 1973.
Source: American Telephone and Telegraph Company.

Experience has shown that individual participants include people who, because of the costs and effort involved in making purchases in the regular market, might not otherwise invest further in stocks at all. Furthermore, by adding to the supply of shares already in the hands of the public, this ownership eventually leads to new business for brokers when those shares are ultimately resold. Thus, reinvestment plans provide investors with an easy way to buy more stock while leading to new business for brokers when the shares are sold again.

COMMON FEATURES OF REINVESTMENT PLANS

Although the features of all reinvestment plans are more or less standard, it is important to distinguish between the plans that offer *new* shares and those that offer *existing* shares. The latter are by far the more numerous. Indeed, among the hundreds of businesses that sponsor dividend reinvestment plans, less than 5 percent—perhaps 35 firms—use their plans to raise equity capital through the sale of new shares of stock, and most of those that do are capital-intensive utility companies.

Of 100 businesses surveyed in 1976, nearly eight out of ten identified the improvement of shareholder relations as a primary objective of their plans.[3] Other objectives, as noted in Table 1, were identified as:

Table 1. Survey of 100 companies sponsoring reinvestment programs

Objectives of programs	Number of mentions
Improving shareholder relationships	79
Stabilizing the stockholder base	26
Increasing market support for shares	20
Raising equity capital	12
Reducing costs	6

Source: The Conference Board.

stabilizing the stockholder base, supporting the market price of the company's stock, and reducing the administrative costs of mailing dividend checks and stock certificates. These are valid business reasons for inaugurating dividend reinvestment plans. For the most part, capital formation has not been viewed as a major consideration.

Aside from the obvious differences between new and existing share plans, these features are more or less common among the current corporate investment plans:

1. Reinvestment of all dividends to purchase full and fractional shares.
2. Investment of cash payments on an average of $1,000 a month.
3. A combination of the first two options—investment of dividends and cash payments.
4. Preparation of cumulative stock ownership and tax records for participants.[4]

Also standard among many companies offering new shares is the absence of service fees or commissions on stock transactions. Among a few, a discount on stock purchased with reinvested dividends is an appealing feature to institutional and individual investors, despite the tax treatment applied to the discount.[5] The tax treatment—taxing the discount as ordinary income rather than as a capital gain—is an example of the lack of incentive to equity investment inherent in the nation's present tax laws.

In AT&T's case, the discount and savings on brokerage commissions make investment in additional shares of our common stock especially appealing to large insurance companies, banks, and brokers owning AT&T stock in their own or beneficial owners' names. In 1976, following the start of the 5 percent discount on shares bought with reinvested stock, almost 20 percent of the $432 million raised through the AT&T plan was supplied by institutions which were able to save upward of 6 percent on their stock purchases—the discount plus savings on a broker's commission.

Discount or not, savings on the purchase of stock have always been a primary attraction of reinvestment plans. Small shareowners, for example, can save as much as 40 percent of a broker's commission if they buy already issued shares through a reinvestment plan rather than individually through a broker.[6] But savings are not the only attraction: shareowners can also buy fractional shares that produce dividends, just as do full shares; their stock and tax records are produced automatically; and investment is largely automatic, meaning that stock purchases are made regularly and conveniently without further action by the shareowner.

Even so, the latest estimates of stockholder participation indicate that investor interest in reinvestment plans varies widely. As mentioned earlier, not quite one in four shareowners participates in AT&T's plan, for example. In 1976 participation in 93 of the companies that sponsor reinvestment plans ranged from 1.4 percent to 19.5 percent of the stockholders eligible to enroll,[7] as shown in Chart 4. And of 22 million owners of stock in companies offering reinvestment plans, only an estimated 1.5 million are now enrolled, as shown in Chart 5.

Chart 4. Stockholder participation in 93 reinvestment programs

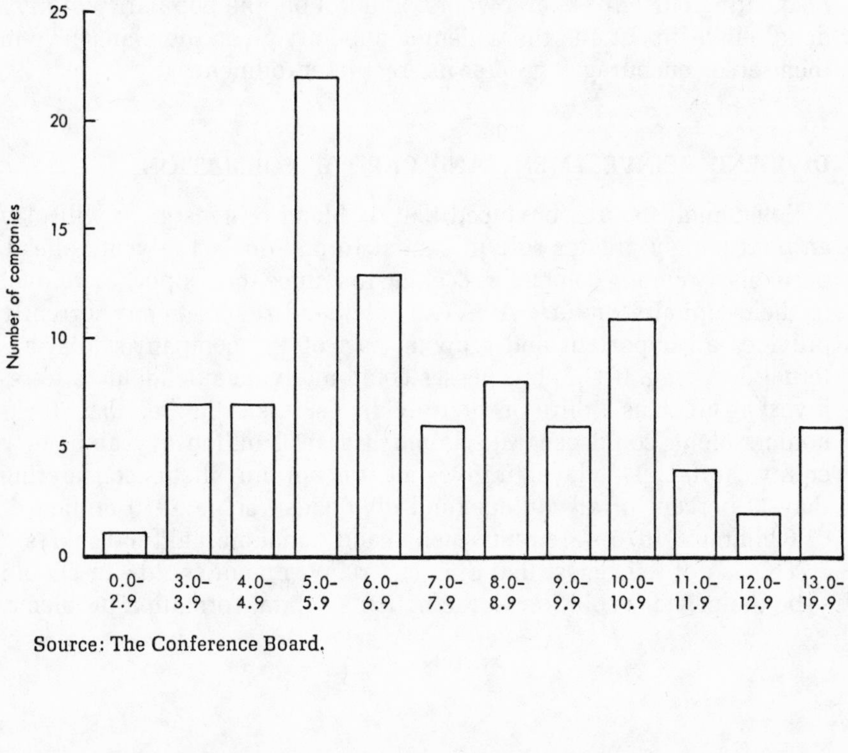

Source: The Conference Board.

248

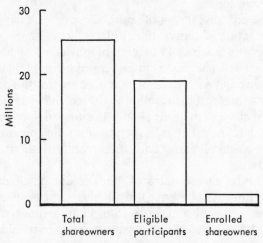

Chart 5.   U.S. shareowners and their participation in dividend reinvestment plans

Source: The Conference Board.

At the same time, participation is on the rise.[8] A recent survey of businesses with reinvestment plans suggests that those with higher participation are the more vigorous in soliciting new—and periodically resoliciting current—shareowners. In addition, the popularity of dividend reinvestment and the widening publicity given the plans have in themselves encouraged greater interest in enrollment.

DIVIDEND REINVESTMENT AND CAPITAL FORMATION

Some analysts are convinced that dividend reinvestment will play an increasingly greater role in capital formation in the years ahead, particularly among companies seeking to reduce the proportion of debt in their capital structure. At AT&T, dividend reinvestment currently provides an important and growing part of the company's total external financing. If U.S. businesses could motivate stockholders to reinvest as much as a third of their dividends, it is estimated that stockholders alone could generate as much as $10 billion a year in new equity capital.[9] This level of investment is not unrealistic, considering that 60 percent of all mutual fund dividends—some $950 million of $1.6 billion in 1976—are reinvested in additional mutual fund shares.[10]

This is not to suggest that dividend reinvestment could—or should—be the primary solution to the nation's capital formation problems.

It is, however, a step in the right direction because it appeals to the small investor to enlarge his or her stake in American enterprise. And it permits small shareowners to do so automatically and regularly, in whatever amounts they choose, and at relatively low cost, especially in those plans which have reduced or eliminated service fees and commissions. In this way, whether they invest in new or existing shares, shareowners make a contribution to capital formation. The important thing is that dividend dollars are being used to make equity investments—that is, being saved rather than being spent.

THE FUTURE OF CORPORATE DIVIDEND REINVESTMENT

The recent increase of interest in reinvestment plans has led to sanguine growth estimates for this type of investment program.[11] This much is clear: the number of participants and the number of plans continue to grow; and among companies offering new shares, equity investment is on the rise. In the case of AT&T's plan, for example, investment and enrollment have never once declined in any of the eight years that the plan has been in operation. Since 1969, there has been a 14-fold rise in shareowner investment in the plan and a 4-fold rise in enrollment.

Encouraging as these signs are, however, a survey of companies sponsoring reinvestment plans suggests that the growth potential is not unlimited. Some businesses fear high administrative costs and low participation. Still others express a more philosophic concern: they are convinced that investment in stock without regard to market price is fundamentally unwise. There is also the matter of investors' desire to diversify.

The prospects for plans that sell new shares appear to be brighter, if only because individuals—the backbone of most reinvestment programs—can purchase stock through them free of service fees or commissions. The extension of such plans, however, hinges upon the return of large numbers of small shareowners to the market.

Crucial to the extension of reinvestment plans, of course, is the profit performance of business. Basic to the success of any reinvestment plan is the underlying demand for a company's stock. This demand rests in turn upon corporate earnings levels that are comparable to those of other companies with which the corporation must compete for equity investment in the capital markets. Without rates of return —and the prospect of continuing earnings improvement—comparable to those of rival investment choices, no plan, however convenient, can expect to attract continuing investment interest.

TAX POLICY BARRIERS TO REINVESTMENT

The future of dividend reinvestment would seem more assured if current tax disincentives to investment—high capital gains taxes and immediate taxation of dividends even when automatically reinvested —were removed. Of all the barriers to the extension of these plans, none is more formidable than the fact that, although they provide no cash flow to the shareowners, automatically reinvested dividends are immediately taxable as personal income. As one utility executive said recently, "Unless there are tax incentives to participate in dividend investment programs, we do not foresee such programs becoming significant factors in the capital markets." Others in a nationwide survey concurred in the view that the answer to further expansion is a change in tax policies that apply to reinvested dividends and dividend income.[12]

Under current tax laws, a stockholder who reinvests dividends must report them as ordinary income—subject, of course, to the individual $100 dividend exclusion. However, for dividends that are reinvested automatically, the shareowners receive no cash flow with which to pay those taxes. Because such tax treatment tends to discourage participation in reinvestment plans—and more important, because it discourages capital investment—the leaders of some of the nation's largest corporations have testified before the tax-writing committees of Congress in support of deferring the taxation of reinvested dividends until the stock purchased is sold.[13] Such a deferral would, of course, match the payment of taxes with the actual receipt of the cash income on which the tax is based.

There is even a good deal of logic for going farther and treating reinvested dividends in the same way as retained earnings are treated for tax purposes. Doing so would reduce the cost basis for the stock held as dividends were automatically reinvested, and would apply capital gains taxes at the time the stock was sold. In effect, this method would provide the same treatment for earnings reinvested at the discretion of the individual shareowner as is now applied to earnings reinvested at the discretion of corporate management. Such a policy would be a powerful incentive both for increasing participation in dividend reinvestment plans and for increasing capital formation itself.

The primary objection to deferring the taxation of reinvested dividends is the prospect of lost federal tax revenues, but the following factors suggest that the actual losses might not be as large as is generally expected:

First, a high percentage of common stock is held by tax-exempt institutions and trusts.

Second, almost a third of all dividends are currently tax-free as a result of the current dividend exclusion.

Third, the terms of any dividend reinvestment credit or exclusion might be drawn to limit tax revenue losses to an economically and politically acceptable level.[14]

And fourth, the economic stimulus to jobs and capital formation of such a step would probably offset any losses in tax revenues.

CONCLUSION

The nation's need for new equity capital has never been greater than it is today. Indeed, it is the prime requisite for increasing job opportunities in the United States. And it is essential to the maintenance of our nation's world economic leadership in its third century.

Already dividend reinvestment plans have proven to be an effective and popular means of stimulating the efficient formation of new equity capital for the U.S. economy. It is an idea whose time is "now." In the years ahead, dividend reinvestment programs will, I believe, become a major part of this country's equity growth processes.

NOTES

1. Patrick J. Davey, *Dividend Reinvestment Program* (New York: The Conference Board, 1976), report no. 699, p. 1.
2. "Dividend Reinvestment: A Growing Source of New Capital," *Bell Telephone Magazine,* November–December 1974, p. 8.
3. Davey, *Dividend Reinvestment,* p. 6.
4. Mark J. Appelman, *The Corporate Shareholder,* August 15, 1974, pp. 1–4.
5. "Companies Make It Easier to Reinvest Dividends" (New York: Standard & Poor's Corporation, 1976).
6. Appelman, *Corporate Shareholder,* p. 1.
7. Davey, *Dividend Reinvestment,* p. 10.
8. Ibid., p. 12.
9. Charles D. Kuehner, "Capital Formation—A New Approach via Dividend Reinvestment," speech given to the National Investment Relations Institute, May 20, 1975.
10. News release, Investment Company Institute, Washington, D.C., April 1, 1977.
11. Davey, *Dividend Reinvestment,* pp. 43–47.
12. Ibid., pp. 13–16.
13. Robert N. Flint, AT&T vice president and comptroller, statement submitted to the Ways and Means Committee, U.S. House of Representatives, July 23, 1975.
14. Eugene M. Lerner, "On Utility Financing," *Public Utilities Fortnightly,* May 8, 1975, p. 30.

Chapter 19

HOW INSURANCE COMPANIES CONTRIBUTE TO CAPITAL AND JOB FORMATION

*Donald S. MacNaughton**

INTRODUCTION

The great capital shortage debate in the United States is concerned with the adequacy of expected aggregate savings relative to the nation's projected capital requirements. The implications of a capital-short economy for sustaining real economic growth and job formation are obvious. No modern industrial nation can hope to achieve sustainable growth and to fully employ its labor force without an adequate capital base and the incentives to insure that this adequacy is maintained in the future. Although rigorous analysis has been applied to this problem, its usual macroeconomic orientation has often masked important micro considerations. For example, both opponents and proponents of the capital shortage thesis seem to be preoccupied with the equating of aggregate demand and supply. Hence they often do not seriously consider the specific roles that financial intermediaries play in the capital formation process. It would appear that too little has been said about how financial institutions may encourage higher levels of savings and capital formation by offering innovative products and services and by creative approaches to channeling savings flow to the ultimate capital investor. Although advances in financial technology alone cannot provide a total solution to any threatened capital gap, the increasing efficiency with which financial resources have been

---

* Chairman and Chief Executive Officer, Prudential Insurance Company of America.

allocated has made a significant contribution to capital and job formation in the past and can do so in the future, given an accommodating political and economic environment.

This chapter will investigate the role of the insurance industry in the economy and how it functions within the saving-investment process. It will discuss the role of insurance in society and, where possible, it will quantify the industry's impact on capital and job formation. Subsequent sections will examine how the life industry accumulates private savings and how it allocates these investable funds among competing financial assets. Then a brief review of property-casualty company investment activity will be presented, followed by some concluding remarks concerning the future prospects of the insurance industry.

THE ROLE OF THE INSURANCE INSTITUTION IN SOCIETY

The role of the insurance industry is critical to the capital formation process even though the individual insurance companies do relatively little direct physical investment themselves. The insurance industry's greatest contribution to capital formation is through the risk-bearing function. The importance of insurance in providing relief from fear of financial losses due to a host of contingencies has led to the industry's being termed the "handmaiden" of commerce. In this respect the insurance product facilitates the flow of savings into physical and human capital by insuring such investment against physical perils and financial uncertainties. A rational investor, institutional or individual, would not think of making a financial commitment if a venture were not properly protected against insurable risks.

In today's modern economy, the insurance technique, that is, the spreading of economic losses by the pooling of risks, facilitates the conduct of virtually every commercial and industrial activity. For example, even such a commonplace transaction as granting a home mortgage would not take place in the form familiar to us if it were not possible to insure the property against fire or other natural disasters and the mortgagee against loss of income due to death or disability.

The insurance industry also aids economic activity by providing the financial security that allows individuals to pursue their career and family goals to the best of their ability and initiative. There is a relation between the productivity and general well-being of labor and the personal financial security which life insurance companies provide through life and health insurance and private pension plans. Life insurance creates an immediate estate, thereby ensuring that family members will be able to pursue their individual goals even in the event of the premature death of the breadwinner. In like manner, health insurance and disability income coverage remove the threat of financial catastrophe due to medical expenses and loss of income arising out of accident or sickness. Similarly, the accumulation of pension benefits adds the security of knowing that the cessation of earned income at retirement will not be a serious financial burden.

Insurance companies, and particularly those in the life insurance industry, also play an important role as financial intermediaries. Through this function they lubricate the wheels of the production process by providing an efficient mechanism for channeling private savings to the ultimate capital investor. Furthermore, because of the long-term nature of many life insurance and pension obligations, life insurance companies are able to commit the bulk of their investable funds to long-term financing which is vital for capital investment.

With this broad outline of the basic nature of the insurance mechanism as background, it is possible to set out in more detail how the insurance industry contributes directly to capital and job formation.

THE JOB-CREATING NATURE OF INSURANCE INDUSTRY INVESTMENT ACTIVITY

Insurance company investments in their own plant, equipment, and office buildings provide the physical capital base that supports the industry's ever-increasing work force. In 1975, the industry directly employed over 1.6 million persons. This represented, however, only a fraction of the industry's overall impact on the employment of human and physical capital.

The industry's major contribution to job formation undoubtedly arises out of its risk-bearing function, which greatly narrows the degree of uncertainty surrounding all forms of economic activity. However, the pervasive financial security created by insurance activities is primarily an intangible whose influence cannot be measured in the customary terms of dollars, jobs, or physical units.

Narrower in scope but somewhat more susceptible to quantification is the industry's contribution to job formation through its role as a financial intermediary in directing the flow of investable funds into a whole spectrum of capital projects. Even in this area, however, conceptual problems and data limitations prevent establishing a straightforward relationship between financial flows and investment and job formation. For example, the Bureau of Labor Statistics has developed a methodology that relates the jobs required to produce a specified amount of capital investment in plant or equipment.[1] This procedure, however, cannot be simply applied to financial flows from insurance companies because there is no way of knowing how much of a given year's investable funds is channeled in new capital projects and how much goes to support or refinance existing capital stock. In the latter case the industry's financing activity tends to support current employment levels, whereas in the former case such activity tends to stimulate new employment opportunities. Even if this particular problem could somehow be overcome, determining the amount of *permanent* direct and indirect employment created as a result of financing, say, the building of a new plant presents even more formidable difficulties.

Although we lack a precise measure of the job impact of insurance industry investment flows, the general principal that investment is required to create employment certainly does hold. In the economy as a whole, the dollar amount of business physical capital (land, inventory, plant and equipment) in existence per private sector employee has grown steadily since 1948, and in the last five years alone the increase has averaged 7½ percent per annum. To illustrate this in dollar terms, capital per employed worker amounted to $47,000 in 1975. This represented a sizable increase from about $33,000 in 1970, or an additional $14,000 per employee in just five years.[2]

These figures strongly suggest that the insurance industry will have to continue to be a major supplier of long-term financial capital if the nation is to achieve and sustain the amount of business physical investment needed for a high level of employment. Thus, the remainder of this chapter will focus in more detail on the insurance industry's contribution to the overall flow of financial capital.

HOW LIFE INSURANCE COMPANIES ATTRACT SAVINGS

The life insurance industry is an important thrift institution since, in meeting the demands for individual financial security, it attracts and invests personal savings. In contrast, property-casualty companies do not directly compete for savings dollars. Their funds for investment arise primarily from their capital and surplus, reserves for prepaid premiums, and loss reserves needed to support underwriting activities. A closer examination of life insurance products reveals how they attract savings of a contractual nature and provide an important source of financial capital.

The "whole-life" policy with cash values remains the major life insurance product despite an increased reliance on term insurance. The whole-life policy form creates a reservoir of funds which represent accumulated premiums and investment income and which act as the reserves to meet future obligations. This pool of funds arises because premiums paid during the early years of the contract exceed the sums immediately needed for benefits and expenses. In later years, when mortality costs exceed periodic premium payments, the shortfall is made up by earlier premium surpluses and the investment income derived therefrom. In addition to whole-life policies, other basic forms of reserve-generating individual contracts include endowment and retirement income life insurance and annuities. Even term life and health insurance sold on either an individual or group basis generate some reserves, but the savings element in these types of contracts is insignificant compared with their protection features.

The life insurance industry's other major reserve-generating product is group pension plans (including profit-sharing and thrift plans), and this business has experienced dynamic growth in the last 20 years. Unlike Social Security, insured pension plans generate a large reserve of investable funds and represent an important vehicle through which private savings are accumulated.

With the relaxing of certain legal and regulatory limitations in the 1950s and 1960s, life insurance companies were able to compete more aggressively and successfully with banks and other financial institutions for pension fund business. Three developments in particular directly strengthened the competitive atmosphere in the pension market and increased the saving alternatives available to the public. One was the Life Insurance Company Income Tax Act of 1959, which largely exempted from federal income tax the investment earnings credited to insured qualified pension plan reserves, thus paralleling the tax treatment of self-insured, trusteed plans. The second development was the so-called new money or investment year method of crediting investment returns to group annuity contributions at the yields currently obtainable on new investments. This supplanted the traditional method of crediting earnings on the basis of the average yield on the insurer's total existing portfolio.

Equally significant, if not more significant, was the introduction of "separate accounts" for the purpose of investing pension funds. These separate accounts are not subject to the same investment regulatory limitations as the general asset account, particularly with reference to the percentage of assets that may be invested in common stocks. The separate account innovation was originally designed to increase the industry's investment flexibility in providing common stock investments for pension funds, but today we find insurers offering pooled separate accounts in publicly traded bonds, private placements, short-term money market instruments, real estate mortgages and properties, and even accounts especially tailored for larger employers.

As Chart 1 shows, both the life insurance and pension reserves of life companies have shown rather steady growth since 1955, although the trend for pension reserves has been somewhat erratic. Between 1955 and 1960 group pension reserves grew at close to an 11 percent annual rate and then slowed during the 1960s due to intense competition from banks before the separate account concept was fully accepted by state insurance departments and marketed by the life insurance companies. By 1971 all states permitted separate accounts, and this universal acceptance is in part reflected in the over 11 percent growth in insured pension reserves recorded over the 1970–75 period. In addition, insured pension growth has been stimulated by the passage of the Employee Retirement Income Security Act of 1974 (ERISA),

Chart 1. Growth in total life reserves and policy loans

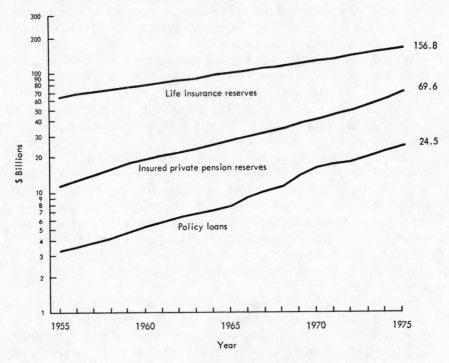

| | Growth rates (annual averages) | | |
	Life reserves	Insured private pension reserves	Policy loans
1955–60	4.4%	10.7%	9.7%
1960–65	4.7	7.7	8.0
1965–70	4.5	8.2	15.9
1970–75	5.0	11.4	8.8

Reserves and policy loans are measured at book value, using the level of outstandings in 1953 as a base and adding subsequent annual dollar flows to obtain the level of outstandings in each succeeding year.

Source: Division of Research and Statistics, Board of Governors of the Federal Reserve System, *Flow of Funds*, September 1976.

which overall has served to encourage the funding of employee plans and has also specifically provided for individual retirement programs for the self-employed and employees not covered under a private plan.

Although the investable funds of the life industry have continued to grow substantially, there have been serious leakages in the form of policy loans that have interrupted the smooth flow of life insurance funds into the capital markets. As Chart 1 indicates, policy loan growth accelerated markedly during the 1965–70 period. Although the rate of growth slowed over the subsequent five-year period, the absolute increase continued to be significant. For example, the increase in policy loans between 1970 and 1975 was equal to the $8.4 billion increase recorded between 1965 and 1970. Policy loans have increased in response to the secular rise in interest rates, which encourages policyholders to borrow against cash values at mandated rates which are below market. This form of disintermediation tends to reinforce upward long-term interest rate pressures to the extent that it reduces the available pool of loanable funds.

THE IMPACT OF PUBLIC PENSION SYSTEMS ON PRIVATE SAVINGS

Along with the inflationary environment of the U.S. economy, the dramatic growth of public income maintenance systems, and especially Social Security, has affected private savings flows. Unlike many private plans which meet strict funding requirements, Social Security is, in effect, currently on a "pay-as-you-go" basis, which means that employee and employer contributions are redistributed to recipients who tend to consume all or most of the income they receive. In addition to this bypassing of the saving-investment process in favor of current consumption, there is concern that other forms of personal savings have been adversely affected by the increasing benefits that public systems offer. The evidence is somewhat mixed as to how seriously public pension schemes have reduced the flow of savings into private capital, but there is ample room for fear that demographic and benefit trends could lead to a significant reduction in the savings rate in the future.[3]

FINANCIAL INVESTMENT BY THE INSURANCE INDUSTRY

Basic investment objectives

The basic investment strategies of life insurance and property-casualty insurance companies differ significantly, and this is quite apparent in the distribution of assets for each type of insurer, as shown in Table 1. Though each attempts in some sense to maximize total return, the operating and regulatory constraints imposed by the characteristics of the different insurance products, and reflected in the liability structure in each type of institution, dictate different investment patterns.

Perhaps the most critical factor is the greater need for liquidity by property-casualty companies because of the short-term duration of their contracts and the unpredictable and catastrophic nature of many of the natural perils against which they insure. The property-casualty insurers also find that the difficulties of predicting the severity of physical damage and legal liability losses are compounded during periods of high rates of inflation. Life insurance companies, on the other hand, protect against contingencies which in the aggregate are fairly predictable, and the benefits paid upon the occurrence of such contingencies are generally expressed in fixed-dollar amounts.

These distinguishing characteristics explain why the property-casualty insurers concentrate their holdings in marketable, publicly issued corporate bonds and in state and local government securities rather than in the nonmarketable, private placement corporate debt which is so prevalent in the invested assets of life insurance companies.[4] The greater need of the property-casualty companies for liquidity also explains why they invest very little in real estate mortgages, which have traditionally been an important outlet for life insurance funds.

Table 1. Asset distribution of the U.S. insurance industry, 1975

	Life insurance companies	Property-casualty insurance companies
U.S. and foreign government bonds	3.6%	8.9%
State and local government bonds	1.6	35.4
Corporate bonds	36.6*	12.5
Common stock	7.0	21.7
Preferred stock	2.7	3.3
Mortgages	30.8	0.2
Real estate	3.3	1.7
Policy loans	8.5	—
Other assets†	5.9	16.3
Total assets	100.0%	100.0%
Total assets (billions)	$289.3	$94.0
Surplus as percentage of assets	6.7%	26.9%

* Approximately 85 percent of life insurance assets in the bond category are private placement corporate debt.

† Cash, receivables (premiums and interest), and other miscellaneous assets.

Sources: *Life Insurance Fact Book*, 1976 ed. (New York: American Council of Life Insurance, 1976); *Best's Fire and Casualty Aggregates and Averages*, 1976 ed. (New York: Alfred M. Best Co., Inc., 1976).

The larger proportion of common stock in property-casualty companies is predominantly due to the typically larger surplus-to-asset positions required to support their type of business. As shown in Table 1, the surplus ratio of property-casualty companies is approximately four times that of life insurance companies. This obviously allows greater exposure to fluctuations of stocks which are valued at market in the statements of both types of insurance companies. Another reason why common stock has been a favored investment, at least until very recently, is that it was thought to provide a hedge against the inflationary trends in physical damage and liability losses.

Investment activity of life insurance companies

Life companies are principally suppliers of long-term funds, and their participation in the major sectors of the capital markets since 1955 is charted in Chart 2. Also shown are the underlying annual rates of change of life company holdings and the total outstanding for each asset category for selected time periods.[5] Several important patterns in life company investments are evident from these data:

1. A steady decline from 61 percent to 33 percent in the ratio of life company bond holdings to total bonds outstanding from 1955 to 1975.
2. Increasing participation in the stock market, rising to a shade under 9.0 percent in 1975.
3. A relatively constant 30 percent share of total nonresidential mortgages since 1955.
4. A gradual decline in the multifamily mortgage ratio from 1955 to 1963, followed by a rising ratio which reached a maximum of about 27 percent in 1969 and then declined to about 20 percent over the 1973–75 period.
5. A declining participation in mortgages on one–four-family homes since 1955, with the decline becoming more pronounced after 1965, as the industry was actually disinvesting in this instrument.

Some of the reasons for these investment patterns are suggested in the following sections on the three major outlets for the investable funds of life insurers.

Corporate bonds

The decline in the relative importance of life company holdings of corporate bonds since the 1950s, shown in Chart 2, has been due to at least three significant developments. One is the rapid growth in state

Chart 2. Ratio of selected life company assets to total assets outstanding

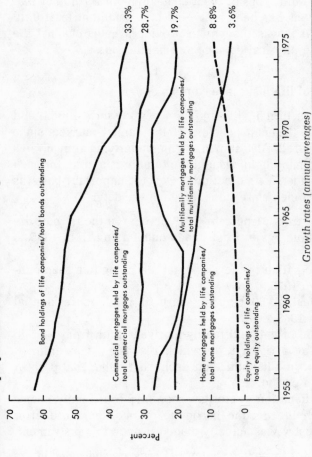

Growth rates (annual averages)

	Total bonds outstanding	Life company bonds	Total home mortgages outstanding	Life company home mortgages	Total multifamily mortgages outstanding	Life company multifamily mortgages	Total commercial mortgages outstanding	Life company commercial mortgages	Total equities outstanding	Life company equity holdings
1955-60	8.2%	5.3%	10.0%	7.1%	9.0%	1.7%	11.5%	11.0%	2.0%	4.2%
1960-65	6.2	4.9	9.2	3.5	13.0	17.9	10.7	10.8	1.5	10.8
1965-70	10.5	4.0	6.2	-2.0	9.5	12.7	9.0	9.1	3.2	15.6
1970-75	9.5	7.3	10.6	-8.0	10.7	4.3	13.0	11.8	3.9	17.2

Bond holdings of life companies/total bonds outstanding — 33.3%

Commercial mortgages held by life companies/total commercial mortgages outstanding — 28.7%

Multifamily mortgages held by life companies/total multifamily mortgages outstanding — 19.7%

Home mortgages held by life companies/total home mortgages outstanding — 8.8%

Equity holdings of life companies/total equity outstanding — 3.6%

Assets are measured at book value using the level of outstandings in 1953 as a base and adding subsequent annual dollar flows to obtain the level of outstandings in each succeeding year.

Source: Division of Research and Statistics, Board of Governors of the Federal Reserve System, Flow of Funds, September 1976.

and local government retirement funds, which invest heavily in corporate bonds. A second influence was the tight money and "credit crunch" conditions in the mid-1960s and the late 1960s, which diverted life insurance company investable funds to policy loans. The third factor is the very large increase in corporate bond issues after 1965, especially those publicly issued, which exceeded the growth in life company investable funds.

Despite the downward trend in their share of total bonds, life insurance companies are still the largest institutional investors in corporate bonds, holding about one third of the total outstanding. In addition, life insurance companies currently purchase between 25 percent and 30 percent of the annual net new corporate debt issues with a maturity of more than one year. Moreover, life companies play a special role in the corporate bond market by virtue of being the major takers of privately placed debt—that sold directly to investor-lenders rather than issued through the public market. Typically over 90 percent of total bond acquisitions by the life insurance industry are private placements, and this represents roughly four fifths of all corporate debt placed privately each year.

Because private placements allow flexibility in tailoring loan terms to specific borrower needs and facilitate the forward commitment of funds, large companies are able to use them as an alternative to publicly issued bonds. The private placement instrument is also an important source of long-term financing for small- and medium-sized companies, especially new firms and firms without the earnings history and credit rating required for access to the public market. Indeed, there are times when credit market conditions are such that providing long-term debt financing to lower-rated and smaller companies is left almost entirely to the life insurance industry. For example, of the over $6.9 billion in new bond authorizations made by life companies in 1975 (a period when many lower-rated companies had very limited access to the public credit market) over 90 percent represented funds extended to companies whose quality was the equivalent of a Moody's A rating or lower.

Chart 3 shows the breakdown of all public and private bond and note financing by industry for selected years. Of all the industries shown, the manufacturing sector places the greatest reliance on the private market in terms of amount, while the percentage of financing done privately is greatest for the transportation industry. The aggregated "other" category, which includes extractive, commercial, sales, and finance companies, generally fund over 30 percent of their debt privately. The significance of the private placement market in key in-

Chart 3. Percentage distribution of bond and note financing between the public and private market

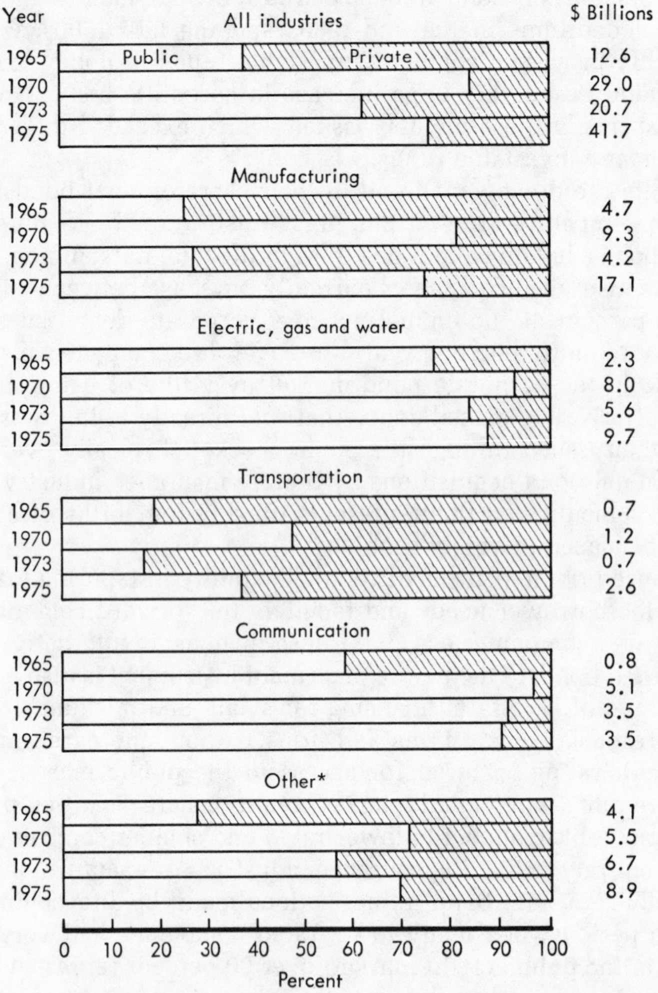

* The other category includes the following industrial classifications: extractive, sales and consumer finance, financial and real estate, commercial, and other.

Source: Securities and Exchange Commission, Office of Economic Research, Branch of Securities Offerings and Studies, April 9, 1976.

dustrial sectors is apparent from these data. It is evident, then, tha through their specialized role as lenders in the private market, life insurance companies have been instrumental in the capital formation process by providing long-term funds to virtually all of the nation's growing industries.

Mortgage loans and real estate

Life companies have traditionally been active participants in the financing and the direct purchase of real estate. Of the major holders of mortgage debt, life companies rank third behind savings and loan associations and commercial banks. In addition, life companies were pioneers in the construction of large-scale apartment complexes under their ownership and have encouraged the building and financing of a variety of real estate projects by purchasing them from developers and leasing them back for management. In recent years, the direct owner-ship of income-producing commercial and industrial properties and the development of real estate have taken on much greater signifi-cance, largely in response to the desire for a better measure of pro-tection against inflation.

The distribution of mortgage debt held by life companies has altered considerably over time. Net new home mortgage financing (one–four-family housing), after growing strongly during the 1950s declined and became negative after 1966, when loan repayments began to exceed new investments and the level of industry holdings fell. This reduced participation was due to a shift in the interest rate structure in which a host of factors converged to make yields on home mortgages in-creasingly less attractive than those on multifamily and nonresiden-tial mortgages and corporate bonds.

Despite a de-emphasis of residential mortgage lending in recent years, the life insurance industry has made a significant effort to meet the serious problems of housing in inner-city areas. In 1967 the life industry set up the Urban Investment Program, which committed $1 billion to assist in financing housing and creating jobs for low-income families in inner-city neighborhoods. In 1969 an additional $1 billion was made available, and by 1972 the program had essentially accom-plished its objectives. In the end, total life company investments pro-duced some 116,000 housing units, 60 day-care centers, and 40 nursing homes. In addition, it is estimated that 40,000 to 50,000 jobs were cre-ated or retained in the cities.[6]

Unlike the downward trend in its share of residential mortgage financing, the life company share of total commercial and industrial mortgages has remained at a nearly constant 30 percent of the total outstanding, as shown in Chart 2. The forward commitment process used by insurers has been an integral part of this activity because of the long time span involved in planning and constructing commercial properties. Indeed, such commitments for permanent mortgage financing are generally a prerequisite for the short-term financing of commercial and residential construction. Life insurance companies have become active in residential construction, in the direct ownership of income-producing properties, and in real estate development through joint ventures, subsidiaries, and affiliated companies. At the end of 1975 life company holdings of directly owned real estate amounted to $9.6 billion, and their investments in this area have increased an average 8.8 percent annually since 1970. Of the 1975 figure about 69 percent represented commercial and residential properties, while about 22 percent was accounted for by home and branch office buildings, with the remainder in other types of real estate.

This major participation of life insurance companies in the commercial mortgage and real estate markets has facilitated capital formation by adding to the capacity to produce goods and services. Moreover, life insurers, unlike other types of mortgage lenders, operate in a national market contributing to a flow of mortgage funds to the areas where needs and demands are the greatest.

Common stocks

In recent years, life company equity purchases have demonstrated remarkable growth, especially in contrast to the relatively minor role equities traditionally played in the portfolios of life insurance institutions. The legal restrictions on common stocks held as general account assets were relaxed, beginning in the 1950s. As a result, life companies stepped up their general account purchases as investment policy began to reflect the view that stocks offered a greater total return (capital gains and dividends) than did bonds and mortgages and were a better hedge against inflation—the latter notion recently having lost some of its earlier preeminence. An additional stimulus to equity investment occurred in the early 1960s, when the states began to further liberalize legal restraints on equity holdings by permitting life companies to institute separate accounts for the investment of pension plan assets in common stocks.

Chart 4 shows the rapid growth of equities held in the general and separate accounts of life insurance companies. The data reflect the substantial shift in investment policy since the mid-1950s which increased general account holdings of common stocks before separate account stock acquisitions became significant. Indeed, during the

Chart 4.   Distribution of total life equity holdings between general and separate accounts

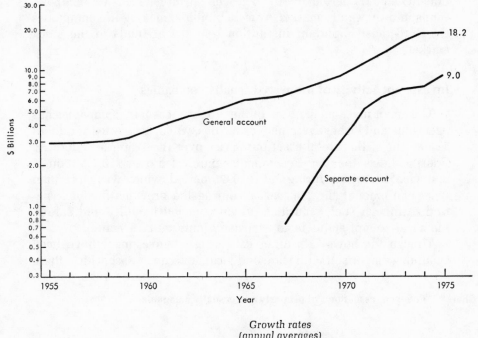

	Growth rates (annual averages)	
	General account	Separate account*
1955–60	4.2%	—
1960–65	10.9	—
1965–70	8.8	65.0%
1970–75	14.9	23.0

* Separate account data begin in 1967.

Common stock holdings are measured at book value, using the level of outstandings in 1953 as a base and adding subsequent annual dollar flows to obtain the level of outstandings in each succeeding year. To calculate the book value of equity holdings in the general account, the ratio of the market value of equities in the general account to the total market value of equities was multiplied by the computed book value of total equity holdings. A similar calculation was made to obtain the book value of separate account equity holdings.

Sources: Division of Research and Statistics, Board of Governors of the Federal Reserve System, *Flow of Funds,* September 1976; American Council of Life Insurance, *Life Insurance Fact Book* (New York: 1976).

1960–65 period the average annual growth in general account equity holdings was 11 percent, more than twice the rate of increase registered in the previous five years. However, the most rapid rate of increase in equity purchases took place when separate accounts gained universal acceptance within the life industry. During the 1970–75 period separate account acquisitions increased by over 23 percent an-

268

nually, as compared with 15 percent for the general account acquisitions. Over this period the average annual infusion of life company funds into the equity markets was $3.0 billion, making life companies the third most important institutional source of funds to the stock market.

Investment activity of property-casualty companies

The major investment outlet of the property-casualty companies has been state and local government securities, which accounted for about 52 percent of their total asset purchases over the 1955–75 period. As Chart 5 shows, the nonlife companies purchased over $16.5 billion of municipal securities during the 1970–75 period, which was more than twice the amount they purchased during the previous five-year period. Although such securities provide needed liquidity and safety, their tax-exempt status is an especially important attraction.

Though the flows into other categories of investment have been small by comparison with state and local government securities, there

Chart 5. Five-year asset flows of property and casualty companies

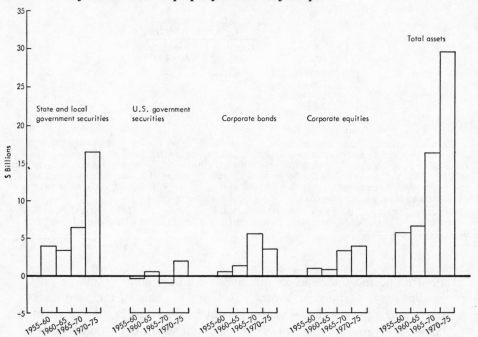

Source: Division of Research and Statistics, Board of Governors of the Federal Reserve System *Flow of Funds,* September 1976.

have been some notable shifts in investment policies over the past 25 years. Since 1965, for example, property-casualty companies have increased their participation in the equity and bond markets, though their flow of funds into corporate bonds was $2.0 billion lower in 1970–75 than in the prior five-year period. Not readily apparent from these data is the current very cautious attitude with regard to common stocks induced by the disastrous experience of 1973–74. While double-digit inflation was contributing to soaring underwriting losses, the accompanying two-year plunge in common stock values was seriously eroding the surplus positions of the property-casualty companies.

In the remaining asset category, property-casualty insurers were net liquidators of federal government securities through 1970, when this trend was reversed. Most of the $2.0 billion increase during the 1970–75 period, however, occurred in 1975, when credit demands by the federal government and the credit agencies it sponsored were the highest in U.S. history.

THE INSURANCE INDUSTRY'S FUTURE ROLE

Looking to the future, insurance companies will continue to make important contributions to capital and job formation through their risk-bearing and financial investment functions. These contributions will occur against a background of continuing innovations in financial security products, marketing techniques, and investment practices, which are too numerous to cover in any detail.

Significant within the risk-bearing role will be a trend toward product design and marketing distribution based on a life cycle concept and/or policyholder account selling on an all-lines basis. Given this approach, the distinctions among life, health, retirement and property-casualty coverages will eventually blur and protection might even conceivably include contingencies not now normally insured. Ideally, the ultimate objective is an insurance product or package designed to provide protection against loss of income or property, regardless of how it is caused, but this is unlikely to be achieved soon. Insurance companies will continue to modify and broaden their activities in the financial security and services area, but the basic features of today's insurance products and marketing systems are likely to remain dominant in the foreseeable fture. One possible exception is health insurance, in which enactment of certain forms of national health insurance plans could cause a radical departure from current insurance practices.

The property-casualty companies' direct role as financial intermediaries in the saving-investment process will continue to be based on the growth of their prepaid premium and loss reserves rather than that of a distinct savings function. On the other hand, a number of important developments involving products will attract savings dollars to life insurance companies.

Individual life insurance products will continue to serve a broad market in meeting the needs of the increasing numbers of families and individuals who are in a financial position to create an estate through life insurance. Life sales will also get an extra boost over the next several years from demographic developments producing a rapid increase in persons in the prime insurance buying ages. Moreover, recent pension reform legislation encourages vast numbers of previously excluded individuals to save through qualified pension products, and the life insurers have introduced flexible individual life insurance and annuity plans designed especially for this growing individual retirement market.

Still, group life insurance and group pensions will continue to account for an increasing share of the total life insurance business. Through their expertise and experience with group arrangements, the life insurance companies are well equipped to encourage and participate in the trend toward collective personal savings and insurance coverage. Appropriate savings and insurance plans can be marketed and administered efficiently on a payroll-related basis and in conjunction with an advanced computer technology that allows extremely flexible options. These plans will also provide expanded markets for the services of the large professional investment staffs of life insurance companies. For example, the separate account innovation now applies to a wide range of investment vehicles, inducing some group pension clients to turn to the industry for discretionary asset management.

In summary, given these developments and many others too numerous to mention, the insurance industry's future contribution to capital and job formation should be significant. The degree to which the industry is successful, however, and the adequacy of the nation's capital formation in total obviously depend on important broad economic policy considerations. We now have more than ample evidence that the U.S. economy, its financial system, and its insurance industry do not function efficiently in periods of high and accelerating rates of inflation or when competition and innovation are blunted by undue government interference in the marketplace.

To be consistent with a high rate of capital and job formation, economic policy must be designed to control inflation and avoid excessive government intervention. Such policy, in turn, requires widespread recognition that encouraging economic growth through private investment and savings is as much a national priority as the more politically popular human concerns of income security, income redistribution, consumer rights, environmental safeguards, and health care and maintenance, which have been the driving forces in the rising share of government in the economy. The inevitable trade-offs that have to be made among these competing priorities will most likely be the final determinants of the adequacy of capital and job formation in meeting America's third-century challenge.

NOTES

1. U.S. Department of Labor, Bureau of Labor Statistics, *Factbook for Estimating the Manpower Needs of Federal Programs,* bulletin 1832 (Washington, D.C., 1975).
2. The Conference Board, *The National Wealth of the United States* (New York: 1976); and U.S. Department of Labor statistics contained in *Employment and Training Report of the President* (Washington, D.C.: 1976).
3. For example, one authority notes that the impact of Social Security on private savings has been neutral because to date the negative impact of Social Security benefits has been offset by the extension of the retirement years, which has forced individuals to save more during their working lives for any given level of desired retirement income. It is concluded that "whereas the forces have just offset one another in the past, it is unlikely that this balance will continue in the future. The extraordinary decline in labor force participation of the aged appears to have slowed, while the pace of benefit increases seems to have accelerated. This means that the net effect of social security in the future may be a serious decline in the savings rate, *all other factors held constant* (emphasis added)." See Alicia Munnel, "The Impact of Social Security on Personal Savings," *National Tax Journal,* vol. 26 (October 1974), p. 553.
4. Life insurers are not able to take full advantage of the tax-exempt feature of state and local securities because of the specialized tax treatment afforded life insurance companies.
5. An expanded treatment of this subject is found in George A. Bishop, *Capital Formation through Life Insurance* (Homewood, Ill.: Richard D. Irwin, 1976).
6. Institute of Life Insurance, Clearinghouse on Corporate Social Responsibility, *A Report on the $2 Billion Urban Investment Program of the Life Insurance Business, 1967–1972* (New York: The Institute, 1973).

Chapter 20

PROMOTING STOCK OWNERSHIP
BY INDIVIDUALS

*Donald T. Regan**

A unique characteristic of U.S. economic life is the widespread ownership of corporate stock, especially by individuals of relatively modest means. This development, so different from European experience, has been in evidence throughout this century, or even before, but its most dramatic growth has come since World War II. Contributing factors include the rapid postwar economic growth and high per capita income; the growing diffusion of wealth among the American people; and the vigorous emergence of publicly owned corporations as a central force in the U.S. economy and society.

Stock ownership—and the opportunity it affords to share in the profitable growth of a successful business enterprise—has proved particularly well suited to the entrepreneurial spirit and social mobility of the American people. Equally important, a corporation's ability to issue securities makes possible the quick mobilization of capital, contributing to the dynamic quality of the economy itself. In many respects, we benefit from a self-reinforcing system. The resources and social characteristics of the United States favor the development of widespread stock ownership, and this in turn encourages further economic betterment for the country.

STOCK OWNERSHIP IN THE UNITED STATES
AND ABROAD

Older industrial countries, by contrast, continue to be characterized by more highly stratified societies and generally less expansive econ-

---

* Chairman and Chief Executive Officer, Merrill Lynch & Co., Inc.

omies. Although the corporate (joint stock) form of business organization became fairly common in Europe in the 17th and 18th centuries, public participation in corporate shares never developed on the U.S. scale. Shares were ordinarily owned only by the more affluent classes. Only recently has the development of a more broadly based middle class—and, no doubt, the example of America—led to the expansion of stockholder rolls abroad.

In the United States, the latest benchmark for the total number of individual shareowners was 25.2 million as of mid-1975.[1] That represented a four-fold increase from the 6.5 million in the first New York Stock Exchange shareowner tally, in 1952. But it was 5.6 million fewer than the record 30.9 million posted in the 1970 census. The latest census represented 11.8 percent of the total U.S. population, compared with only 4.2 percent in 1952, though down from the 15.1 percent of 1970.

The periodic New York Stock Exchange surveys are generally considered the most comprehensive set of statistics available on the U.S. investor population, though their scope is limited. Counted are owners of stocks and mutual funds, but not any other investment vehicles.

Chart 1.   U.S. shareowner population

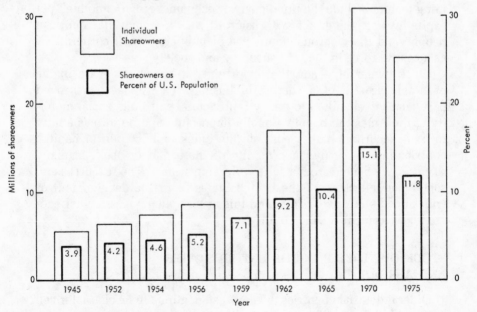

Figure inset in each lower bar is percentage of total U.S. population.

Sources: NYSE censuses for 1952 and 1956–75; NYSE staff estimate for 1954; Federal Reserve Board estimate for 1945.

And, of course, many tens of millions of Americans have a strong but indirect stake in stock investments through pension funds and the like; such indirect interest has expanded tremendously in the past two decades, both because of the great growth of such funds and because of the increased institutional interest in common stock investments.

Observers of the securities industry attributed the decline in stock ownership between 1970 and 1975 to two principal factors: the sharp downturn in most stock prices in the early 70s and the hyperinflation and deep recession which the price slump reflected. There was a particularly severe decline in the number of mutual fund participants. In part this undoubtedly reflected discouragement with the performance of the funds in a severe bear market. But another factor was that many who began specific-purpose mutual fund programs in the 50s and early 60s had now reached the retirement or college years for which they had invested.

Even taking these defections into account, the proportion of Americans who own equities is still much greater than that of most other countries. Although the foreign data are far more sketchy, and such figures as are available are often not strictly comparable with either those of the NYSE or those of other foreign countries, the fundamental difference is unmistakable.[2]

In Britain, for example, the current "best estimate" indicates that 2.5 million individuals own stock, or only 4½ percent of the total population. This figure only includes direct owners, and not investors in mutual funds.

France has an estimated 4.5 million stock investors, some 8.6 percent of the population. However, this does count mutual fund owners; in fact, the great majority of these French investors participate exclusively through mutual funds. Only 1.5 million, or under 3 percent, own stock in individual corporations.

Surprisingly, only some 3.6 million West Germans, or 6.2 percent of the population, own stock, including about 2.5 million direct investors in corporations. The rest of the total is made up of mutual fund owners and employees with stock in their own companies.

The biggest push of all toward popular stockownership has come in Japan. Although, again, the figures are not completely comparable, reports indicate that there are about 18.8 million individual Japanese shareholders. This represents some 14 percent of the population. Thus the amazing postwar development of Japan has made it the one country which matches and possibly exceeds the United States proportion of citizen-stockholders. Or perhaps we should reverse the reasoning and conclude that the wide participation of individual investors at least contributed to Japan's "economic miracle."

THE MAJOR POSTWAR STIMULI TO STOCK
MARKET INVESTMENTS

The rapid growth in stock ownership by individual investors in the United States in the 50s and 60s was triggered in the first instance by the dramatic rise in U.S. economic activity following World War II. The war years of 1942–45 were themselves accompanied by a bull market of no small magnitude. From a low of 92 in 1942, the Dow Jones industrial average moved up almost relentlessly to a high of 212 in 1946, as production boomed and considerable amounts of savings, denied normal spending outlets, were channeled into stocks. A period of indecision followed while industry headed back to a peacetime footing (the dreaded postwar depression never occurred). This proved to be simply the launching pad for a spectacular surge in market activity and prices that carried through the 50s and well into the 60s, peaking at 995.15, within an eyelash of the magical 1,000 on the Dow, in February 1966.

The market's upward momentum emitted vibrations that impelled more and more people to invest in stocks. But there were other basic forces at work as well. Federal securities reform legislation enacted in the early 30s unquestionably helped to reestablish stock ownership as an accepted investment medium for the American public. Equally important was a sustained marketing drive on the part of the securities industry itself.

MAKING THE INDIVIDUAL FEEL WELCOME

Wall Street initiatives to widen individual stock ownership took a number of forms. Even before World War II, Merrill Lynch began its pioneering campaign to "bring Wall Street to Main Street" and to make it easier for the average American to invest, and invest intelligently. Extensive educational efforts were launched, including such booklets and brochures as "How to Invest" and "How to Read a Financial Report."

In the early 50s the New York Stock Exchange began to take on an active role. In 1954 it launched an advertising and promotion campaign on behalf of its membership, built on the theme: "Own Your Share of American Business." This reinforced what was already the start of the American public's lengthy (even if not yet fully perceived) romance with stocks. The program was "devoted to improving the public's appreciation of common stocks and the character and function of the Exchange and its members."[3] In the first year, full-page ads appeared every other week in 532 newspapers serving 43 million readers. Member firms were urged in addition to utilize the "Own Your Share of American Business" theme on their own letterheads, business cards, brochures, and other promotional materials. By the time the campaign ended several years later, any Americans who were unfamiliar with the advantages of share ownership and the basic function of the stock market clearly had not looked at a newspaper.

Members of the securities industry meanwhile moved aggressively so they could deliver investment services to an ever-increasing range of customers in this country. In many cases, firms also established facilities to meet increased interest in U.S. securities among investors abroad. From 1950 to 1965, the Exchange community's period of greatest growth, the number of branch offices of member firms more than doubled, to 3,521, while the number of registered representatives nearly tripled, to 33,800.[4]

INDIVIDUAL VERSUS INSTITUTIONAL MARKET PARTICIPATION

Even before the recent, and quite likely temporary, decline in the number of individual shareholders, during the first half of the 70s, the proportion of New York Stock Exchange trading by individuals had begun to taper off. The reason, of course, was that the market activity of institutional investors grew so swiftly. Specifically, institutional investment activity rose from 31 percent of public trading volume in 1963 to 57 percent in early 1976. Conversely, the individual share declined from 69 percent to 43 percent. However, the total volume of trading grew tremendously in those years. Consequently, in absolute terms, individual activity accounted for about 6.5 million daily shares in 1963 but almost three times as much, 18.8 million shares, in the 1976 period.[5] Individual trading, in other words, has been accounting for a smaller slice of a much bigger pie—so the net result has been a far larger piece.

How significant is the 18 percent drop in individual shareholders chronicled in the latest NYSE census? Is it an aberration or a portent of the future? Would it have occurred if the surveyed period had not coincided with a combination of unusually adverse circumstances— bear market, oil upheaval, double-digit inflation, deep recession? Although some storm factors remain—particularly the discouraging tax treatment of investors—the general atmosphere has cleared. So it would at the very least be premature to conclude that we have been witnessing the start of a long-term trend toward fewer shareowners.

Economic recovery is under way; many corporations have strengthened their balance sheets and have improved yields on their outstand-

Chart 2. Individual participation in the stock market

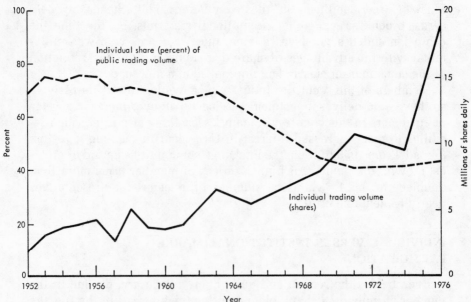

Source: New York Stock Exchange, *Public Transaction Study, 1976.* Based on shares bought and sold on the NYSE.

ing shares through higher dividends. Individual investors are not un-aware of these developments, and some who have been on the sidelines have begun to edge back into the marketplace.

THE IMPORTANCE OF THE INDIVIDUAL

That, it may be said, is fine for brokers. But from the standpoint of the American economy, does it really matter whether individuals re-main in the market? All the evidence says yes. In short, the importance of the *individual's* role in the capital-raising mechanism cannot be un-derestimated. Individuals still hold by far the largest proportion of outstanding stock.[6] And direct investments by individuals contribute billions in new capital each year and provide liquidity for the entire market. What is often ignored is that you cannot induce new capital investment simply by making a new securities issue more attractive. It is just as important for capital-raising to have a readily accessible (and fairly taxed) secondary market. The reason is simple. For inves-tors to be willing to purchase newly issued shares, they must be secure in the knowledge that they can dispose of those shares at a competitive price at some future time. It is this liquidity, provided through the continuous auction process on the trading floor of the exchanges, that frees up much of the capital for still newer investment.

Investment institutions as a group represent a challenge to the marketplace, and to the securities firms servicing them. This reflects the usually more active operations of institutions and size of the assets they own. Still, the investment pools managed by institutions are basically oriented toward the individual in the sense that many millions of people (employees, fund shareholders, policyholders, and others) are the beneficial owners of the assets.

NON-STOCK INVESTMENTS

The individual investor's involvement in the capital-raising process is scarcely confined only to stocks. This has been especially evident during and since the bear markets following 1968, which caused individuals to be increasingly attracted by the safety-of-principal feature and relatively high yields of fixed-income securities. Progressive securities firms have catered to these investor interests by establishing or expanding facilities for bond research and trading, and even more important, by developing new instruments to make it easier for the individual investor to participate.

As recently as 1968, some 45 percent of the total financial assets of individuals (actually the Federal Reserve's "household sector," which also includes personal trusts and nonprofit organizations) consisted of corporate equities; by 1976, equities represented only 26 percent of their holdings (see Chart 3). During the same period, the household group's holdings of corporate and foreign bonds increased from less than 1 percent to 2.6 percent of total financial assets. Perhaps even more indicative of the increased interest of individuals in bonds, in 1968 these bond investments represented only a 9 percent share of their total debt and credit instrument holdings, whereas by 1976 this ratio had jumped to 20 percent.

A particularly significant new instrument is the "unit trust," a packaged portfolio made up of either tax-exempt municipal bonds or corporate bonds or in some cases preferred stocks. These trusts enable the investor, through just a $1,000 unit, to share in an income-yielding investment which otherwise would usually be available only in lots of $10,000 to $100,000 or more; furthermore, the unit trust investors get the advantages of risk-spreading diversification and monthly interest checks. And while these trusts are not suited for use as trading

Chart 3. Equities in relation to other financial holdings

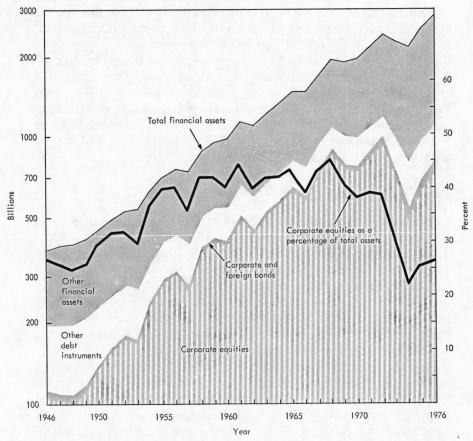

Includes households, personal trusts, and nonprofit organization; 1976 figures preliminary
Source: Board of Governors of the Federal Reserve System, flow of funds accounts.

vehicles, secondary markets are maintained in them so that the investors can readily get their funds out again when they want to—a vitally important protective factor for the small investor.

The burgeoning of the unit trusts serves to illustrate two key characteristics of the securities industry. First, it illustrates the industry's inherent flexibility, adaptability, and—to the surprise of those who consider the industry irretrievably stodgy—creativity, which brings quick response to changing investor needs and styles.

And second, it illustrates the industry's recognition that a successful market system must foster maximum liquidity. It's this reassuring knowledge that you can always get out again that gives the investor the confidence to purchase newly issued securities—or, as in the case of unit trusts, securities packages.

LIQUIDITY ESSENTIAL TO MAKE INVESTMENTS FLOW

It bears reemphasizing. Again and again, the question is put: Granted that we need more investors of all types to provide corporations with additional funds, what has that to do with making it easier or more attractive for investors to trade in already outstanding securities? And the answer remains: It has everything to do with successful new capital-raising—you won't want to commit new funds unless you have confidence that you can get out again through a fair and orderly market —and also unless you have confidence that the tax collector won't turn your risk into an impossible odds proposition.

That's why we must constantly seek to improve the efficiency of the securities markets. The United States already has the best and most efficient markets in the world. But this is no excuse for standing pat; we must work to make them better yet, and to meet the expanding needs of a dynamic economy.

MAKING THE BEST MARKET BETTER

Fundamentally, all investors should be able to get the best possible price (whether they buy or sell), the most efficient and economical execution of their orders, and effective safeguards against manipulation, deceit, and unfair dealings. And clearly, an effective market must be a truly competitive one. Major strides toward fuller competition were taken with the abolition of fixed commission rates and the elimination of the required imposition of an odd-lot differential on trades of less than 100 shares.

Now we are moving toward a National Market System, which should provide the best possible service for investors through competing market makers and competing markets. As in all major developments, there is bitter argument about how to implement such a system and what it should do—and there are those who still hope that the entire idea will just quietly go away. But a coordinated National Market System is inevitable. And whatever its details, we feel that it must include a method whereby all investors, small or large, individual or institutional, will be able to have their order executed at the most favorable price available on any market anywhere in the system. The securities companies handling the order for the customer may act as brokers (that is, agents) or dealers (buying or selling out of their own inventory or for their own account). But it will in essence be a true "auction" market, because the buying customer will get the stock at the lowest price at which anyone is willing to offer it. Likewise, the seller will receive the highest price anyone is willing to bid.

In such a market the continuous interaction of orders—large and small—will nurture maximum liquidity and encourage investment to make America's dynamic brand of capitalism work.

FAITH IN A SOUND ECONOMY IS A MAJOR INVESTMENT INCENTIVE

There are, of course, other underlying requisites if we are to encourage the widest possible stock ownership by individuals. Former SEC Commissioner A. A. Sommer, Jr., has summed the matter up cogently: "If people are to undertake the risks of equity investments they must have a basic confidence in the future of the economy, believe there is a reasonable prospect of gain commensurate with the risk, and [possess] a conviction that the success of their investment [in the present environment] is not likely to be nullified by the forces of inflation."[7]

Confidence in the economy presupposes, of course, a pattern of continued long-term economic growth and political stability. It also assumes governmental policies to support, not restrain, these objectives. One important national priority should be to encourage some shifts toward increased savings and investments, though this entails forgoing some immediate consumption. Within a short time, the "multiplier effect" would increase both income and consumer spending. Thus, the real gain in capital investment would spur productivity growth, high employment, and environmental improvement. The added investment outlays, moreover, would go a long way toward combating economic instability and inflation.

ALLEVIATING TAX DISCOURAGEMENTS

Furthering these objectives calls for significant federal tax reforms. A major shortcoming of the present system centers on inequities in the capital gains tax; this tax acts as a brake on investment because upon disposing of securities, investors are taxed heavily on any gains —even those which largely reflect inflation—but are allowed only very limited relief in case of losses. Investors are penalized severely when they simply act to switch investments as their needs change.

The double taxation of corporate dividends similarly continues to be inequitable and unsettling. A corporation's interest payments on debt are clearly an unavoidable cost of carrying on the business and hence a deductible expense. But dividends—though from a practical *standpoint just as much an essential business cost—must be paid from already-taxed income.* This inevitably skews the corporate balance sheet toward a higher ratio of debt versus equity than is desirable for national fiscal soundness or than would exist if corporations could treat all capital costs—whether debt or equity—equally. And from the investor's standpoint, having the return on the investment taxed twice obviously means that the attractiveness of the investment has been reduced.

The Tax Reform Act of 1976 provided some minor benefits, especially through somewhat more liberal capital loss provisions. But it also created major new handicaps for the investor through severe capital gains treatment. *The central problem remains: the need for realistic tax reform to reduce the present bias against savings and capital accumulation.*

Here, then, are the paving blocks for the road to increased individual participation in the securities markets—stable economic, social, and political conditions; fairer tax treatment of investors and investments; and a more competitive, efficient, and credible market system. To achieve these conditions will require a commitment to long-term objectives as well as to the challenges that are closer at hand.

ECONOMICALLY EDUCATED CITIZENS

One key longer range effort must be to educate everyone in our society as to how the economy works and how investing fits into the process. A meaningful program of economic education must begin in the schools. Primary-grade children acting out real-life situations, such as going to the store or earning money at simple chores, can begin to learn the fundamentals of what makes the economy tick—notably the role of profits in allocating resources in a free enterprise system and, most important, how profits in turn encourage investments which help create jobs and prompt further economic growth. The programs should become more extensive and sophisticated as the students advance on the educational scale.

At the same time opportunities for economic education must be made available to the adult public, so that producers in society can better understand the role and workings of the securities markets and how various kinds of investments help individuals meet differing investment needs and objectives.

On a more pragmatic level, investors should be made aware of how the ready availability of specific investment information about industries and individual companies can assist them in making intelligent decisions in buying and selling securities.

Basically these varied efforts have a common goal—to carve out a more hospitable environment in which the individual investor of moderate means can find an effective position in the marketplace.

It is important to note that despite the sharp and often painful fluctuations of the stock market, conservative investment programs stressing "total return" (that is, a combination of dividend receipts and gains from market appreciation) have proved rewarding over the years. As illustrated in Chart 4, which uses the Standard & Poor's 500-stock index as an example, dividends for this large stock group have increased almost uninterruptedly over the years. Earnings (which, over the long run, form the major base for stock valuation) have also shown strong growth over the years. And as a measure of investment growth, if the dividends were reinvested annually, the 500-stock group would have shown a 15-fold increase in value in this 24-year period.

INVITING GREATER INVESTOR PARTICIPATION

Many securities firms have devised means of encouraging wider participation by individual investors through a simplified, low-cost investment service. An example of such an approach is Merrill Lynch's "Sharebuilder Plan." Programs such as these enable individuals to make a series of small periodic investments, often $50 a month or less, as well as isolated "one-time" purchases. The operating principle underlying such plans is that streamlined processing—with orders filled at the opening price the business day after they are received—makes it possible to charge low rates for the service.

Changes in Wall Street rules also made it possible for Merrill Lynch and other firms to initiate odd-lot programs which enabled investors to avoid the 12½ cents a share odd-lot differential that had traditionally been charged on purchases and sales of less than 100 shares.

There are a number of other methods of encouraging investment by investors of modest means. In particular, programs that can be administered on a group basis can benefit from economies of scale which are ordinarily shared with the consumers of the services. These economies of scale include dividend reinvestment programs, which are normally administered by financial institutions on behalf of corporations, and employee stock purchase programs. The latter programs are of two kinds: the conventional type, usually involving payroll deductions, and the more recent, federally sanctioned, company-sponsored "Employee Stock Ownership Plans" (ESOPs), whereby stock allocated in trust to employees by the company can be funded by tax-aided borrowings. Other group-type services provided individuals by invest-

Chart 4. Investment return and the market (based on Standard & Poor's 500-stock index)

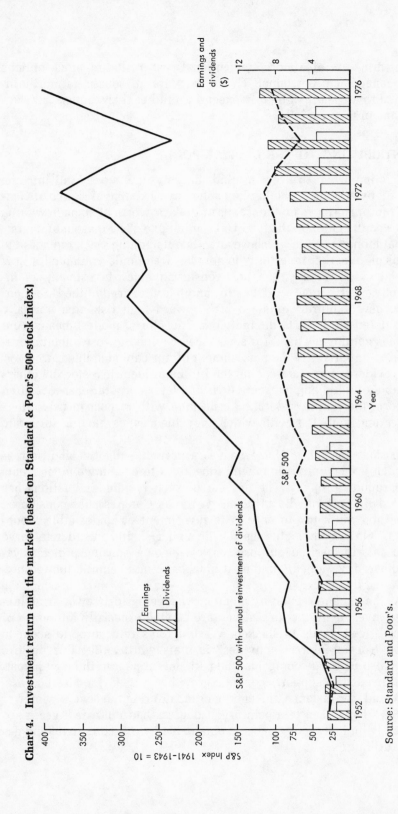

Source: Standard and Poor's.

ment firms are of a more conventional cast, including stock options for management personnel. These plans are, of course, primarily intended to attract high-quality executives rather than to raise substantial amounts of capital.

CONTRIBUTING TO THE CAPITAL POOL

It is important to keep in mind that any new money put into the market by anyone—whether he or she buys a couple of shares of General Motors or picks up thousands of dollars' worth of some new issue —is a contribution to the total U.S. capital pool. The reason, of course, is that money used to purchase already outstanding stock replaces the funds of an earlier investor who now has free funds available for new investment. Thus, even the most conservative new investment can indirectly contribute toward meeting another vital need of the U.S. economy: new venture capital—a high reward–high risk area normally considered off limits to the individual investor of modest means. And there is continuous need for such "seed capital" to foster the innovations so important to the nourishment of our capitalist system.

Providers of venture-capital tend to be affluent investors or others capable of assuming substantial risks. Major corporations, too, often perform the role of risk-taker, especially with respect to new enterprises and activities with which they themselves have a corporate affiliation.

In some instances, Uncle Sam is a partner—albeit a silent one— through tax law provisions with incentives to encourage investments in particular projects. The number of such tax-aided situations has been dwindling rapidly in recent years, as Congress has considered more and more tax incentives to investment as undesirable "loopholes." Only a few activities remain under shelter in order to serve such socially desired purposes as low-income housing projects; yet even here investors are finding it tougher going to extract limited tax-sheltered income.

As the tax and regulatory mood moves increasingly away from tax-aided investment, the flow of venture capital, especially into areas of special need, tends to slacken. Washington's reluctance to seem to favor "special-interest activities" is praiseworthy. But this posture must also be balanced against the national interest in the new investment needed to support economic growth.

Would, for instance, the energy crunch during the severe winter of 1976–77 have been less painful if Congress had not a few years ago severely limited the tax benefits obtainable by investors in oil and gas well drilling?

Tax incentives, to be sure, are a privilege under law and should be subject to continuous governmental reappraisal and review. And undoubtedly, except for some special situations which require unusual help, the economy and the nation would be best served not by trying to pick and choose areas where investment capital gets a tax welcome, but by simply making it more attractive to invest in general. *The real tax loopholes are those which make it so unattractive to invest that investors don't bother to put their money to work—and so there's no tax to collect on profits or on the income from the jobs that would have been created by investment. Those are the tax-swallowing loopholes that our citizens simply can't afford.*

Instead, let us remember that, as noted at the outset of this chapter, widening stock ownership by individuals has long been a hallmark of the American way of life and has added a solid dimension to U.S. democratic ideals. This widespread ownership of "the means of production" has not only fueled the enormous growth of the American economy, but has significantly contributed to the stability and health of U.S. society at large.

That's why we must all bend every effort to encourage individual investment as an invitation to further economic and national growth in our nation's third century.

NOTES

1. New York Stock Exchange, *Shareownership—1975,* the seventh shareownership census, released December 9, 1975.
2. Foreign data, obtained privately from local sources, usually represent informed estimates. Also, the data for any one country are often not directly comparable to those for the others.

    The British estimates were obtained from the statistical unit of the London Stock Exchange, which stresses that no hard data are available. The estimates exclude mutual funds as well as indirect holdings through pension trusts and the like; the latter are, of course, also excluded from the U.S. study.

    The French report indicates that two thirds of estimated stock investors participate solely through mutual funds, unit trusts, and so on. The mutual fund and unit trust sector is believed to be so large because it includes employee profit-sharing funds, which are usually invested in local mutual fund shares.

    The West German estimates include 2.5 million holders of shares in various corporations; 900,000 participants in investment companies; and 500,000 who hold so-called Belegschaftsactien (job stocks) in the companies they work for. Since the total German investor population is figured at 3.6 million, there is probably some overlap among the three subcategories.

    The Japanese data were obtained from the Japan Stock Dealers Association, which says that the most recent figures are for December 1975.

    Some earlier estimates and comments on foreign stock ownership may be found in Chase Manhattan Bank, *Listing on European Stock Exchanges* (New York: 1967).

3. G. Keith Funston, president, *Letter to Members of the New York Stock Exchange,* February 26, 1954.
4. New York Stock Exchange, *1976 Fact Book,* p. 82.
5. New York Stock Exchange, *Public Transaction Study, 1976.*
6. The New York Stock Exchange has made periodic estimates of the total holdings of listed stocks by major institutions, including insurance companies, mutual funds, pension funds, and nonprofit institutions. The holdings of these institutions for the 1973–75 period consistently averaged around 32 percent of the total market value of all Exchange-listed stocks (up from 23 percent in 1965 and 15 percent in 1949). However, the Exchange notes that it has not been able to estimate the holdings of a number of institutional categories, including bank-administered personal trusts and foreign institutions, and concludes that total institutional holdings would probably come close to half of the total NYSE market value.
7. A. A. Sommer, Jr., former SEC Commissioner, *Can the SEC Help the Capital Crunch?* address delivered at National Investor Relations Institute, Washington, D.C., September 29, 1975.

Chapter 21

TAX REFORMS REQUIRED FOR CAPITAL AND JOB FORMATION

*William E. Simon**

There is no subject more central to our hopes for the future than our ability and our willingness to meet the capital investment needs of coming years. Those needs are impressively large, and they will demand a full-scale effort. The record shows that:

■ During the 1960s and 1970s the United States has had the worst record of capital investment among the major industrialized nations of the Free World.

■ Correspondingly, our records of productivity growth and overall economic growth during this period were also among the lowest of the major industrialized nations.

■ As other nations have channeled relatively more of their resources into capital investment and have acquired more modern plant and equipment, they have eroded our competitive edge in world markets.

■ Our record on capital investments reflects the heavy emphasis we are placing on personal consumption and government spending as opposed to savings and private capital formation.

■ Our record also reflects a long-term decline in corporate profits since the mid-1960s.

■ Although the U.S. economy remains sufficiently large and dynamic to overcome the sluggish investment record of recent years, our future economic growth will be tied much more directly to the adequacy of our capital investments.

---

* Secretary of the Treasury, 1972–77.

- Estimates of future needs vary, but it is clear that in coming years we will have to devote more of our national resources to capital investment than we have in the recent past.
- It is an economic fact of life that increased productivity is the only way to increase our standard of living. For the sake of future economic growth—jobs, real income, and reasonable price stability—the inescapable conclusion is that government policies must become more supportive of capital investment. We must make a fundamental shift in our domestic policies away from continued growth in personal consumption and government spending and toward greater savings, capital formation, and investment.

Some analysts have concluded that it will not be possible to meet our future capital investment needs. I disagree. I firmly believe that we are capable of achieving our basic investment goals, but I also believe that these goals represent one of the most formidable economic challenges of the decade ahead.

GOVERNMENT TAX POLICIES

Although our economy is capable of financing its large private capital investment requirements, our success in meeting those requirements is heavily dependent upon the effects of government policies. Federal tax policies affect capital investment decisions by determining the aftertax earnings available for investment and by establishing incentives or disincentives for future investment.

Table 1 shows that our tax system—like any arrangement that relies on income taxes—is biased against savings, the obvious prerequisite for future investment. Tax changes will increase savings only to the extent that they remove the disincentives created by existing taxes. Thus, the fundamental element in any tax proposal to increase saving, is a net reduction in the tax on the income from savings. There are different mechanisms for achieving that net reduction, and they have different advantages and disadvantages. *But the active ingredient is the final net reduction, and there is no way to escape that fact.*

I have long been a proponent of comprehensive reform of the federal tax system. Tax reform that will reduce the bias against savings and consequently stimulate capital formation would logically build upon those measures of the present law that are conducive to capital formation.

1. The investment tax credit (ITC). Empirical studies indicate that the amount of investment in machinery and equipment has in-

Table 1. Comparison of general tax revenue sources, 1971

Tax revenue by type	United States Value ($ millions)	Percent of total	France Value (francs millions)	Percent of total	Germany Value (DM millions)	Percent of total	United Kingdom Value (pounds millions)	Percent of total	Canada Value (C$ millions)	Percent of total	Japan Value (yen millions)	Percent of total
Corporate income and profit*	30,234	10.4	18,747	5.8	11,655	4.5	1,558	7.8	3,080	10.2	2,977	18.8
Household income and profit*	98,176	33.6	32,492	10.1	70,295	26.9	6,668	33.2	10,221	33.9	3,802	24.0
Consumption taxes†	52,698	18.1	112,139	34.8	73,425	28.1	5,340	26.6	8,660	28.7	3,289	20.7
Social security contributions	60,286	20.7	134,802	41.9	88,430	33.8	2,828	14.1	2,463	8.2	3,174	20.0
Other taxes	50,301	17.2	23,916	7.4	17,655	6.7	3,685	18.3	5,710	19.0	2,612	16.5
Total	291,695	100.0	322,096	100.0	261,460	100.0	20,079	100.0	30,134	100.0	15,854	100.0

Comparison excluding social security distributions

Tax revenue by type	United States Value ($ millions)	Percent of total	France Value (francs millions)	Percent of total	Germany Value (DM millions)	Percent of total	United Kingdom Value (pounds millions)	Percent of total	Canada Value (C$ millions)	Percent of total	Japan Value (yen millions)	Percent of total
Corporate income and profit*		13.1		10.0		6.8		9.0		11.1		23.5
Household income and profit*		42.4		17.3		40.6		38.6		37.0		30.0
Consumption taxes†		22.8		59.9		42.4		31.0		31.3		25.9
Other taxes		21.7		12.8		10.2		21.4		20.6		20.6
Total	231,409	100.0	187,294	100.0	173,030	100.0	17,251	100.0	27,671	100.0	12,660	100.0

* Includes capital gains.

† Defined as taxes levied on transactions in goods and services on the basis of such intrinsic characteristics as value, weight, strength, and so on. The source document provides further elaboration concerning tax category definitions.

Source: Organization for Economic Cooperation and Development, Revenue statistics of OECD member countries, 1965–71.

creased when ITC has been in effect and has declined when ITC was suspended or repealed. To realize the full potential of ITC in stimulating capital investment it should be increased to 12 percent and made a permanent feature of the tax law.

2. Depreciation allowances. The amount of capital recovery charges permitted for tax purposes strongly influences the aftertax earnings available for private investment. In the past 20 years great strides have been made in quickening the pace of capital recovery through the enactment of tax depreciation provisions, such as accelerated depreciation, the asset guideline lives system, and the asset depreciation range (ADR) system.

The figures summarized in Chart 1 indicate that American firms using both ADR and ITC can recover only 55 percent of the value of new investments during the first three years. By comparison a greater capital recovery rate is permitted by some of our major international trading partners, such as Canada (100 percent), France (90.3 percent),

Chart 1. Capital recovery in the first three years: Major international trading partners

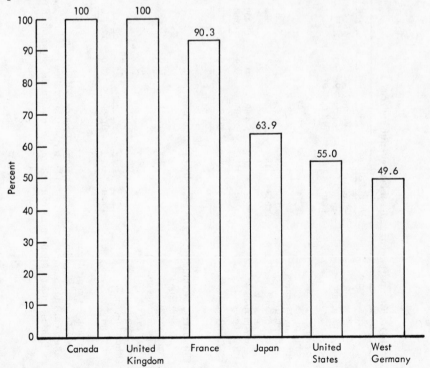

Source: Arthur Andersen & Company.

and Japan (63.9 percent). Although the U.S. position becomes more comparable by the seventh year, further liberalization, fervently desired by many business groups, is a legitimate consideration that should be part of ongoing general tax reform analysis. A larger point to be considered in this context is the impact of inflation on capital recovery. The purpose of depreciation is to provide for the timely recovery of capital invested in plant assets. But in an inflationary environment, depreciation allowances based on original cost do not recover the actual economic cost of plant and equipment being consumed in current production, and foster erosion of the capital base.

3. Corporate income tax rate.   Since 1950 the corporate income tax rate has vacillated slightly above or below the 50 percent level. In 1975 the corporate surtax exemption was doubled to $50,000 and the "normal" tax rate was reduced from 22 percent to 20 percent on the first $25,000 of corporate earnings. Those changes, though temporary, nonetheless provided welcome relief to small business. However, they had little impact on the great bulk of corporate income which is subject to the corporate surtax.

AN INNOVATIVE PROPOSAL FOR INCREASING SAVING AND INVESTMENT

The most important step our nation can take to achieve greater savings through the tax system is to move toward elimination of the double tax which is now imposed on income from assets used in the corporate form of business. Integration of the individual and corporate income tax structure ought to be included as part of a federal tax reform program that: (1) would not subvert the progressivity of our income tax system; (2) would not create increases in budget deficits subtracting from the pool of private savings even as tax measures are causing additions to it; and (3) would encourage greater savings by individual taxpayers, and in particular, would broaden the ownership of stocks by middle- and lower-income persons.

Under our present system of taxation, income earned by corporations is taxed twice: first to the corporation and then again to the shareholder, if and when it is distributed as a dividend or realized on the sale of stock. The existence of the two-tier tax has a number of perverse results:

1. It creates double taxation, which is inherently inequitable when other kinds of income are taxed only once.

2. It slows the flow of savings into new corporate equity investments because those savings will have to earn a higher level of pretax income in order to produce the required return. This causes an

efficiency loss for everyone. It erects an extra cost barrier for consumers because the prices they pay for the goods the corporation produces must be high enough to cover two taxes rather than one.

3. It creates a systematic bias against lower-bracket taxpayers owning corporate stock. This seems generally undesirable both economically and socially. West Germany has a system which partially eliminates the two-tier tax, and it is giving serious consideration to its complete elimination. The bias against low-income shareowners is illustrated in Table 2.

Table 2. Taxation of $100 of corporate income under present law: 100 percent dividend payout

1.	Shareowner's marginal tax rate	14%	32%	70%
2.	Corporate income	$100	$100	$100
3.	Corporate tax	48	48	48
4.	Corporate aftertax income	52	52	52
5.	Dividend	52	52	52
6.	Retained earnings	0	0	0
7.	Shareowner's tax on dividend	7.28	16.64	36.40
8.	Total tax on corporate income (line 3 + line 7)	55.28	64.64	84.40
9.	Effective tax rate (line 8 ÷ line 2)	55.3%	64.6%	84.4%
10.	Ratio of effective tax rate to individual marginal rate (line 9 : line 1)	4:1	2:1	1.2:1

4. The double tax on corporate profits applies only to the income attributable to equity investment. Corporations must earn enough gross income to cover the interest payments made to compensate bondholders and other creditors for the savings which they have supplied. But interest payments are deductible corporate expenses and thus are not included in the net income which is taxable to the corporation. The fact that interest income on debt is taxed only once, whereas income in equity investment is taxed twice, creates a very heavy bias toward debt financing. Thus, the double corporate tax has contributed to the steep and dangerous increase in debt ratios in recent years. But, as is quite universally agreed, a high debt ratio restricts a company's ability to attract new capital—essential for financing new jobs and economic growth.

5. It creates a market bias against stocks with high-percent dividend payouts—the stocks which have traditionally appealed to investors of modest means. So long as earnings are retained, that is not paid out by

the company, the second tax is avoided. If the stock of such a company is ultimately sold, the sales price will be greater because of the rein-vested earnings (unless those earnings have been unwisely invested by the corporation), but that tax is imposed at half rates, and a stock-holder may avoid it entirely if the asset is held until his or her death. Thus, the stocks of utilities supplying life's basic necessities, such as water, gas, electricity, and telephones, which have traditionally relied on high dividend payouts, are placed at a substantial disadvantage. This stems from the double tax imposed on their income (corporate tax and ordinary income tax on dividends), which is greater than the double tax on companies which do not distribute earnings (corporate tax and capital gains tax or no tax).

6. It places a heavy penalty on corporate decisions to distribute earnings to shareowners as dividends. In an ideal, free market, the tax system would be neutral with respect to the retention or distribution of corporate earnings. Corporation managers would retain earnings if they could use them productively. But stockholders would call for larger distributions when it appeared that the money could be invested for a better return in some other company or enterprise. Thus, capital markets would be generally more competitive. The current tax penalty on paying out earnings puts corporate managers under great pressure to do almost anything productive with retained earnings rather than pay them out. The double corporate tax thus "locks in" corporate capital and keeps it out of the capital markets where it is most needed.

Mechanisms to remove the double tax

For many years our system of imposing a double tax on corporate profits has been referred to as the "classical" system of corporate tax-ation. So long as tax rates at the corporate level remained relatively low, the system did not create undue mischief. In the United States, the corporate tax rate was less than 15 percent as late as 1935; it rose to 40 percent during World War II, dropped back to 38 percent in the last of the 1940s, and rose again to 52 percent during the Korean War. The current 48 percent rate was enacted in 1965. Thus, basically, it was only as recently as the Korean War in the early 1950s that corporate rates reached their present high levels. Similarly, corporate rates have been rising in other countries, but not so fast as in the United States. Today, virtually all of our major trading partners have a system which eliminates much of the double tax. Such systems are in effect in Canada, the United Kingdom, France, West Germany, Belgium, Italy, Japan, and Iran. The European Economic Community has adopted a resolution urging all of its members to adopt such systems and is at present engaged in an effort to promote greater uniformity of existing systems and to harmonize the differences that remain.

The existing systems all operate with one of two basic mechanisms: a stockholder credit or a dividend deduction (including its variant, the "split rate" system). Under both mechanisms, taxes are imposed at both the corporate and the individual level. However, an adjustment to prevent doubling up is made at the time the income is distributed to shareowners. It would be theoretically possible to tax all earnings initially and directly to the ultimate owners, the stockholders, regardless of whether or not the earnings were distributed. However desirable such a system might be theoretically, it would present practical problems, and although Canada considered such a system, no country has, in fact, adopted one.

The dividend deduction method

Under the dividend deduction method (Table 3), the corporation is allowed a deduction for all or part of any dividend distributions which it makes. The deduction, in effect, reverses the tax which the corporation previously paid on such income. Assume, for example, that a corporation earned $100 and is subject to a corporate tax rate of 48 percent. If it pays a dividend of $100, a full deduction will completely eliminate taxable income. Stockholders will pay tax on the $100 dis-

Table 3. Dividend deduction system

		Dividend deduction	
	Present law	100 percent payout	60 percent payout
Corporate level			
1. Net income	$100	$100	$100
2. Dividend	52	100	60
3. Dividend deduction	—	100	60
4. Taxable income	100	0	40
5. Tax (48 percent)	48	0	19.20
6. Retained earnings	0	0	20.80
Individual level			
7. Dividend	52	100	60
8. Tax (30 percent)	15.60	30	18
9. Total tax	63.60	30	37.20
Effective rate (9 ÷ 1)	63.6%	30%	37.2

tributed, but the corporation, having distributed everything, will pay
no tax. If the corporation distributes $60, it will pay tax on $40, that is,
on the earnings not distributed. The stockholders will pay tax on the
$60 which is distributed. Thus, whether the tax reduction dollars ac-
tually end up in the hands of the corporation or its shareholders will
depend importantly upon the corporation's need for new capital spending for growth and plant modernization.

The stockholder credit method

Under the stockholder credit method (Table 4), the corporation gets
no deduction, but the shareholder is given a credit to compensate for
the tax which the corporation has already paid. Taking the same corporation as an example, it earns $100, pays a $48 tax, and has $52 left. If
the entire $52 is distributed, the stockholder is treated as if he had
originally received the same amount of gross income as the corporation, that is, $100, and is given a credit for the tax the corporation has
already paid, that is, $48. If that $52 is distributed to the shareholder,
he "grosses it up" by the amount of tax attributable to the $52 he re-
ceived, that is, by $48. This produces a "grossed-up" amount equal to
the gross income which was earned by the corporation. He then reports that $100 in his income and is allowed a credit for the $48 which
the corporation paid. If he is in a 50 percent tax bracket, he will have a

Table 4. Stockholder credit system

	Present law		Stockholder credit	
Corporate level				
1. Net income	$100		$100	
2. Tax	48		48	
3. Dividend	52		52	
4. Retained earnings	0		0	
	50 percent bracket	20 percent bracket	50 percent bracket	20 percent bracket
Individual level				
5. Dividend	52	52	52	52
6. Gross-up (line 2 above)	—	—	48	48
7. Taxable income	52	52	100	100
8. Tax before credit	26	10.40	50	20
9. Credit (line 2 above)	—	—	48	48
10. Tax after credit	26	10.40	2	(28)
11. Total tax (line 2 + line 10)	74	58.40	50	20
Effective rate (line 11 ÷ line 1)	74%	58.4%	50%	20%

gross tax liability of $50, a credit of $48 for the tax paid by the corporation, and a tax bill of $2. On the other hand, if he is in a 20 percent tax bracket, he will have a gross tax liability of $20, the same credit of $48, and will get a refund of the difference, $28.

If the stockholder credit system were instituted, the initial result would be to put all of the cash tax savings in the hands of shareholders, as the corporation would continue to pay corporate tax and the adjustment mechanism is a credit which goes to the shareholders.

You will note that in the case of a total distribution the two systems produce the same result: the corporation has nothing left, and the entire $100 has, in effect, been taxed at the shareholders' rates. With less than total distributions, there are "first instance" differences. In the first instance, the dividend deduction is an adjustment at the corporate level, whereas the stockholder credit is an adjustment at the stockholder level and is reflected in increased cash flow to stockholders. However, by appropriate changes in the levels of dividend declaration, either mechanism can be tailored to produce the same result vis-à-vis the corporation and its shareholders—that is, the same tax benefit can be divided in the same manner between the corporation and its shareholder in either case. Thus, the two systems are economically the same.

The revenue implications of eliminating the double corporate tax

The nation clearly cannot afford to eliminate the double corporate tax completely in any short period of years, for the federal revenue losses would be too great. At 1978 revenue levels, a complete deduction for dividends paid would create a revenue loss of approximately $17 billion. A stockholder credit would produce the same revenue loss of approximately $17 billion if the credit were extended to tax-exempt and foreign stockholders, and approximately $13 billion if the credit were not extended to such stockholders.

Recommended mechanism: A combination of dividend deductions and stockholder credits

I believe that Congress should eliminate the double taxation of income from savings invested in corporate form in a deliberate six-year transition. In this manner the natural growth of the economy (encouraged by the increasing reduction of tax on income from corporate sources) should provide sufficient incremental tax revenue to ameliorate the revenue loss arising from the gradual elimination of the double taxation of corporate income.

The specific mechanism that I favor for the elimination of double taxation is a combination of the dividend deduction and the stockholder credit (see Table 5). This approach has two major advantages:

1. Use of the dividend deduction would create additional cash flow at the corporate level, and help provide the capital business needs for increased spending on new plant and equipment.

2. Use of the stockholder credit mechanism permits flexibility with respect to tax-exempt and foreign stockholders. I do not believe that the stockholder credit should be extended to them. Like other stockholders, however, they will benefit indirectly from the dividend deduction at the corporate level. Thus, the tax burden on income going to such stockholders would be reduced, but would not be totally eliminated. That seems an appropriate way to deal with them, and it significantly reduces the revenue loss. Moreover, bilaterally negotiated tax treaties can and should accommodate the concerns of foreign stockholders.

Table 5.   Half dividend deduction/half stockholder credit

		Present law	Half/half method
Corporate level			
1.	Net income	$100	$100
2.	Dividend	52	68
3.	Dividend deduction	—	34
4.	Taxable income	100	66
5.	Tax	48	31.68
6.	Retained earnings	0	0.32
Individual level			
7.	Dividend	52	68
8.	Gross-up (50 percent of line 7)	—	34
9.	Taxable income	52	102
10.	Tax before credit (30 percent)	15.60	30.60
11.	Credit (line 8 above)	—	34
12.	Tax after credit	15.60	(3.40)
13.	Total tax (line 5 + line 12)	63.60	28.28
	Effective rate (line 13 ÷ line 1)	63.6%	28.3%

Note: As indicated in the text, the combination of a 50 percent dividend deduction and a 50 percent stockholder credit, when combined with a 48 percent corporate tax rate, more than eliminates the double tax. It is recommended that the percentage of dividends deductible be reduced appropriately.

The dividend deduction

Approximately half of the total reduction would be accomplished by a dividend deduction. Thus, ultimately there would be a deduction for roughly 50 percent of the dividends distributed. The reason I say "roughly 50 percent," rather than exactly 50 percent, is that by making it slightly less, it is possible to make the stockholder credit mechanism far simpler for individual stockholders.

This proposal would entail a dividend deduction for the first year at a percentage level which would produce a net reduction of approximately $2.5 billion in corporate tax liabilities for that year. Additional dividend deductions required to bring the total deduction up to approximately 50 percent of dividends distributed would be phased in during the next five years, causing the revenue loss to increase at a rate of about $1.3 billion a year (at 1978 levels).

The stockholder credit

The balance of the double tax would be eliminated by a stockholder credit to be phased in equally over a five-year period. This would cause a revenue loss in each of those years, increasing at the rate of about $0.6 billion a year (at 1978 levels).

The stockholder credit should not be made available to tax-exempt or foreign stockholders (in the absence of tax treaty provision), for giving the credit would completely eliminate the tax on the income accruing to those classes.

The credit mechanism would be extremely simple. The stockholder would "gross-up" his dividend by adding to his taxable income an amount equal to 50 percent of the dividends he receives and would then take a tax credit equal to the gross-up. As a matter of arithmetic, the combination of a 50 percent dividends-paid deduction and a 50 percent gross-up and credit, when combined with a 48 percent corporate rate, would more than eliminate the double tax. One or the other must be adjusted slightly. In terms of tax return simplicity, it is obviously very desirable for tens of millions of shareholders to use a gross-up and credit of 50 percent rather than an odd percentage which requires more complicated arithmetic. Therefore, I recommend that the required compensating adjustment be made by reducing somewhat the percentage of deductible dividends. It is for this reason that I suggested earlier that the dividend deduction might ultimately be for slightly less than 50 percent of the dividend.

Relief for all savers, not just stockholders

It should be strongly emphasized that the elimination of the double tax on corporate income would produce benefits which would be quickly distributed by market forces across the income from all forms of saving and investment. The benefits do not come to rest in the hands of stockholders. This is not a program for big business. It is a program to benefit *all savers*. This is an absolutely fundamental point, and one on which we all have an obligation to educate the public.

The elimination of double taxation of corporate income has major implications for an efficient capital formation process. Several observations should be made.

First, it is erroneous to think of the corporate tax as primarily affecting stockholders. A significant increase in the corporate tax will, in the first instance, significantly affect existing stockholders. But in the longer run, the equalization process will come into play and depositors in savings accounts and other kinds of investors will help bear the economic incidence of the tax. Other investors will benefit similarly by decreases in the corporate tax.

Second, the price charged by corporations to their customers must be adequate to provide funds to cover the two-tier tax and still leave investors with a competitive return. That necessarily means that prices for goods produced by corporations must be relatively higher than prices for goods produced in the noncorporate sector. That, in turn, discourages consumers from purchasing goods produced in the corporate sector, causing them to spend less of their money on such goods than they would if taxes were neutral with respect to different kinds of investment. If the extra tax burden on corporate investment were eliminated, that bias would disappear and there would be a greater demand for corporate goods and services. People would be able to have more of the things they prefer, and the efficiency of our stock of capital would be increased. The real income of the nation would rise significantly, as more desired output was substituted for less desired output. Thus, the double tax is a barrier to the most efficient use of existing capital. Getting more out of the capital we already have is as good as having more capital. In fact it is better, because in order to get more capital we must give up some current consumption, which need not be the case if we are only increasing the efficiency of what we already have.

Third, the existence of the two-tier tax is directly responsible for much of the dangerous growth in debt-equity ratios. If a company wishes to expand, it must consider what goods it can sell and what prices it will be able to charge in order to provide an adequate return on its new investment. To the extent that net expansion is financed with debt, after the costs have been covered, $1 of additional price will provide $1 of return to the investor. In the case of equity, however, the company must charge $2 to provide $1 of return. With that kind of a tax premium on debt as compared with equity, the pressure for greater debt is tremendous.

Benefits of the proposed change

The elimination of double taxation of corporate income would provide major national economic benefits.

1. The net tax reductions on the income from saving will increase the rewards for saving and will thus increase the total amount which people and institutions will be willing and able to save. That will produce benefits for everybody, not just for savers, in the form of increased growth, more jobs, and greater prosperity generally.
2. It will eliminate the existing tax discrimination in favor of debt as compared with equity financing and strike at the heart of the debt-equity problem.
3. It will make American businesses better able to compete against foreign companies for which the cost of capital has already been reduced by elimination of the double tax. In addition, increased returns on savings in the United States will help attract additional foreign savings.
4. It will greatly improve the efficiency of the process by which capital is allocated and thus will produce the equivalent of perhaps 0.5 percent increase in our national income.
5. It will make the capital markets more competitive. Corporate managers will have to demonstrate to stockholders that they can do a better job of investing profits than the shareholders can do for themselves. It will eliminate the tax penalty which at present induces corporate managers to "lock in" corporate capital and keep it out of the capital markets.
6. It will be an immediate and major assist for equity financing. Businesses which have lost access to equity markets will again be able to compete.
7. It will be a great help to utilities and other industries whose investors rely upon steady dividends.
8. It will greatly reduce the tensions and distortions which follow from the present large differential between the tax rates on capital gain and the tax rates on other income.

THE GOALS

The proposed tax reforms to increase saving and investment have the following goals:

Jobs. Increased saving is the quickest and most direct way to put resources at the disposal of those persons who will use them to expand business operations and jobs. Placing equal amounts at the disposal of individuals who will simply spend them would in due course—as they spent it—increase business income, but it would do so less quickly, and with much less assurance that the proceeds would be used for new investment.

Debt-equity ratios.   Additional saving must be made available for equity investments. Steeply climbing debt ratios have left our businesses highly vulnerable to any adverse change in the business climate and have handcuffed them in their ability to expand and modernize.

Productivity and real wages.   Increased saving will make possible the increased investment in capacity that enables workers to turn out more goods and services. Without modernization and new investment, that will not happen. In turn, increased productivity permits wages to increase—in real terms, not just dollars—and helps suppress inflation.

Inflation.   Increased saving and investment, by increasing productivity and the amount of goods and services produced, helps keep prices down. Increased productivity also lets an employer raise wages without also raising prices to his customers. It is our chief insurance against having wage demands turn into a wage-price spiral.

Chapter 22

THE GOVERNMENT'S ROLE IN THE CAPITAL FORMATION PROCESS

*W. Michael Blumenthal**

In analyzing what the federal government can do to promote capital formation, it is best to begin at the beginning.

And the beginning, in my view, is to remind ourselves of the simple, yet oft-overlooked, proposition that our free enterprise economy can grow and remain healthy, and can do the job of providing enough employment for all, only if we ensure that enough private capital flows into financial markets to finance the plant and equipment, the research and development, and the entrepreneurial activities of larger and smaller companies alike.

If that is not the case—and there is increasing concern that it may not be—nothing else that the government can do in shaping an economic program will succeed. An adequate flow of capital is the life-blood of our economy. Without it, our economy cannot function for long, and our many political, social, and cultural goals will remain unfulfilled.

Has there been a shortage of capital? There is no simple answer to that question.

THE NEED TO DEFINE TERMS

To begin with, difficulties arise simply in defining what we are talking about. There has been a lot of debate in recent years as to whether there is or will be a "capital shortage." But it's not always clear what kind of capital the participants in these debates are referring to. Is it a

---

* Secretary of the Treasury.

shortage of financial capital—of means of financing outlays for bricks and mortar? Or is it a shortage of the physical capital itself—the stock of physical assets with which to produce the stream of goods and services called the gross national product? Too often, the debate slips back and forth between the two without regard for the fact that they are distinct—albeit interrelated—concepts.

PHYSICAL CAPITAL

Turning first to physical capital and looking at current numbers on capacity utilization—imperfect as they are—one might be tempted to describe our current stock of plant and equipment as adequate. With operating rates for manufacturing as a whole in the low 80 percent range, there is little to suggest a present shortage. Moreover, the share of total output dedicated to new business fixed investment has been somewhat higher in the past decade than in the preceding two decades —10 percent of real GNP as against 9 percent earlier.

What, then, suggests a shortage of the physical capital required to sustain the balanced, noninflationary growth we are all seeking?

To begin with, some industries appear to be nearing the point at which capacity could constrain production. There are at least half a dozen, including food processing, petroleum refining, and mining, in which current operating rates are edging close to those that prevailed during the most recent period of high utilization (1973). Moreover, a number of studies have pointed to potential capacity problems in other industries, where even moderate sustained growth in economic activity can push them to their capacity ceilings, creating "bottleneck" situations long before the total economy fully utilizes its resources.

THE GROWTH OF FACTOR INPUTS

Second, we have to look to the changing balance between factor inputs, that is, the balance between growth in the stock of physical capital and growth in the stock of human capital. Respectable though recent growth rates in physical capital may be by historical standards, capital stock has not grown commensurately with the growth of the labor force. In the first half of this decade, the average amount of business capital per worker grew at only half the rate at which it had been growing in the 50s and 60s. *In other words, we were not providing tools of production as fast as the growth in workers to use them.*

This shortfall in the availability of capital for the growing labor force has had unpleasant ramifications for the economy. It has contributed in an important degree to the slowing of productivity gains in recent years, a period when output per worker has risen far more slowly than in the 1950s and 1960s. Diminishing rates of gain in productivity put upward pressure on prices, limit improvement in living standards, adversely affect profits, lower incentives for capital investment, and reduce the possibilities for creating jobs in the private sector.

INCREASING INVESTMENT'S SHARE OF GNP

It is therefore quite clear that if we are to move toward a full-employment economy over the balance of this decade, investment in productive capacity will have to absorb a higher proportion of our national output. We will have to achieve a better balance in distributing the results of economic growth between current consumption and investing for even greater future growth.

How do we accomplish this clearly desirable social goal? The first prerequisite for an adequate volume of capital formation, as we see it, is to ensure a sound economy overall, stable and growing, one in which investors can have confidence.

There appears to have been some concern lately as to whether the policies of our federal government will meet this need, concern that the government's efforts to reduce unemployment will be pursued without sufficient regard for the need to reduce inflation, to bring the federal budget into balance, and to provide the predictability and stability that are the sine qua non for the nation's economic health.

Let me stress that you need not have the slightest doubt about our intentions and policies in this regard. President Carter is not a spender —far from it. He is dedicated to a policy of prudence, frugality, and the elimination of wasteful expenditures at all levels. He firmly believes in the need for a vigorous attack on inflation, and he sees this need as just as important as the attack on unemployment.

As for myself, I assure you that I did not take this job to participate in an Administration that fails to address itself vigorously to the danger of inflation.

I accepted this assignment precisely *because* I viewed licking inflation and unemployment as linked; *because* I saw in this my greatest challenge as secretary of the Treasury; *because* I believe that it is possible to do the job; *because* I believe that the time to do it is now; and —above all—*because* we now have a president who will fully back and, indeed, insist on sound policies to make it happen.

The time has come, I believe, to separate myth from reality, and to focus attention on the realities of the Administration's emerging economic policies instead of on slogans and fears unsupported by facts.

ADMINISTRATION POLICIES

Since this is so vital a matter, allow me to focus on a few points with clarity.

1. *This is an Administration dedicated to eliminating budget deficits.* The deficits for fiscal year 1977 and fiscal year 1978 are largely inherited. Their cause lies in large measure in a sluggish level of economic activity. For example, if industrial capacity utilization were now at, say, 86 and 88 percent instead of the present 80 percent; if, then, unemployment were not 7½ to 8 percent but more like 5½ to 6 percent; then $20 billion or so in additional revenues would be available.

Three further comments about the budget:

First, I regard the FY 77 and FY 78 deficit targets as representing outside limits. I expect the actual numbers to come in below them.

Second, work on the FY 79 budget is beginning. With zero-base budgeting as a tool, it is our firm intention that the FY 79 budget deficit will be appreciably lower than the previous year's. New programs will not be funded through increased deficit spending, but rather through the growth in revenues from an expanding economy. Our goal is budget balance by FY 81.

Third, the projected deficits for FY 77 and FY 78, and the significantly smaller deficit projected for FY 79, need not be inflationary in an economy with much unused capacity, nor need they lead to appreciably higher interest rates in an economy currently awash in liquidity.

2. *This is not an Administration that talks about inflation but will do nothing about it.* We are putting in place an anti-inflation program which the president and the secretary of the Treasury and the rest of the Carter Administration team will back with vigor.

THE ADMINISTRATION PROGRAM—WHAT IT WILL NOT BE

First of all, let me spell out what the Administration's program will *not* be.

1. *It will not be based on controls—actual, standby, or any other kind.*

I know of nothing less likely to give us growth with stability than saddling this country and our free market economy with that kind of bureaucratic nightmare.

If anyone had any doubts on that score, the previous Administration's efforts—and failures—in this regard in the early 70s should have dispelled them. The Carter Administration has no intention whatsoever of repeating that folly.

2. *It will not be a program concentrated largely on other forms of incomes policy.*

Management, labor, and consumers must cooperate with the government in the anti-inflationary fight—it is clearly in their self-interest to do so. But in our view this is best achieved if neither direct controls nor indirect coercion is involved.

It is missing the point, therefore, to get involved in debates over buzzwords and catchphrases which divert attention from the realities.

I don't know what "jawboning" means precisely. No doubt it implies different things to different people. Rest assured on one point: if it means that labor or management is to be strong-armed or pressured into complying with arbitrary government guidelines, we will have none of it.

Nor do I believe that it is useful to waste our energies on fruitless arguments about the pros and cons of imprecise concepts, such as "prenotification" on wages and prices—voluntary or otherwise.

What is there to argue about? The expiration date of the major labor contracts is a matter of public record. Doesn't this give all the prenotification needed?

On the price front, I am equally confident that major U.S. industrial leaders, who see the importance of containing inflation as clearly as anyone, will, in the kind of cooperative program we plan to develop, weigh carefully and be prepared to discuss with us the implications of various price options. This pattern has already begun, and it can continue—if we all keep our wits about us.

THE ANTI-INFLATION GOAL

At this point, a logical question is, "What *will* the Administration's anti-inflation program involve?"

First, a prompt review of all government regulations which create bottlenecks, restrict output, or are otherwise inflationary. This has already begun. We are exploring alternatives to regulations which impose exceptionally stringent technological standards on industry without regard to economic criteria, which, indeed, may prove perverse in result because they inhibit industry from adopting more efficient technologies.

We are examining the need for cost-plus or cost-reimbursing contractual arrangements in government purchases, which tend to reduce normal business cost-minimizing incentives. We are examining government price-fixing, which protects inefficient producers against competition and reduces consumers' ability to choose between lower prices and extra services. And we are trying to place a quantitative cost tag on all federal actions which affect prices, so that better cost/benefit analyses can be derived.

Second, a policy on international trade that provides help and protection to industries and workers hurt by imports, but does so in ways which do not result in inflationary price increases borne by the consumer. We plan to develop new ideas of how to improve our competitiveness, emphasizing programs of structural reforms that will lower costs and increase productivity. This, rather than price-raising restrictions which hurt the consumer, is the right approach and the one we intend to promote.

Third, the presentation to Congress this year of a comprehensive proposal for major tax reform, designed to promote business investment to achieve increased productivity.

Fourth, a review of unnecessary and costly reporting requirements imposed on business by the government, requirements which raise costs without really meeting any vital needs. Lawyers and accountants do not need this kind of lifetime employment guarantee to keep them busy and productive.

Fifth, an effort to create an effective system to analyze the economic impact of each major new federal legislative or regulatory effort. This has not been handled adequately in the past—and we aim to do something about it.

Sixth, improvement of the operation of the Council on Wage and Price Stability, not to control or coerce, but to provide the data and the research to identify bottlenecks and economic problem areas ahead of time, particularly those which limit productivity and fuel inflationary flames.

Seventh, the organization of a labor-management committee, consisting of outstanding labor and management representatives who, together with members of the Administration, can serve as a forum for the candid and thorough discussion of labor and management perspectives on the major issues relating to inflation, productivity, employment, and related economic questions.

Eighth, along with all this, a clear identification of the goals and targets to be achieved as we strive to balance the budget and simultaneously reduce unemployment and inflation. This set of objectives can then form the basis for enlisting labor, management, consumers, and all levels of government in common commitment and a cooperative effort to achieve our economic goals.

We are now beginning to put the parts of this program into effect. One thing is certain: we are in dead earnest. If we are to succeed, a common effort and, no doubt, a common sacrifice will be required. But we will work hard at it, and we aim to succeed.

ENSURING A GREATER FLOW OF INVESTMENT CAPITAL

If we can do the things I have just outlined, one of the critical prerequisites for ensuring a much greater flow of capital will have been achieved.

But, of course, that will not be enough.

After all, the rate of capital investment depends in the final analysis not so much on inflation rates as on the rate of return anticipated for that investment.

In this regard, we appreciate the pressure on business executives to halt the decline in profits and profit margins. *The record is quite clear: whether measured in terms of share of national income or in terms of ratios to sales, corporate profits and profit margins have been declining since the mid-60s.* We are aware of this erosion, and we understand that last year's rise in profits and margins was a cyclical response characteristic of the early stages of a cycle recovery, and not necessarily a permanent reversal of the downward trend.

But we do not believe that the way to break this trend is through inflationary price markups; indeed, price markups of that sort would, in all likelihood, have the opposite effect. The path to sustained recovery in profits is through investment in more efficient production techniques, for gains in productivity are highly correlated with gains in profits.

SUPPORTING THE REQUIRED GROWTH OF INVESTMENT

Now let me turn to the other major concern about the capital formation process, the adequacy of the flow of financial capital to support the required growth in investment.

Our financial system is justifiably renowned for its capacity, scope, richness of form, and resilience. It functions with remarkable efficiency in gathering the savings of the public and transforming these into the means of financing private investment. Nevertheless, there are areas in which improvements can be made to ensure that the insufficient availability of financing—in both amount and form—does not become an impediment to the necessary growth in our capital stock.

312

DEBT VERSUS EQUITY

One fundamental problem is the tilt of the system toward financing through debt instruments. Savers appear, in general, to prefer acquiring financial assets of fixed nominal value and fixed income return— a preference that persists despite the postwar erosion in the purchasing power of fixed-value claims. Moreover, our tax system encourages the financing of investment through debt instruments.

Over the longer run, this is not the ideal arrangement; there are limits to which it is prudent or even feasible to pile increasing amounts of debt on a very slowly growing equity base. A debt-heavy financial structure increases the vulnerability of the business enterprise to cyclical fluctuations in income. It limits the venturesomeness of investment, for lenders cannot in good conscience underwrite the risks appropriate to an equity participant. And it inhibits economic growth, because growth depends very much on willingness to risk investment in new products and new processes.

Moreover, the emphasis on debt financing raises particular problems for smaller and newer enterprises, which often lack the track record necessary to attract adequate amounts of financing from lenders, and must therefore fight for access to pools of equity financing.

Many proposals have been advanced to modify the tax structure in order to achieve more evenhanded treatment of alternative means of financing investment, and to improve the functioning of securities markets with respect to small businesses. These proposals are all under active study. And business leaders' advice on how best to achieve these objectives will be actively solicited.

FINANCIAL INTERMEDIARIES AND PUBLIC SECURITIES MARKETS

Any review of the adequacy of our system for financing capital formation must, of course, address the operations of the principal channels through which savings flow into investment—financial intermediaries and public securities markets.

The transformation of savings into investment in our country occurs principally through the intermediation of financial institutions. In 1976, over two thirds of the $250 billion advanced in credit markets was supplied by banking, thrift, and insurance institutions. The question is whether the panoply of government legislation and regulation is helping or hindering the achievement of maximum efficiency in the allocation of these funds.

What we must do now is reevaluate the complex of government

rules, regulations, and procedures affecting financial intermediaries to ensure that there are not, in our regulatory structure, any factors inhibiting the sustained flow of financing for investment. We do not need yet another commission or yet another round of extensive studies. We will, however, seek the counsel of business leaders as our own ideas develop.

At the same time, we will be reevaluating the efficiency with which our public securities markets meet the needs of savers, borrowers, and risk-takers. Our country is fortunate to have such well-functioning securities markets, very much the product of the leadership provided by the Securities and Exchange Commission for more than four decades. The reputation that the SEC has earned for fiercely guarding the rights of the investing public is a major element in our success in transforming the savings of individuals into the financing of private investment.

The SEC's expertise and its insights into the operation of the securities markets will be an important contribution to our review of the saving/investment process.

Let me, then, summarize quickly how I see the capital formation problem, and what this Administration proposes to do about it.

SUMMARY

We do have a capital shortage, in the sense that the growth of physical plant and equipment is lagging behind the rate of expansion required to reach a full-employment economy. That situation must be corrected, for unless it is, we can expect to experience persistently unsatisfactory productivity increases, rising unit costs, and a continuation of the unemployment which is in large measure a result of these two factors.

Chapter 23

THE VITAL ROLE OF CONGRESS

*Charls E. Walker**

As the authors of the preceding chapters have demonstrated, "America's third-century challenge" to create adequate capital and jobs will be truly monumental. This chapter recognizes the elementary fact that the federal government, especially Congress, will play a crucial role in meeting that challenge. Indeed, it is not too much to say that congressional actions in the years ahead will be the *deciding* factor in success or failure.

Because of the conviction of knowledgeable observers that tax policy is probably the single most important governmental influence on the rate of capital and job formation, this chapter will be devoted largely to the "how" of reducing the bias in the federal tax structure. This bias now favors consumption over saving and productive investment. However, tax policy is not the sole area in which congressional actions are important. Three others that come most quickly to mind are stabilization policy, the federal budget, and the regulation of business.

Stabilization policy

One need only examine the economic record of the traumatic decade ushered in by the Vietnam War to comprehend the importance of effective federal stabilization policies to achieving a high and sustained rate of capital formation. The commitment of large amounts of resources to productive investment involves considerable risk. If the decision-maker is confused and uncertain about the effectiveness of stabilization policy—fearing, for example, that "stop-go" policies will dominate and that "stagflation" will be the likely result—then such

---

* Chairman, American Council for Capital Formation.

commitments are bound to be scaled down, if not inordinately post-poned or canceled.

A discussion of the use of federal stabilization policies to achieve a high rate of noninflationary growth is beyond the scope of this chapter. Suffice it to say that, if the promise of success in this respect is absent, the pace of capital and job formation is bound to be slow and the chances of meeting the third-century challenge of jobs and capital formation are damaged significantly.

Budget policy

In the two decades ending with fiscal year 1978, the federal budget was in surplus only twice. Even in those instances the surplus was small. Net deficits over the 20 years approached $375 billion, the exact figure depending on the final outcome for fiscal year 1978. Moreover, the deficits do not include "off-budget" financing, federally guaranteed loans, and so on. In calendar year 1976, the total funds "*raised* under federal auspices" amounted to more than 40 percent of the funds advanced in domestic credit markets (including equities). Reflecting this, a new phrase, federal *crowding out*, has recently been added to the language.

What all this means is that in recent years the federal government has become a gigantic borrower in the same financial markets where industry must obtain the debt and equity funds that support capital formation. Therefore, if the long string of federal deficits could be converted into surpluses, or even reduced significantly, the availability of funds to the private sector and for capital formation and jobs would be greatly increased.

What are the chances? There are some reasons for guarded optimism, even though the natural proclivity of Congress is to spend big and tax small. Optimism arises from the early success of the congressional budget process under legislation enacted in 1974. Only time will tell whether Congress can ultimately slow the rate of increase in federal spending, thereby permitting revenues to "catch up." But the public pressure that led to the legislation—based upon the conviction that "big spending" causes "big deficits" which result in "big inflation" —is likely to remain strong. Congress may therefore be forced to retrench, however reluctantly. A good starting point is the billions being spent on subsidies and assorted social programs which, because they ultimately increase taxes on the productive sector of society, have the end result of actually impeding economic progress.

Still, the third-century challenge is not likely to be met through a long string of large federal surpluses. We shall do well to get back to balance (over the business cycle) and stay there.

Government regulation of business

Ubiquitous and rapidly expanding government regulation of industry looms as a major deterrent to capital and job formation. It is especially ironic that the red tape of regulation is most damaging in the very area where new investment is so badly needed—energy. Experts estimate that the decade now required to conceive, design, and construct a nuclear power plant could be reduced by several years if it were not necessary to run the obstacle course of federal, state, and local regulations.

Since government regulatory agencies are likely to continue on their present course, only Congress can restore the "rule of reason" to government regulation of industry. Will it do so? Only time will tell, but increasing analysis of the problem by scholars (including analysis of the hidden "costs" of excessive regulation), coupled with increasing public attention to a growing list of "horror stories," gives some cause for optimism. This optimism would be especially justified if business leaders were to develop and implement an effective legislative program—one similar in form, but not in content, to that described for tax policy in the remaining pages of this chapter.

PRODUCTIVE TAX REFORM: AN IMPOSSIBLE DREAM?

Many business and financial leaders are convinced that truly productive tax reform—structural changes in tax laws to promote capital and job formation—is an impossible dream. They point to the demonstrably low level of economic understanding on the part of the American people—most of whom think that business profits per sales dollar is about 30 cents (six times the actual amount) and few of whom have the foggiest idea of what capital formation really means. Only in rare cases do Americans see any connection between the rate of capital formation and growth in jobs, output, and living standards.

But the outlook is *not* bleak. To be sure, economic illiteracy is a major problem, but there is evidence that the American people, congressmen and other federal officials, and even the press, the unions, and so-called public interest groups increasingly recognize that this nation faces a serious problem with respect to capital formation.

Consider first a survey in 1976 by the highly respected *Cambridge Report*. The first conclusion of the survey confirms the views of the skeptics; the word *capital* (and, therefore, the concept of capital formation) is understood by only a handful of Americans. Nevertheless, as is shown in Chart 1, 25 percent believed that there was a "very serious" problem involved in "raising the dollars needed for business investment" in the years ahead, and 39 percent thought that the problem was

Chart 1. Capital shortage facing U.S. industry—General public

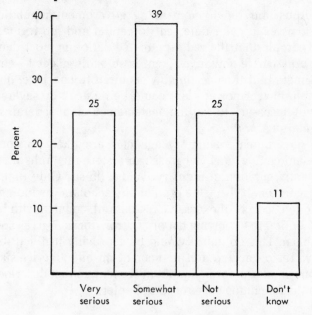

"Do you think there is a problem with raising the dollars needed for business investment?"

Source: *The Cambridge Report,* first quarter (Cambridge, Mass.: Cambridge Reports, Inc., 1976).

"somewhat serious." Some 64 percent therefore believed that there was a problem that was at least "serious," and only 25 percent denied that the problem was "serious." The rest "did not know." Also encouraging, 72 percent favored private investment over government investment, and two thirds of those respondents stated that they would favor the private route even though that meant higher corporate profits. This last point is especially impressive when it is recognized that almost half of the respondents believed that corporate profits were too high.

This concern is reflected in Washington. In 1975 still another highly respected polling firm, the Opinion Research Corporation, reported to its clients on interviews on the subject with "thoughtleaders" in the nation's capital. The results were as encouraging as they were surprising. The question was framed as follows: "How serious do you think the shortage of investment capital facing U.S. industry will be over the next ten years or so? Will the capital shortage be very serious, somewhat serious, slightly serious, or don't you believe industry faces a capital shortage?" The "thoughtleaders" consisted of three groups: legislators; officials of the executive branch and regulatory agencies; and a combination of unions, public interest organizations, and press and other media. The results are shown in Chart 2.

Most significant, of course, was the whopping response from 95 percent of the legislators that the problem was at least "serious," with 57 percent stating that it was "very serious" and 21 percent stating that it was "somewhat serious." And perhaps the most surprising set of responses came from the "union/public interest/media group,"

Chart 2.   Capital shortage facing U.S. industry—"Thoughtleaders"

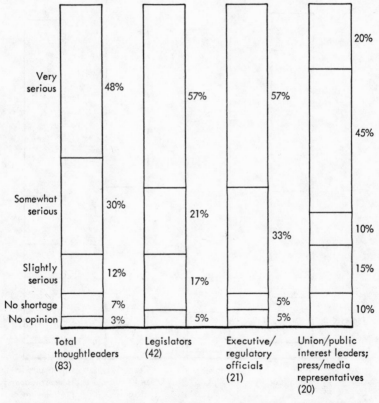

"How serious do you think the shortage of investment capital facing U.S. industry will be over the next ten years or so? Will the capital shortage be very serious, somewhat serious, slightly serious, or don't you believe industry faces a capital shortage?"

320

with 65 percent stating that the problem was either "very serious" or "somewhat serious," and only 15 percent believing that there was no capital shortage.

Even more significant is Chart 3, which shows that 55 percent of the "thoughtleaders," including half of the Congress and more than half of the union/public interest/media group, believed that "the federal tax laws ... hurt ... the capital situation facing U.S. industry."

Chart 3.   Effect of tax laws on the capital situation

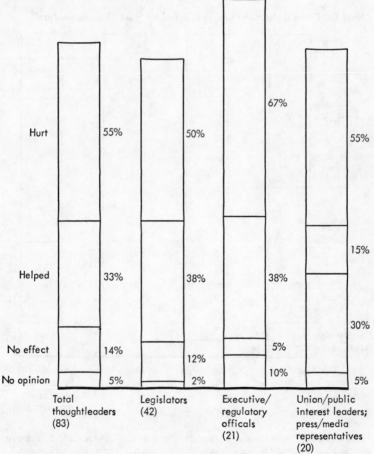

"Have the federal tax laws helped, hurt, or had no effect on the capital situation facing U.S. industry?"

Percentages total more than 100 because of multiple answers where respondents felt that the tax laws had helped the capital situation in some ways and hurt it in other ways.

Impediments to productive reform

Given these views, why hasn't Congress enacted a whole panoply of tax measures to promote capital formation? Why hasn't the corporate income tax been reduced, if not eliminated, since it is clearly a drag on economic growth and since its incidence may be such as to result in a highly regressive impact? Why haven't the depreciation, that is, capital recovery, rules been liberalized in the manner of our major competitors abroad? Why hasn't the investment tax credit been improved and made permanent? Why did Congress, in the early 1970s to the mid-1970s, in effect almost double the capital gains tax for many individuals?

There are several reasons. And if the advocates of tax changes for capital formation are to succeed, they must understand those reasons, develop good answers, and then seek out means of obtaining the agreement of majorities in the tax-writing committees and in Congress as a whole.

One reason advanced in the past, but which has lost its punch, is that "this nation faces no capital formation problem." The surveys cited above demonstrate that both the public and "thoughtleaders" agree that there is a serious problem. The real task is not to arouse concern; the concern is there. *The task is to convince Congress that productive tax reform will help solve the capital and job formation problem. To do this, the business and financial community must markedly improve its efforts in public education and legislative action.*

The core of the problem is that the very tax actions which will help capital and job formation involve reductions for the businesses which invest in new plant and equipment. Reductions are likewise in order for individuals who are in a position to save portions of their income. In short, tax reform must focus on eliminating tax penalties on the corporate leaders and the "fat cats" whom some newspaper cartoonists like to portray as corpulent, balding, vested, middle-aged men wearing dollar signs.

To make matters worse, the press and many politicians believe that:

1. The federal tax system is shot through with "billions upon billions" of dollars in "loopholes" just ripe for the closing (with the revenue pickup available to reduce taxes on the middle- and low-income brackets).
2. Virtually, all of the rich "get away with murder" when it comes to paying taxes, paying none at all or at least paying percentages of their income smaller than those paid by the poor (a regressive system).

3. Taxes can be levied on corporations with no ultimate impact on people, a convenient means of shifting the burden from the "little man" to "big business."
4. The government can't afford the revenue loss from business tax cuts.

These widely held views are wrong. Data, experience, and expert opinion tell a very different story. It is that story which the advocates of productive tax reform must comprehend and then use effectively with the public and Congress.

EXPLODING THE MYTHS

The American Council for Capital Formation has developed a careful and comprehensive refutation of these allegations.[1] Space does not permit its repetition here, but the highlights of that refutation can be covered as a basis for a recommended action program to obtain legislation.

Charge 1. The federal tax system is shot through with billions upon billions of dollars in tax loopholes.

Short answer. The overwhelming majority of the provisions in question are not "loopholes" at all, but provisions of the tax code which provide some reductions in rates for activities that Congress has found to be socially or economically desirable. Contrary to the popular view, preferences for individuals far exceed those for corporations, and it is mainly low- and middle-income taxpayers who benefit (for example, homeowners, from interest and property tax deductions; workers, from such things as tax-free unemployment compensation and tax-exempt contributions by employers to medical insurance and pension plans; and the elderly, from tax-free Social Security benefits). The largest business "preference" is, of course, the investment tax credit. But this device promotes capital and job formation, and moreover, as noted below, its repeal could actually cause losses, not gains, in federal revenues.

Since the preferences are, in general, defensible, efforts to reduce them and use the revenues to reduce taxes in the lower-income brackets, such as have been made in the past, are likely to bear little fruit.

Charge 2. Many people with high incomes pay no federal income taxes. Moreover, the system is regressive.

Short answer. According to Treasury studies, in 1975 taxpayers with incomes of $200,000 or over paid an average effective rate of 35 percent, and half of such taxpayers paid 40 percent or more. Only 182 high-income individuals paid no federal income taxes, and this resulted from large deductions in that year, usually for interest. In addition, the federal individual income tax system is not regressive. It is nicely progressive, ranging from average effective rates of less than zero (for some who claim the earned income credit), to about 10 percent in the lowest bracket, to 40 percent and upward in the high brackets.

Charge 3.   Business can be taxed without affecting people with low or middle incomes.

Short answer.   Corporations do not pay taxes—people do. Taxes paid by business are in some combination ultimately passed forward to consumers or backward to "factors of production," that is, wage earners and the suppliers of the savings to pay for new plant and equipment. To the extent that such taxes are passed forward, they are doubtless regressive, since people with low incomes spend a larger portion of their earnings on products of industry than do those with high incomes. If they are passed backward, workers earn less and capital formation is impeded.

The important point is that newspaper headlines or television "leads" referring to a big cut in taxes "for business" are misleading. Such reductions are in reality reductions for people—consumers, workers, savers, and investors.

Charge 4.   The government cannot afford the revenue losses resulting from cuts in business taxes, losses that would simply drive up federal deficits and increase the burden on capital markets.

Short answer.   As has been proved consistently since World War II—especially in the early years of the Kennedy Administration—soundly conceived business tax cuts do not reduce federal revenues; they tend to increase them. Taxes are a drag on business activity. When business taxes are reduced, the aftertax return to a firm for successful expansion increases. Profits tend to rise—which encourages further business expansion—and the government obtains a significant increase in business tax payments. Employment and payrolls increase, so that the taxable income of workers also goes up, with still another boost to federal revenue.

This relationship is demonstrated vividly in Chart 4. As can be seen, the major business tax cuts in 1948, 1964, and 1971 were followed by rapid growth in federal revenues (shaded areas).[2]

A PROGRAM OF INFORMATION AND ACTION

Quite clearly, the problem is one of convincing people of the benefits in terms of jobs, growth, and living standards that flow from increased capital formation. And when it comes to tax measures to pro-

Chart 4.   Federal government receipts (seasonally adjusted annual rates, quarterly; NIA basis)

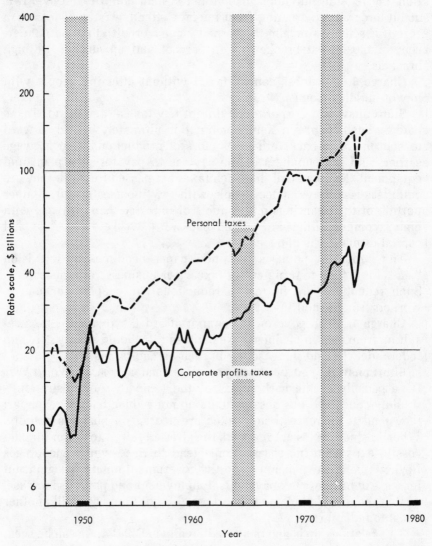

mote such expansion, refutation of the false charges discussed above provides the most promising route.

How can this be done? What communications devices and routes are available? Will Congress react? How can the whole process be speeded sufficiently to meet "America's third-century challenge"?

The most difficult problem raised by these questions—but at the same time the most important—is the manner in which Congress should be approached and persuaded. In this respect, there has been a very big change in the past decade or so. Throughout much of our history, including the periods of Sam Rayburn's leadership in the House of Representatives and Lyndon Johnson's in the Senate (until 1961, in both instances), congressional leadership played a very important, and at times an overpowering, role with respect to tax legislation. But in recent years, the force of leadership in the Congress has decreased, as has the number of "followers"; more and more members are assertive of their individual prerogatives, as opposed to party loyalty or direction from a president of their own party. The result is that "grass roots" contacts are the key to affecting legislation. Needless to say, that makes the task of those who support tax measures for capital and job formation infinitely more difficult, for the simple reason (already noted) that the typical voter views such measures as "handouts" to "big business" and "fat cats."

The man on the street

Raising the level of economic understanding among the electorate is a monumental undertaking, but it is of great importance. *Quite simply, if the typical voter does not sooner or later come to understand the "hows" and "whys" of a market economy, our economic system can be voted down the drain.* Fortunately, energetic individuals have recognized this problem, and effective programs (primarily under the leadership of the prestigious Joint Council on Economic Education and its affiliates) are being pushed vigorously.

One of the most important things that the business community can do to help speed this process (in addition to providing financial and volunteer support for the programs of the Joint Council) is to set up economic education programs for its employees. Several companies have enjoyed considerable success in this respect. There are major pitfalls, however, and the cautious executive will contact the headquarters of the Joint Council before he takes any such steps.[3]

Still, if early action is to be obtained, other measures are necessary. Two important aspects involve the press and organized labor.

The press

More and more corporations have been using paid advertisements to raise the level of public economic understanding and to make the case for capital and job formation. These advertisements have generally been constructive; alone, however, they are insufficient. Somehow or other, reporters and editorial writers must be convinced that a genuine problem exists; that the United States individual income tax system is not a "disgrace" but is basically fair; that the rich do pay heavy taxes; that business as such pays no taxes, but is simply a surrogate collector for the Internal Revenue Service; and that soundly conceived business tax reductions tend to raise rather than lose government revenue. How can this be done?

First, advocates of capital and job formation must master the arguments and be certain of the facts. As noted earlier, the American Council for Capital Formation has prepared material for this purpose. Armed with such material, business and financial leaders should use every opportunity to make their case with editorial boards, financial editors and writers, and general reporters (including broadcast journalists). The time is especially ripe for such an approach; as more and more journalists recognized that perhaps the biggest "story" of the 1970s involved economics, they quickly concluded that they were miserably prepared to deal with it. They want and need help, and if that help is based on facts and reasoned argument, good journalists will give it every consideration.

What will this achieve? Certainly not overnight passage of tax measures to promote capital and job formation. But the tone of news stories and the opinions of editorialists should change for the better. And even if the only success is to convince reporters and editors that a congressman does not deserve to be designated a "tax reformer" simply because of a professed desire to raise taxes on business and the well-to-do, the effort will be worthwhile.

Organized labor

On major issues, Congress sooner or later responds to the will of the people. But on what appear to be narrower matters, the influence that can be exerted on Congress by so-called interest groups is likely to be crucial to the life or death of a legislative proposal. And so it is with many aspects of business taxation. For example, on the simple and straightforward issue of promoting capital and job formation by cutting the corporate tax rate, the vast majority of voters would doubtless respond negatively. But when such relatively arcane issues as the investment tax credit, depreciation procedures, integration of the individual and corporate income taxes, and treatment of foreign source corporate income come up, the typical voter usually expresses little understanding or interest. Consequently, the attitude of organized labor on tax changes for capital and job formation is of utmost importance. This is because organized labor is, at this writing, the single most powerful "interest group" affecting Congress. Unfortunately, labor's attitude has been largely negative. But is the situation hopeless? Not by any means.

The first point that should be emphasized is that, in contrast to organized labor in some other nations, organized labor in this country is in favor of our type of economic system and in fact works actively to further the goals of the Joint Council on Economic Education. Moreover, there is no class distinction here; workers know that they can move up into higher income ranges.

Second, the fact is that the ultimate interests of business and labor are identical on the vast majority of the legislative issues which they fight out in Congress. Such issues include jobs, a healthy economy, price stability, and international competitiveness. Sooner or later, business and labor must recognize this fact. And when that happens, positive congressional measures to promote capital formation should be forthcoming.

This may happen sooner than many people think. One reason is a "changing of the guard" among union leaders. Another is the increased willingness of top leaders from labor and business to sit down and air their differences of public policy issues. Such quiet discussion led to some very promising agreements on capital formation measures in the mid-1970s; it can do so again.

Needless to say, labor leaders cannot get too far ahead of their members. This is all the more reason why the business community should make a heavy and continuing commitment to increasing economic understanding, not just in the schools but also among adults.

THE BOTTOM LINE

There are promising signs that America will meet its third-century challenge on capital and job formation. Among the most encouraging signs is the willingness of business leaders to recognize the social responsibilities of their organizations and, more important, to do something about those responsibilities. Moreover, chief executive officers have come to understand that even though their subordinates can provide invaluable staff assistance, it is up to the leader to carry the message to the press, the public, and Congress. Today's chief executive officer, in other words, is convinced that what is truly in the public interest, although perhaps disturbing in the short run, is in the long run good for the company. It is this recognition, and the will to do something about it, that provides the solid basis for optimism—the optimism that is an appropriate concluding note to this compendium.

We can meet America's third-century challenge.

NOTES

1. The American Council for Capital Formation is located at 1425 K Street, N.W., Washington, D.C. 20005.
2. Opponents of business tax cuts to promote economic growth argue that post-war reductions occurred during business recoveries, when federal revenues would be expected to rise. *Answer:* Yes, but the business tax cuts were significant contributors to those recoveries. In this respect, the 1971 cut is most interesting. Although the cuts (restoration of the investment tax credit and congressional validation of accelerated depreciation) were assured politically as early as November 1971, few economists recognized that business was recovering strongly until well into 1972.
3. The Joint Council on Economic Education is located at 1212 Avenue of the Americas, New York, New York 10036.